מסורה

ArtScroll Series®

Rabbi Nosson Scherman / Rabbi Meir Zlotowitz

General Editors

SPECIAL SUPPLEMENT:
The Mitzvah of Ahavas Yisrael

Refining the way we speak:
An inspiring blend of
laws, stories and insights

Rabbi Shimon Finkelman

The Gift of Speech

Published by

Mesorah Publications, ltd

FIRST EDITION
First Impression … September 2000

Published and Distributed by
MESORAH PUBLICATIONS, LTD.
4401 Second Avenue / Brooklyn, N.Y 11232

Distributed in Europe by
LEHMANNS
Unit E, Viking Industrial Park
Rolling Mill Road NE32 3DP
Jarow, Tyne & Wear,
England

Distributed in Australia and New Zealand by
GOLDS WORLD OF JUDAICA
3-13 William Street
Balaclava, Melbourne 3183
Victoria Australia

Distributed in Israel by
SIFRIATI / A. GITLER
10 Hashomer Street
Bnei Brak 51361

Distributed in South Africa by
KOLLEL BOOKSHOP
Shop 8A Norwood Hypermarket
Norwood 2196, Johannesburg, South Africa

ARTSCROLL SERIES®
THE GIFT OF SPEECH
© *Copyright 2000, by* MESORAH PUBLICATIONS, Ltd.
4401 Second Avenue / Brooklyn, N.Y. 11232 / (718) 921-9000 / www.artscroll.com

ISBN:
1-57819-471-7 (hard cover)
1-57819-472-5 (paperback)

Typography by CompuScribe at ArtScroll Studios, Ltd.

Printed in the United States of America by Noble Book Press Corp.
Bound by Sefercraft, Quality Bookbinders, Ltd., Brooklyn N.Y. 11232

This book is dedicated in memory of five precious *neshamos* who were taken from this world in their youth:

רייזל ע״ה בת ר׳ דוד משה נ״י
רבקה אסתר ע״ה בת ר׳ דוד משה נ״י
אליהו יצחק ע״ה בן ר׳ דוד משה נ״י
PILLER

ברכה יטא ע״ה בת ר׳ שמואל נח נ״י
MERMELSTEIN

דוד מרדכי ע״ה בן ר׳ אשר יעקב צבי נ״י
MOSKOWITZ

Their years were short, but their days were filled with spiritual accomplishment.
May their memories inspire us all to give meaning to our lives and use the gift of speech for its intended purpose.

And in memory of

ר׳ רפאל בן ר׳ ניסן אייזק
RABBI RAPHAEL ANDRUSIER ז״ל

Softspokenness was his trademark. He had only good things to say to people and about people, and he epitomized the teaching
הוי מקבל את כל האדם בספר פנים יפות.

ת. נ. צ. ב. ה.

May the lessons gleaned from this volume be a source of merit for them.

מכתב הסכמה וברכה
מאת הרב מתתי' חיים סלומון שליט"א
משגיח רוחני דבית מדרש גבוה דלייקוואד

בס"ד
מוש"ק פרשת עקב תשנ"ס

מיום שהוריד השי"ת רוח ממרום על קדוש ישראל מרן רשכבה"ג בעל חפץ חיים זצוק"ל להעיר כלל ישראל על גודל עון לשה"ר ורכילות ושנאת חנם כדי להחזיר עטרה ליושנה לבנות ההנרסות מחורבן בית מקדשנו אשר היא בית חיינו ולמהר גאולתנו ופדות נפשנו על ידי התעוררות רבים לחזור בתשובה שלמה על עונות הנ"ל ולקים כראוי מצות ואהבת לרעך כמוך כמבואר בכמה מקומות בספריו הנפלאים, מאז ועד היום שמעו רבים לקולו ונתרבו ספרים וקונטרסים כולם בנויים על יסודותיו החזקים לבאר ולחזק ולקרב ולמשוך לב ישראל לאביהם שבשמים כל אחד בסגנון שלו בהלכה ובאגדה בלה"ק ובכמה לשונות בכמה מדינות ולכל אחד מהמחברים והמאספים זכות גדולה עד לשמים, ה' ישלם שכרם.

ועתה קם איש צנוע הוי'ה כמוהר"ר שמעון פינקלמאן שליט"א אשר כבר איתמחי גברא כבקי בספרי החי"ח זצוק"ל על הלכות לשון הרע ושמירת הלשון ואתמחי קמיע כסופר מהיר לחבר ספר ללמוד כסדר בכל יום ויום, ועוד ידו נטויה לקרב אל המלאכה לחבר ספר שלם כדי שיהיו מצות אלו לנחלת כל ישראל מפשוטי עם עד נבונים ומצעירי הצאן עד זקניהם ע"י שילוב מיוחד של הלכות ואגדות במשלים ודוגמאות ומעשים יום יומיים אשר כל אחד ואחד ימצא בה טעם ומתיקות להביאו שישתמש במתנה טובה זו של כח הדיבור אשר חנן אלוקים ויחד בה האדם -- רק לטובה.

אחשוב שכדאי להעתיק פה דברי רבנו יונה בשערי תשובה (שער ג' סוף ס' רי') אשר דבריו הקדושים מאירים עינים לראות עד כמה השי"י רוצה שנהי מדברים ולא כאלמים חיו וז"ל שם:

ואמרו רבותינו (ילקוט תהילים תשכא) כנסת ישראל בקולה אהובה ובקולה שנואה -- שנאמר (שה"ש ב' ידי) השמיעיני את קולך כי קולך ערב, ובקולה שנואה -- שנאמר (ירמי' יב' ח') נתנה עלי בקולה על כן שנאתיה, וזהו שנאמר (משלי יח' כא') מות וחיים ביד הלשון ואהבה יאכל פריה, פירוש ואהביה יאכל פריה, אוהב הלשון והוא האיש החפץ לדבר תמיד, העצה הנכונה אליו שיאכל פריה, שלא ידבר בדברי בטלה אך בדברי תורה חכמה ומוסר, והבאת שלום בין אדם לחבירו, ולהצדיק הרבים, ולשבח הטוב, ולגנות את הרע, ולקנא את האמת, כי זכיות אין קץ יוכל לקנות לנפשו בלשונו, וכאשר הקדים כי "חיים ביד הלשון." עכ"ל הטהור.

ישמשו דברי רבנו יונה הנ"ל כהקדמה והסכמה לספר בהיר זה, וכברכה להרהמ"ח שליט"א אשר זכה וזיכה את הרבים זכות הרבים תלוי בו.

אמלין יב גלקי !

מתי חיים סלומון.

Table of Contents

Preface 9

Acknowledgments 11

1 Word Power 15
The "Chazzan" of Shaarei Chesed / When Everyone's a Loser / Word Disease / The Power of One Word

2 Destruction and Rebuilding 20
Destroyers of Communism / Points to Ponder / The Board Meeting / The Manchester Rosh Yeshivah / A "Business Proposition"

3 The Truth Hurts 31
The Hotel Manager / See the Good / Nothing New / A Moment of Victory

4 The Benefit of the Doubt 37
A Special Worker / Surprise / A Case in Point / Measure for Measure

5 A Shameful Mistake 44
A Reason to Weep / Tea, Anyone? / A Time to Be Silent / Reb Yaakov's Concern / No Strength to Shame

6 Painful Words 50
"I Didn't Mean it" / Practical Jokes / Sensitive Souls / Thoughtful Silence / Inward and Outward

7 Put-downs 58
Trust in Hashem / The Right Approach / The Ravages of Jealousy / The Prayer of R' Nechunia / Bad Humor

8 Not-So-Innocent Remarks 64
Negative Comments / Loose Tongues

9 "In My Opinion…" 68
The Chofetz Chaim and the Cook / Speech Analysts / Watch
Your Praise

10 **Common Misconceptions** 73
"And There We Were…" / "…Eighteen Hundred Dollars!" / "…I
Always Find Food on the Table" / "Now, Naftali's Brother…" /
Double Identity / Silent Lashon Hara / Hidden Lashon Hara

11 **Bad News** 81
The Big Lie / Disparaging Torah Scholars / A Thoughtless
Remark / When Great Men Disagree / Living Scrolls / Highway
Robbery

12 **Wholesale Destruction** 90
The Truth Be Told / "The Shopping Bag Ladies" / His Second
Mistake / A First-hand Lesson

13 **Playing with Fire** 96
The Real Enemy / Real Strength / In the Way of Moshe / The Only
Solution / Sign of True Love / Sound Advice / Seek Peace

14 **When Bad is Good** 106
Risky Partnerships / Two Sides of a Coin / An Innocent Victim /
A "Sticky" Situation / The Way to Criticize / The Seventh
Condition / A Quick Review

15 **Family Talk** 115
Chaim's Mistakes / Yaffa's Humor / Between Husband and Wife /
One Small Spark / Another Exception / A Place for the
Shechinah

16 **Rechilus** 124
Third-party Support / In All Circumstances / When the Stakes
Are High / For the Sake of Peace / Shame of Honor

17 **Shades of Ill Will** 132
Causing Distress / Avak Rechilus / Unfortunate and Avoidable

18 **Repairing the Damage** 137
"I Have Sinned" / Between Man and Man / R' Elyah Lopian / A
Child's Regret

19 **The Art of Not Listening** 144
A Time to Leave / Of Fingers and Ear Lobes / On the Battlefront
/ Against the Current / Air Pollution / Strategies / Corrupted
Speech

20 Listening vs. Accepting   154
The Death of Gedaliah / Exceptions / A General Rule

21 Squandering One's Wealth   161
A Frightening Exchange / A Jew's Craft / Turning Point / Prayer
Bashing / In Hashem's Palace / Lashon Hara in Shul / The
Tosafos Yom Tov's Prayer

22 Nothing but the Truth   171
Language of the Heart

23 Fine Tuning   176
A Hidden Flaw / The Right Expression / A Tzaddik's Wish

24 The Right Word   181
"Good Morning" / A Letter to Ben / A Good Listener

THE MITZVAH OF AHAVAS YISRAEL

1 "...As Yourself"   191
A Heartless Request / A Helping Hand / Visitors for Bentzy /
Prayer Preparation

2 Three Levels of Love   200
A Good Friend / Level Two / Never Too Busy / A Model for All /
The Highest Level / Hillel's Rule

3 The Great Rule   209
All-encompassing / The Totality of Torah / Love Your Fellow,
Love Hashem / The Power of Unity / With One Heart / "I Am
Hashem"

4 Children of One Father   217
Those Who Are Distant / A Praiseworthy Jew / For His Enemy's
Sake / "Reb Shmuel" / A Higher Purpose

5 Lessons of Greatness   227
The Hostage Crisis / Everyone's Friend (I) / Everyone's Friend
(II) / For Those Who Caused Him Pain / No Time to Rest / For
Every Jewish Child / A Hug for Life

Sources   241

Preface

To the words וַיְהִי הָאָדָם לְנֶפֶשׁ חַיָּה, *And man became a living soul* (*Bereishis* 2:7), *Targum Onkeles* translates: "And man became a speaking spirit." The gift of speech, an expression of man's intellect, is what distinguishes him from all other creatures. Abuse of this gift is the primary cause of strife, hurt and *sinas chinam* (baseless hatred) which, our Sages inform us, was the primary cause of the Destruction of the Second *Beis HaMikdash* and the subsequent exile in which we still languish. If we truly wish to witness the end of this exile through the coming of Mashiach, then it is imperative that we strive to refine our speech to the best of our ability.

During the past two decades, the Torah world has experienced a spiritual awakening in the area of *shemiras halashon*, the requirement that a Jew "guard his tongue" and ensure that his words are in consonance with *Halachah*. Rabbi Yisrael Meir HaKohen, זצ"ל, (the "Chofetz Chaim") collected these laws from the vast body of Oral Law and organized them into the code that he entitled *Sefer Chofetz Chaim*. He also authored a companion volume, *Sefer Shemiras HaLashon*, which presents the *hashkafah* (ethical and philosophical concepts) forming the underlying basis for these laws. For decades, however, relatively few people studied these works, and many seemed unaware that the laws of *shemiras halashon* were Biblically mandated and required of everyone.

Then the Manchester *Rosh Yeshivah*, the *gaon* and *tzaddik* Rabbi Yehudah Zev Segal, זצ״ל, appeared on the scene. He instructed his *talmidim* to undertake daily study of both *Sefer Chofetz Chaim* and *Sefer Shemiras HaLashon*, and he composed a daily calendar, whereby these works could be completed thrice annually. Rabbi Segal would quote the Chofetz Chaim, saying that the proliferation of troubles and suffering among the Jewish people in recent times was largely due to the sins of *lashon hara* and *sinas chinam* (baseless hatred). Conversely, he would assure those who sought his blessings and prayers that there are few sources of merit equal to that of *shemiras halashon.*

Rabbi Segal's disciples spread his message so that today, largely due to Rabbi Segal's influence, the Chofetz Chaim's works are studied in Torah communities throughout the world and *shemiras halashon* is no longer what the Chofetz Chaim called a *"meis mitzvah,"* a *mitzvah* which is neglected and even ignored. During the past twenty-five years, a number of works have popularized the concept and made the laws of *shemiras halashon* accessible to the English reader. The first such work was *Guard Your Tongue* by Rabbi Zelig Pliskin. I have had the *zechus* to collaborate on two such works, both of them joint ventures of ArtScroll/Mesorah and the Chofetz Chaim Heritage Foundation: *Chofetz Chaim: A Lesson a Day* and *Chofetz Chaim: A Daily Companion.*

This book, *The Gift of Speech*, presents a new approach to *shemiras halashon* study. It addresses the basic laws of *hilchos lashon hara* and *rechilus* in an easy-to-read style, blending *halachah* and *hashkafah* with real-life illustrations and stories. The book also deals extensively with other crucial speech-related topics such as: *ona'as devarim* (pain caused by hurtful words), *lashon nekiah* (refined speech), truth, the sin of shaming one's fellow, and the power of speech when employed as a *chesed* tool. Finally, it includes a special section on the *mitzvah* of *ahavas Yisrael*, which is the basis for the *mitzvah* of *shemiras halashon*. However, the book is not meant to preclude the study of the aforementioned works, for it does not present a complete digest of the laws of proper speech.

I am hopeful that readers will find the finished product informative, enjoyable and inspiring and that it will serve to strengthen observance of *shemiras halashon* and spread *ahavas Yisrael.* May it inspire us all to utilize our power of speech to help and encourage others, and to be *mekadesh shem Shamayim.*

Acknowledgments

Rabbi Meir Zlotowitz, upon the suggestion of his son, R' Gedaliah, invited me to undertake a project of this nature. I am grateful to him and to Rabbi Nosson Scherman, who read and commented on the manuscript in its early stages, as I experimented to find the correct style and approach. I take this opportunity to thank Rabbi Scherman for always being available to me for advice and guidance, both on a professional and personal level.

My thanks to R' Avrohom Biderman and Mrs. Rivkah Hamaoui for coordinating the various stages of this project; to R' Eli Kroen and Avrohom Kay for the beautiful cover; to Shaya Sonneschein, Mrs. Toby Goldzweig, Ruchy Reinhold, Hindy Goldner, and Esty Weinberg for their typesetting; and to the rest of the ArtScroll staff.

I am deeply grateful to the Lakewood *Mashgiach,* HaRav Matisyahu Salomon, שליט"א, who took the time to read much of the manuscript and graced this work with his מכתב הסכמה וברכה. May the *Ribono shel Olam* grant him good health and long life, so that he can guide and inspire for many years to come.

My appreciation to Rabbi Arye Beer, who read the manuscript for halachic accuracy and offered some important suggestions.

I am fortunate to be associated with outstanding places of *harbatzas Torah*: Yeshivah Darchei Torah, under the leadership of the *Rosh HaYeshivah*, Rabbi Yaakov Bender, and the *Menahel* of the junior high division, Rabbi Raphael Skaist; and Camp Agudah, where I am privileged to serve under its wonderful Director, Meir Frischman; Head Counselor, Rabbi Simcha Kaufman; and Learning Director, Rabbi Naftali H. Basch. May Hashem grant these great *marbitzei Torah* good health, long life and continued success.*

Neither the power of speech nor the written word is adequate to express my appreciation to my parents, שיחיו, for all that they have done for me. May Hashem grant them good health, long life and much *nachas*.

I am eternally grateful to my parents-in-law and I pray for their continued good health. I am especially grateful for their having raised the true *bas Yisrael* whom Hashem chose as the עזר כנגדי. May Hashem grant my wife, Tova, תחי׳, good health, and long life, and may we have the *zechus* to raise our children to lives of Torah, *yiras shamayim* and *shemiras halashon*.

I thank the *Ribono shel Olam* for permitting me to undertake and complete this project. May the *mitzvos* of *shemiras halashon* and *ahavas Yisrael* lead to the imminent redemption of our beleaguered people, בביאת גואל צדק במהרה בימינו, אמן.

Shimon Finkelman

Erev Rosh Chodesh Elul 5760

---

*Please note: The illustrations in this book involving yeshivos or summer camps are purely fictitious, unless otherwise noted.

Chapter One

Word Power

*R*abban Gamliel, one of the great Sages of the Mishnah, served as *Nasi* (President of the Great *Sanhedrin* and leader of his generation) in the period following the Destruction of the Second *Beis HaMikdash*. Once, Rabban Gamliel sent his wise servant Tavi to the market to purchase some good meat. Tavi returned with a piece of tongue. Later, Rabban Gamliel asked Tavi to purchase some meat of inferior quality, and Tavi again returned with some tongue. Tavi explained that he did this to demonstrate an important lesson to the members of the *Nasi's* household: When we use our tongues in a good way, there is nothing better, and when we use our tongues in a bad way, there is nothing worse. This is what Shlomo *HaMelech* had in mind when he said,[1] "Death and life are in the power of the tongue."[2]

Words can build and words can destroy. A kind word can lift

a person's spirits, and sometimes change his entire life for the better. A nasty comment can hurt a person deeply and sometimes leave permanent scars.

ℰ *The "Chazzan" of Shaarei Chesed*

The following story was related by the renowned *tzaddik*, R' Yaakov Meir Shechter of Jerusalem:

In the last years of his life, the great Torah leader R' Dov Beirish Weidenfeld, known as the Tchebiner *Rav*, resided in Jerusalem's quaint Shaarei Chesed neighborhood. A familiar face in Shaarei Chesed was that of a beggar dressed in strange, raggedy clothing, who would make his way from *shul* to *shul* collecting for himself. The man had a loud, coarse voice, but he considered himself a *chazzan* (cantor) and he loved to sing — much to the dismay of everyone else! He had a special tune for "*Yehalelu,*" the verse which is said when the Torah is returned to the *aron kodesh* following the Torah reading. Whenever there was a *chasan* (groom) in *shul* during the week of *sheva berachos*, the beggar would sing his "*Yehalelu*" in honor of the occasion. The children loved every minute of it and would serve as his "back-up choir," while many of the adults would get upset at the disturbance.

One weekday morning as the Torah reading was coming to a close, the beggar entered the *shul* where the Tchebiner *Rav* was praying. The man approached the *tzaddik* and extended his open hand for a donation. The *Rav* said to him, "I usually give you a few coins. Today, however, I will give you a generous donation — but on one condition. When the *sefer Torah* is returned, I want you to sing the '*Yehalelu*' which we all enjoy so much."

The beggar's face broke into a huge smile, as the others looked on in wonder. The man holding the Torah scroll rose and the beggar began to sing. This time, instead of the children laughing and the adults cringing, everyone sang along in a respectful manner. For weeks afterward, the beggar was in high spirits as he related again and again how the Tchebiner *Rav* had requested that he sing. And everyone else marveled at the sensitivity of this Torah genius who, with but a few words, had gladdened the heart of a man whom everyone else shunned.

Yes, words can build.

But words can also destroy.

♭ *When Everyone's a Loser*

In a certain town in Poland more than a century ago, some prominent Jews became angered over something their *rav* had done. They began to speak against the *rav*, while others came to the *rav's* defense. Soon a full-scale feud erupted. The *rav's* opponents gained the upper hand and the *rav* was forced to leave the town. He died shortly thereafter, a man broken in body and spirit. And terrible misfortunes befell those whose wicked words had caused him so much pain.

As time passed, the feud became a thing of the past. But one young man could not forget it. His name was R' Yisrael Meir Kagan, and in years to come, he would become renowned as "the Chofetz Chaim," which is the name of his classic *sefer* on the laws of forbidden speech. In his memoirs, the Chofetz Chaim's son R' Aryeh Leib wrote:

> It was not long after this episode that my father began to involve himself with studying and compiling the laws of *lashon hara* (evil talk) and *rechilus* (gossip). It is my feeling that this episode is what inspired him to shake heaven and earth concerning the terrible evil of forbidden speech which had become widespread.

The Chofetz Chaim had seen firsthand how *lashon hara* can destroy people's lives, and therefore set for himself the enormous task of compiling a *sefer* of laws concerning what a Jew may and may not say. When *Sefer Chofetz Chaim* was first published in 1873, the legendary R' Yisrael Salanter declared,

"Heaven has prepared a leader who will mend the hearts of his fellow Jews and renew their closeness with Hashem."

ℒ Word Disease

"Quarantine" is a word which all of us dread. In the Torah there is only one situation which is similar to quarantine: that of the *metzora,* a person whose skin developed a patch of white skin called *tzaraas.* A *meztora* was quarantined in the sense that he had to live in isolation, away from his fellow Jews. But his disease was not contagious. It was not caused by any bacteria or germ; it was caused, our Sages taught, by a specific sin. Anyone who was innocent of that sin did not contract *tzaraas.*

Isolation was only part of the *metzora's* fate. The *metzora* was *tamei* (impure) with a most severe type of *tumah* (impurity). Anything he touched became *tamei,* anything upon which he sat or lay became *tamei.* If someone entered a room in which the *metzora* was present, the person became *tamei without even touching the metzora.* No other living person could spread *tumah* in this way.

The *metzora's* appearance resembled that of someone who was mourning the death of a close relative. His clothing was torn, his hair was disheveled and his face was partially concealed by his cloak.

If people would approach him, he was to cry out, "I am *tamei,* I am *tamei!*" He did this for two reasons: so that people would not become *tamei* by touching him, and in order for people to pray for him that he should be cured of his *tzaraas.*

Tzaraas was a punishment for speaking *lashon hara,* one of the worst sins in the Torah. In fact, the word מצרע is a contraction of מוֹצִיא שֵׁם רָע, *one who spreads slander.*[3] It was because he had spoken *lashon hara* that the *metzora's* degree of *tumah* was so severe.

And it was because he had spoken *lashon hara* that he needed others to pray for him. For *Zohar* teaches that a *baal lashon hara* (one who speaks *lashon hara* regularly) contaminates his power of speech so that his words of Torah and *tefillah* (prayer) lose their spiritual power. Therefore, until his *teshuvah* (repentance) is accepted by Hashem, his own prayers will do him little good.[4]

⅃ *The Power of One Word*

Picture a *chasan* and *kallah* during the festive *sheva berachos* week following their wedding. It is the happiest time of their lives. Each day, they are the guests of honor at lavish meals, which are highlighted by lively singing and dancing.

On the third day of *sheva berachos,* the *chasan* wakes up and finds a small white patch of skin on his arm. It looks like *tzaraas.* His first thought is, "Oh, no! What about *sheva berachos*? If this is *tzaraas,* then I have to leave the city and go into isolation!"

He is wrong. The *halachah* states that a person does not become a *metzora* unless a *kohen* examines him, determines that the spot is, indeed, *tzaraas* and pronounces the word "*tamei*" ("you are impure") upon the person.

Without the *kohen* saying those two words, the person cannot become a *metzora.* In the case of a *chasan* and *kallah* during the week of *sheva berachos,* the Torah allows the person to postpone his examination by the *kohen* until the *sheva berachos* week has ended. The same applies to any Jew who finds a patch of possible *tzaraas* on his body during the week of *yom tov.*[5]

However, once the *kohen* does examine him, confirms that the spot is *tzaraas* and declares, "*Tamei!*" the *tumah* (state of impurity) descends upon the person and he immediately becomes a *metzora.*

This, says the *Dubno Maggid,*[6] should be a lesson to the *metzora.* He may have spoken *lashon hara* because he fooled himself by thinking, "What's the big deal if I say something negative about someone? I'm not doing anything to him — I'm just saying words!"

The *metzora* learns that words can be very, very powerful, for it is the pronouncement of one word — "*tamei*" — which spells the difference between his remaining pure and his becoming a *metzora.*

Chapter Two

Destruction and Rebuilding

*I*magine that you are living in the holy city of Jerusalem, some nineteen hundred years ago. Reports begin to filter in to the city that a huge contingent of Roman soldiers is advancing on the city, poised for battle. Thousands of Jews rush to join in the defense of their beloved city in which stands the *Beis HaMikdash,* but the situation seems almost hopeless.

Then, an announcement is heard. The *Nasi* has ordered everyone — men, women and children — to assemble in the city square at an appointed time. The moment arrives and tens of thousands fall silent as the *Nasi* steps onto a platform to address the crowd. He begins:

"My fellow Jews: The situation, as you know, is grim. The Roman armies are nearing the city and it is only a matter of time before the siege of Jerusalem will begin. No one will be able to enter or exit the city. Food will grow scarce. And all the while, the Romans will be preparing for the moment when they will breach the wall which surrounds our beloved city. We are vastly outnumbered, both in numbers and in weaponry.

"But hope is not lost! *Even if a sharp sword is resting on your neck, do not despair of Hashem's mercy.*[1]

"The great sages of our generation have informed me that they know which sin is the primary cause of the terrible situation with which we are now faced. It is *sinas chinam,* senseless hatred, which has brought all this upon us. So many of us are guilty of *lashon hara,* so many speak badly of their neighbors and relate gossip to one another. This has caused ill will and bitterness which does not easily fade.

"In the days of the wicked King Achav, the Jews were guilty of terrible sins — yet they were victorious in battle. And why? Because they lived in peace with one another.[2] They enjoyed real unity. But today, there is no unity.

"My fellow Jews: This is what is needed — now, before it is too late. Stop speaking *lashon hara!* Judge your fellow Jew favorably and fill your hearts with *ahavas Yisrael.* Love peace and pursue it.

"This, and only this, can save our city and our precious *Beis HaMikdash* from destruction."

How would you have responded to the *Nasi's* call? Would you have been ready to do what was necessary to save the *Beis HaMikdash* from destruction?

You now have an opportunity to prove yourself.

Our Sages teach that any generation in which the *Beis HaMikdash* is not rebuilt, is considered as if it destroyed the *Beis HaMikdash.*[3] Why is this so? The Chofetz Chaim explains[4] that if the *Beis HaMikdash* has not yet been rebuilt, this means that the *cause* of its destruction — *sinas chinam* — has not yet been corrected. If *lashon hara* and the hatred which it spawns would not be found among the Jewish people, the glorious days of *Mashiach* would already be upon us. Therefore, each generation that does not rid itself of these terrible sins is considered as if it destroyed the *Beis HaMikdash.*

If we truly want to bring an end to this bitter exile and see the

Beis HaMikdash built in our days, then each of us must do his or her best to master the wonderful quality of *shemiras ha-lashon* (guarding one's tongue).

✒ Destroyers of Communism

You might be thinking: Can *I* make a difference? Is what *I* say or refrain from saying really going to make that much of a difference?

Let us study a bit of recent world history.

In 1917, the Russian Revolution brought Lenin and the Communists to power in what became known as the Soviet Union. For the next seventy years, Russia was a giant prison where people lived in constant fear, where the teaching of Torah and *mitzvos* was a serious crime. In the late 1980's Mikhail Gorbachov's rise to power brought a degree of democratic change, though Communism was still the official party line.

In late summer of 1991, an attempt by hardline Communists to overthrow Gorbachov threatened to turn the clock back to the days of the Cold War and possibly lead to war. Instead, the coup failed miserably within days, but it did serve to force Gorbachov to resign, and along with him the Communist regime disappeared. Jews were free to emigrate from Russia and to spread Torah throughout the former Soviet empire.

What was the spark that set off the chain of events which caused a mighty empire to crumble with hardly a gunshot being fired?

Some historians contend that it all started with the Chernobyl nuclear disaster. Aside from the actual death and destruction, the explosion at Chernobyl awakened the Russian people to the truth — the Soviet "paradise" was far, far from perfect and the propaganda which they had been fed for seventy years was nothing but lies.

Others will contend that the fall of Communism began with Gorbachov's miscalculations. His policies gave his countrymen a taste of democracy and once their appetite was whetted, they would not settle for anything less than total freedom.

R' Shimon Schwab, of blessed memory, took a different view. As he explained:

For more than sixty years, Torah Judaism was almost non-existent in the Soviet Union. As the years passed, Soviet synagogues were used only by the aged, who still recalled the days when the Russian landscape was dotted with thriving Torah communities and yeshivos.

Then, in the late 1970's, a small group of *ba'alei teshuvah*, led by a former mathematics professor, Rabbi Eliyahu Essas, sprang up in the heart of Moscow. These young men and women, numbering perhaps a hundred souls, risked arrest, imprisonment or worse, to be taught Torah in secret, to teach others, to perform circumcisions and observe other *mitzvos*.

It was a Thursday evening in 1980. In a Moscow apartment, forty-five young men had gathered for a lesson in the weekly *parashah*. Suddenly, there was a loud knock on the door. Sixteen members of the KGB (secret police) entered the apartment. The *sefarim* were confiscated and each person had to produce identification which was recorded to be kept on file. R' Essas saw the fear on the faces of some of his students. He wanted to encourage his students, but conversation was absolutely forbidden during a KGB "operation. " So he spoke to a KGB agent instead, in a loud, clear voice that could be heard throughout the apartment.

"You must do your job and I cannot change your mind, but remember — our people existed for 3,000 years before you came on the scene and we will continue to exist long after you are gone. And remember one more thing — the heads of the KGB have disappeared one by one, murdered by their successors. So do what you have to do, but do not be arrogant."

The message got through to R' Essas' students. Their faces brightened; hope replaced fear. Two weeks later when the interrogations had ended, forty-three out forty-five students returned for more Torah classes.[5]

R' Schwab maintained that the collective *mesiras nefesh* (self-sacrifice) of these *ba'alei teshuvah* came before the Throne of Glory in Heaven and caused the mighty Soviet empire to crumble.

One hundred brave Jews, willing to make any sacrifice for Torah, are more powerful than a mighty regime which had millions of soldiers and the most deadly weapons of mass destruction at its disposal.

When we think of *mesiras nefesh,* we think of someone willing to risk his very life. R' Gedaliah Schorr, of blessed memory, said that *mesiras nefesh* can also mean *sacrificing one's desires.*[6] When we overcome our personal desires for the sake of a *mitzvah,* we have achieved something of immeasurable value.

ℒ *Points to Ponder*

As we all know, the desire to speak *lashon hara* can, at times, seem irresistible. It is at such times that we need to remember:

- TALMUD YERUSHALMI STATES:
  The study of Torah equals all mitzvos combined and the speaking of lashon hara equals all sins combined.[7]

- THE VILNA GAON[8] QUOTES A MIDRASH:
  For every moment that a Jew refrains from speaking forbidden words, he earns for himself a hidden spiritual light that is beyond anything that anyone — even the Heavenly angels — can fathom.

- THE CHOFETZ CHAIM QUOTES THE HOLY ZOHAR[9]:
  R' Shimon [bar Yochai] said: Of everything is HaKadosh Baruch Hu forgiving — except for lashon hara.

The Chofetz Chaim explains that when a Jew speaks *lashon hara* on this world, he causes Satan to accuse the Jewish people in Heaven. The Chofetz Chaim[10] offers a parable:

The love of a parent towards a child is very deep. This love often impels a father or mother to make allowances for a child's bad behavior. When a parent is forced to rebuke a child for improper behavior, he or she will do it lovingly, with abundant compassion.

However, if someone reports to a parent that he witnessed how the child quarreled with other children over nothing and even embarrassed them, the parent will feel it necessary to deal with the child in a stronger fashion.

Similarly, Hashem, in His infinite wisdom, has decreed that Satan's power to accuse the Jewish people is directly related to how we speak about each other. When we refrain from speaking badly about one another, then Hashem, like a loving father, is willing to overlook our misdeeds. However, when through *lashon hara* we accuse one another of wrongdoing, we cause Hashem to take note of the wrongdoing which Satan has brought before him.

The Chofetz Chaim continues:

> Hashem acts toward the Jewish people in the way that we act toward one another. If Jews live in peace and harmony with one another, then in Heaven, Satan is not able to indict them. When a person restrains himself from speaking *lashon hara* and awakening bad feelings towards his fellow Jew, then in Heaven the Accuser is unable to accuse.

Therefore, a person who controls his urge to speak *lashon hara* has, through his efforts, awakened Heavenly mercy in a very unique way. And when thousands of Jews work to master the precious quality of *shemiras halashon*, their efforts can awaken a flow of mercy which can break terrible decrees and hasten the Final Redemption.

✍ The Board Meeting

In the course of a lifetime, we are faced with many thousands of tests in the area of forbidden speech. Each time that we are successful in not speaking something forbidden, we earn for ourselves immeasurable reward and we bring the Jewish nation one step closer to the glorious days of *Mashiach*.

And as we pass these tests, we become better, happier people. Consider the following:

Your *shul* (synagogue) has outgrown its quarters. There is a large empty lot ten blocks from where the *shul* stands, which would be a perfect site for a new *shul*. The *shul's* board of directors has scheduled a meeting to vote on whether or not they should purchase the property.

You are a member of the board. The night before the vote, you are visited by a close friend who is a member of the *shul*. He gets straight to the point:

"How do you plan to vote tomorrow night?"

"Actually," you tell him, "I'm not in favor of this purchase. The lot is over-priced and the owner refuses to budge."

"Good, good!" your friend exclaims. "As you know, I live right next door to that empty lot. Now, don't get me wrong, I love our *shul*. But I *don't* want all that noise right outside my window. You know what I mean — people coming and going, cars pulling in and out of the parking lot, late night *simchas*...

"I'm asking you as a personal favor. Do your best to convince the other board members to vote against the purchase. Please tell them my feelings on the matter."

At the meeting, you tell your fellow board members why you oppose the sale, and you also mention your friend's feelings. Nevertheless, the board votes to purchase the lot.

The next day, after the results of the vote are made public, you meet your friend who is fuming with rage. He grabs you by the lapel and shouts: "So they voted in favor of it? I bet you they wouldn't have voted for it if *they* were living next door to that lot!

"Tell me who voted in favor of it! Come on, you're my friend — I want to know who's responsible for this!"

You are now faced with a difficult test. If you don't tell your friend the information that he is seeking, he will probably be angry at you. This might cause great harm to your friendship.

On the other hand, you know that *halachah* forbids you to tell him how the voting went. Board meetings of this nature are private matters and have to remain private, unless everyone present would agree to release the details of the meeting.[11]

More importantly, this is a classic case of *rechilus, lashon hara* which causes bad feelings between people. If you were to tell your friend which board members voted in favor of purchasing the lot, he would be angry at those individuals and might possibly confront them directly. This would cause bad feelings on both sides and could even lead to a full-scale feud.

So what do you do?

The right approach would be to tell your friend, "Listen, you know that I like you a lot and I would love to help you in every possible way. But the laws of *shemiras halashon* require me to keep the details of the meeting confidential.

"I realize that you're upset, but believe me, all the board members took your feelings into consideration before making their decision. They *do* feel bad for you, but they felt that the needs of the community outweighed your personal needs. The *shul* is terribly overcrowded and as expensive as the lot is, it seems to be the best we can get right now.

"Please try to understand their point of view."

Words that are spoken sincerely often have their desired effect. If your friend accepts your words and calms down, then you will have accomplished the great *mitzvah* of maintaining peace in your community.

> Know, my son, that peace is a very special quality, for שלום, *Peace,* is one of the Names of Hashem....[12]

And if your friend rejects your words and instead is upset with you for "taking their side," you can rest assured that by not speaking *rechilus,* you have earned Hashem's love and have brought great benefit not only to your community, but to the entire Jewish nation.

ℒ The Manchester Rosh Yeshivah

R' Yehudah Zev Segal, the late Manchester *Rosh Yeshivah,* was one of the greatest *tzaddikim* of our generation. He was also the person most responsible for the world-wide awakening in our days in the crucial area of *shemiras halashon.*

As a young man, R' Segal thought to himself, "The Chofetz Chaim was the leader and the *tzaddik* of the previous generation, and he devoted himself to the cause of *shemiras halashon.* I must emulate his ways."

In time, he came to view spreading *shemiras halashon* awareness as his life's most important work. It was in 1967 that he began printing the now-famous *shemiras halashon luach* (calendar) for daily study of *Sefer Chofetz Chaim and Sefer Shemiras HaLashon.*[13] R' Segal asked to be buried with a *shemiras halashon luach,* saying, "It will be my passport to *Olam HaBa* (the World to Come)."

Over the years, thousands of Jews from all walks of life and from all over the world came to R' Segal for his blessings, advice and encouragement. In almost every instance, he would encourage the person to accept upon himself daily study of the laws of *shemiras halashon.* He would quote the Chofetz Chaim who maintained that the proliferation of troubles and suffering which had befallen the Jewish people, ר"ל, were due in no small measure to widespread speaking of *lashon hara* and the strife which it causes.

R' Segal also maintained that the Chofetz Chaim, who passed away in 5693 (1933), remains close to our generation from his place in Heaven. R' Segal firmly believed that the Chofetz Chaim will intercede in Heaven on behalf of those who study the laws of *shemiras halashon* and strive to live by them.

R' Segal encouraged the forming of *shemiras halashon* groups (called "*Machsom L'fi*" groups) as a source of merit for the sick and others in need of salvation. When R' Segal was to undergo surgery, he made a point of studying from *Sefer Chofetz Chaim* and *Sefer Shemiras HaLashon* prior to the operation.

He related that a man who had recently passed away appeared to his son in a dream and said, "It was dark for me [in the next world], but the merit of *shemiras halashon* illuminated the way."

ℒ *A "Business Proposition"*

R' Segal would spend the summer recess in Semmering, an Austrian resort. One summer, he undertook to personally raise *tzedakah* funds for a very important cause. To virtually everyone he met, he would explain the urgency of the matter and would request a donation.

One day, a stranger arrived from abroad to visit R' Segal. A *talmid* who knew that the man was wealthy informed R' Segal of this. After greeting the visitor and conversing with him a bit, R' Segal said to him, "I have an excellent business proposition to offer you, one in which you can purchase something of great importance." To the *talmid's* disbelief, R' Segal then explained the importance of studying the laws and concepts of *shemiras halashon*. He introduced the man to the *shemiras halashon* calendar and said that by undertaking such daily study, he would be joining a worldwide study program of immeasurable value.

"Will you join the group?" R' Segal asked warmly.

"Yes," the man replied, "I will start as soon as I return home in two weeks."

R' Segal was not satisfied. *Tzaddikim* of earlier generations taught that when a person is inspired to improve, he must act *immediately;* otherwise, the inspiration may wear off and become forgotten. The man explained that he could not begin study without a copy of *Sefer Chofetz Chaim* and a calendar. R' Segal turned to his *talmid.* "We each have a copy of the *sefer* and study together. Let us give one copy to our guest." The *talmid* agreed, but said that they had already distributed all the calendars which they had brought with them from Manchester, except for one which they themselves used.

R' Segal replied, "To help a Jew begin study of *Sefer Chofetz Chaim* is so important that it is worthwhile to take the time to transcribe the calendar schedule for ourselves and give our guest the calendar." And that is what they did.

R' Segal did not discuss fundraising with the man, because he did not want to risk dampening the man's enthusiasm for his "business proposition" of *shemiras halashon* study.

So, in case you are asking yourself: "Can *I* make a difference? Does what *I* say or refrain from saying really have that much significance?" the answer most certainly is, "*Yes!*"

Chapter Three

The Truth Hurts

"He's only out for the *kavod* (honor)."

"He's loaded with money, but from the amount of *tzedakah* he gives, you'd never know it."

"He is absolutely the most boring speaker I have ever heard."

Such statements are *lashon hara* — *though they may be true.* If they are false, then they would be called *hotza'as shem ra* (slander), a more serious form of *lashon hara.* When a person speaks *lashon hara,* he transgresses the commandment of לֹא תֵלֵךְ רָכִיל בְּעַמֶּךְ, *Do not go as a peddler of gossip among your people,*[1] and he transgresses other *mitzvos* as well. The Chofetz Chaim lists a total of *fourteen* מִצְוֹת עֲשֵׂה (positive commandments) and *seventeen* מִצְוֹת לֹא תַעֲשֶׂה (negative commandments) which one may transgress when speaking *lashon hara*. Is it any wonder that our Sages consider *lashon hara* one of the worst sins of all?

You may be wondering: "I can understand why it is wrong to make *false* negative remarks about people. But what could be wrong about saying something which is one hundred percent *true*?"

R' Akiva taught that the *mitzvah* of וְאָהַבְתָּ לְרֵעֲךָ כָּמוֹךָ, *Love your fellow Jew as yourself*,[2] is a "great rule in the Torah."[3] Hillel the Elder explained this rule by saying, "What you find hurtful, do not do to others."[4]

The Chofetz Chaim elaborates:

> Every person is aware of his own faults, but nevertheless he does not want others to know of even a fraction of them. If it should happen that someone discovers a little of his neighbor's faults and tells of it to others, the neighbor will be thinking anxiously, "If only Hashem will cause them to disregard what he said about me and not believe it!" This is because he does not want them to have a bad opinion of him, though he knows that he has many, many more misdeeds than what was reported about him. The great love which a person feels for himself overrides everything else.
>
> Such great love is *exactly* what the Torah wants us to demonstrate towards our fellow Jew, by protecting his honor in all situations.[5]

The Chofetz Chaim therefore states that every time a person speaks *lashon hara,* he transgresses the *mitzvah* of וְאָהַבְתָּ לְרֵעֲךָ כָּמוֹךָ.

⅍ *The Hotel Manager*

When major surgery left R' Yehudah Segal extremely weak, he had no choice but to travel to a resort area to recuperate. A *talmid* brought the *Rosh Yeshivah* to a kosher hotel and stayed to help him unpack, for Rebbetzin Segal had passed away by that time. The *talmid* was not pleased with the room which R' Segal had been assigned. "I hope that the *Rosh Yeshivah* will not regret his coming here," he remarked. Upon being told the name of the hotel manager, the young man said, "No wonder this place is the way it is!"

R' Segal did not understand. He asked the *talmid* if he meant that there might be a problem with the hotel's standard of *kashrus.* "Oh, no," replied the *talmid,* "what I mean is, now that I know who the manager is, I understand why this place is such a mess!" R' Segal did not reply.

He remained at the hotel for only a short while and then accepted this *talmid's* invitation to recuperate at his home. It was there that R' Segal's health began to inprove. As soon as he regained some of his strength, R' Segal called the *talmid* aside for a private talk. Always careful to criticize in a respectful and loving manner, R' Segal took his *talmid's* hand in his own. But before he could say anything, the *talmid* spoke. "I know what the *Rosh Yeshivah* wishes to discuss. I should not have made that remark concerning the hotel manager. It was pure *lashon hara* and I deeply regret it."

℘ See the Good

There is another fundamental reason why it is wrong to speak *lashon hara,* even though the remark is true. One of our main purposes in being in this world is to develop ourselves into *baalei midos,* people of outstanding character. When we focus on the shortcomings of others, we are making use of a bad *midah.* It is the way of fine people to focus on the good qualities of others and to overlook their faults.

R' Avraham Pam, revered *Rosh Yeshivah* of Mesivta Torah Vodaath, often speaks of his mother, who was an exceptionally righteous woman. R' Pam says that to his mother, the sin of *lashon hara* was not much of a test, because she never wanted to see the faults of others; she focused only on the good in people.

Toward the end of the Second World War, a concentration camp prisoner smuggled a *siddur* into his camp. The news spread among the inmates that they could each use the *siddur* for fifteen minutes a day — but for a hefty price. The man wanted one quarter of a day's rations each time that the *siddur* was used.

At that point, the prisoners were little more than skeletons of their former selves. The meager rations which the Nazis gave them were hardly edible and far smaller than what their tortured bodies actually needed. Yet many of these Jews were willing to part with a quarter of their daily rations each day for the opportunity to pray from that *siddur*.

The owner of the *siddur* now had more food than his shrunken digestive system could handle. Soon after he opened his "rental business," he died.

After the war, the legendary *gaon* and hero of rescue R' Eliezer Silver journeyed from America to Europe to visit the Holocaust survivors in the Displaced Persons camps. R' Silver arranged daily *minyanim* (group prayers) and offered his brokenhearted brothers and sisters badly needed encouragement.

One day, it came to R' Silver's attention that a certain man never came to *minyan*. He was told that the man was "angry" about the fact that, during the war, the man with the *siddur* had demanded rations from his fellow prisoners. R' Silver wasted no time in visiting this man.

He found him sitting alone in his barracks, sullen. Placing his hand on the man's shoulder, R' Silver smiled and gently said, "So I hear that you are angry."

The man replied, "Yes, I certainly am angry. Why should I want to pray, or do any other *mitzvah* for that matter, if a Jew could be so cruel?"

"And that is all you have to tell me?" asked R' Silver, who was still smiling.

"Isn't that enough, Rabbi?" the man retorted.

"Oh, you silly man," R' Silver replied. "You look only at that one person! Why don't you look instead at the many Jews who willingly gave away one-fourth of their rations though they were suffering from malnutrition and desperately needed every morsel of food? What *mesiras nefesh* (self-sacrifice)! *Who is like Your people Israel, one nation on earth.*"[6]

The man began attending *minyan* the very next day. Years later, when retelling this story, the man said, "Ever since that encounter with R' Silver, I try to remember that there are two sides to most situations."

ℒ *Nothing New*

"Everyone knows that Daniel positively has the worst temper in the class! In fact, he probably has the worst temper in the school! Actually, it might very well be that he has the worst temper in the world!

"Do you remember the time he struck out with the bases loaded to end the game? He was so mad that he picked up home plate and flung it as far as he could — right through the window of the principal's office! Boy, was that a scene — I don't think any of us will ever forget it!"

The Chofetz Chaim[7] teaches us that it is forbidden to speak badly of someone even when everyone present knows that the information is true and they are not hearing anything new. He quotes the words of *Rabbeinu Yonah*:[8] "The correct way of behavior is to 'cover up' the mistakes which others make and to praise them for the good things they do. *It is the way of fools* to seek out the mistakes of others and to criticize them."

There is another point to consider. In our example, the students should pause for a moment and ask themselves: "Why, indeed, does Daniel have such a ferocious temper?" Quite possibly he was born that way. Of course, this does not excuse his behavior. If he is hot-tempered, then he must work to control this negative *midah* (trait). But the others in the class should ask themselves another question: "How would we have reacted had we been born with Daniel's temper and struck out with the bases loaded to end the game?" With this thought in mind, anyone would think twice before reminding his friends of Daniel's behavior and having a good laugh at his expense.

ॐ A Moment of Victory

A yeshivah *rebbi* told the following story:

It was the first day of yeshivah when Yitzchak (not his real name) had his first temper tantrum. Upset that he had not won a raffle drawing, Yitzchak almost broke a bookcase in the classroom as his classmates looked on in horror.

Over the next few months, there were other situations where Yitzchak lost himself. His *rebbi* would patiently explain to him that every person faces tests in life, and obviously one of Yitzchak's major tests was to learn to control his anger. Yitzchak would listen respectfully, but when something did not go his way, he almost always flew into a rage.

Then it happened.

One day during class, the *rebbi* watched as another student, without being provoked, crumpled a piece of paper and threw it at Yitzchak, hitting him in the face. The *rebbi* braced himself for the "explosion" — which never came. Yitzchak did not react at all.

When class ended, the *rebbi* called Yitzchak aside. "Do you know, Yitzchak, that today was your best day of the year?"

Yitzchak smiled broadly. "I know. He threw that paper at me and I didn't get mad."

"Yitzchak," his *rebbi* replied affectionately, "you have no idea what a great accomplishment this is. You should feel very proud of yourself."

He certainly did.

And in that moment of triumph over his *yetzer hara,* Yitzchak had, quite possibly, achieved something that no one else in his class had yet to achieve.

Chapter Four

The Benefit of the Doubt

I have a friend who happens to be a terrific speaker. Wherever he goes, *shuls,* schools and organizations ask him to address their members.

It happened once that my friend was asked to deliver a *shiur* (lecture) on the weekly *parashah* in a local *shul.* The members of that *shul* are known to be very punctual and my friend was told that the *shiur* was to be begin at 8:00 *sharp.*

But at 8:00 on the appointed evening, my friend was nowhere to be seen. By 8:10, he still had not arrived. A large crowd was in attendance and was getting restless. Some people were upset. What was the matter with this speaker? How could he be so inconsiderate? Didn't he realize that there were many people who had rushed their Shabbos meal so that they would be on time to hear him speak? Was *their* time any less valuable that *his* time?

The organizer of the *shiur* approached the *rav* of the *shul* and asked that he ascend the podium and deliver a *shiur* in place of the missing lecturer. The *rav* obliged and was about to begin speaking when suddenly the door of the *shul* opened and my friend entered — looking tense and worn out. Entering together with him was a middle-aged man who had obvious difficulty walking.

The organizer hurried over. "Rabbi, where have you been? We were about to start without you!"

My friend explained: "Believe me, it is not my habit to come late to a speaking engagement. I hurried my meal and left myself twenty-five minutes for the fifteen-minute walk to your *shul*.

"Did you notice the middle-aged man who came in with me? He is my guest for Shabbos. He has great difficulty walking and I was sure that he would not want to make the long walk to hear me speak tonight. But when I mentioned the *shiur,* he insisted on coming along! I knew that this would make the walk take at least twice as long, but I had no choice. He would have felt terrible had I told him that he could not accompany me."

Quite often, *lashon hara* results from our failure to judge a fellow Jew favorably. It is a מִצְוַת עֲשֵׂה (positive commandment) to give a person the benefit of the doubt in a situation where his actions can be interpreted either positively or negatively. As the Torah states, בְּצֶדֶק תִּשְׁפֹּט עֲמִיתֶךָ, *Judge your fellow with righteousness*[1] which means הֱוֵי דָן אֶת חֲבֵרְךָ לְכַף זְכוּת, *Judge your friend toward the scale of merit,* that is, give him the benefit of the doubt.[2]

In the above true story, those assembled in *shul* were required by the Torah to give the speaker the benefit of the doubt as the minutes ticked by and he did not appear. Those who spoke critically of him were guilty of speaking *lashon hara* and also transgressed the requirement to be דָן לְכַף זְכוּת.

℘ *A Special Worker*

Our Sages relate the following amazing story:[3]
A Jew from Upper Galilee in northern Israel hired himself out

for three years to a landowner in the south. At the end of the three years, the day before Yom Kippur, the worker asked for his wages so that he could return home and feed his family.

His employer responded: "I have no money."

"Then pay me with fruit," said the worker.

"I have none," came the reply.

"Pay me with land."

"I have none."

"Pay me with livestock."

"I have none."

"Pay me with pillows and blankets."

"I have none."

The worker slung his pack over his shoulder and headed home, deeply disappointed.

When Succos ended, the landowner appeared at his worker's door with full payment for the three years of work, along with three donkeys laden with food, drink and delicacies. The food was brought inside and the two enjoyed a hearty meal together.

When the meal was over and the worker had received his money, the landowner asked him, "When you asked for your earnings and I replied that I had no money, what did you think?"

The worker replied, "I thought that perhaps a deal that you could not pass up had come along and you had used all your cash for that."

"And when I said that I had no land?"

"I thought that perhaps all your land had been leased to others."

"And when I said that I had no fruit?"

"I thought that perhaps you had not had an opportunity to separate *terumos* and *maasros* from your fruits."

"And when I said that I had no pillows and blankets?"

"I thought that perhaps you had dedicated all your possessions to the *Beis HaMikdash*."

The landowner exclaimed, "I make an oath that that is exactly what happened! ... Just as you judged me favorably, so too should Hashem judge you favorably."

Who was this wonderful worker and who was his employer? Our Sages say that the worker was Rabbi Akiva and his employer was Rabbi Eliezer ben Hurkanos.[4] Rabbi Akiva began to study Torah at age forty; this story took place when he was still ignorant of Torah knowledge. As the *Chasam Sofer* points out, we see from this story that even before he began to study Torah, Rabbi Akiva possessed exceptional *midos*. No doubt, Rabbi Akiva's sterling character had a lot to do with his becoming the greatest Torah sage of his generation and one of the greatest of all time. Good character is the foundation upon which one can grow in Torah. In *Pirkei Avos*,[5] the Sages list forty-eight qualities which one needs to make Torah a part of his being. In the words of R' Aharon Kotler,[6] "To attempt to acquire Torah without these qualities ...accomplishes nothing."

✒ Surprise

As we saw in the above story, judging others favorably is not always easy. Many would have found it hard to believe that the landowner, Rabbi Eliezer ben Hurkanos, had actually used up his available cash, leased all his property, dedicated his possessions to the *Beis HaMikdash* and been unable to separate *terumos* and *maasros* from his fruits and vegetables. But that is exactly what had happened and his worker, Akiva ben Yosef, passed a great test in accepting his claims as truth.

We should always bear in mind that in the course of life, the strangest and most unlikely things can sometimes happen.

In Yeshivah Darchei Torah, an eighth grade student once accused his classmate of stealing his snack. Circumstances seemed to indicate that the accusation was valid — until someone noticed a squirrel with the bag of snack hanging from its mouth.[7]

Rabbi Avraham Pam related a true story which happened in a first grade class. A child was missing a toy which he had brought to school that day. The next day, another boy in the class returned the toy, claiming that he had been surprised to find it in his knapsack! This boy adamantly insisted that he had not stolen the toy and that he had no idea how it had found its way into his knapsack — but of course, no one believed him. How, everyone wondered, could the toy have ended up in his knapsack if he had not stolen it?

A long time passed before the truth was discovered. A third boy had stolen the toy. As soon as he came home from school, he regretted what he had done, but he was too ashamed to admit his guilt. He decided to return the toy without having to face the *rebbi* or the toy's owner. The next day, when he was sure that no one was looking, he went over to a knapsack lying in a corner of the room and stuffed the toy into it. When the owner of that knapsack returned the toy to its owner, he was fulfilling the *mitzvah* of *hashavas aveidah* (returning a lost object), while everyone was accusing him of being a thief.

ℒ *A Case in Point*

As we will learn in detail in forthcoming chapters, the Torah forbids us to listen to *lashon hara* and to accept it as fact. Therefore, if someone tells you of an incident which, according to his interpretation, casts someone in a bad light, it is forbidden to believe his interpretation.

The Chofetz Chaim illustrates this law with the following case[8]:

Reuven is walking down the street when he meets Shimon, who is extremely upset. Shimon has just been declared the loser in a *din Torah* (court case) against Levi. Shimon tells the details of the case to Reuven and says, "Did you ever hear something so ridiculous in all your life? It is obvious that I should have won! These *dayanim* (judges) don't know what they're doing! I'm sure that in any other *beis din* (Jewish court) I would have won."

Reuven must tell himself that no matter how convincing Shimon may sound, he is wrong. *Dayanim* are fair, responsible Torah scholars and are surely qualified to judge the cases which are presented to them. It is Shimon's personal interests which are blinding him from seeing the truth. Reuven should attempt to convince Shimon of this. He should also gently reprimand Shimon for speaking disrespectfully of *talmidei chachamim*.

If Reuven agrees with Shimon and sympathizes with his cause, then he is guilty of accepting *lashon hara* and of not giving the judges the benefit of the doubt. In this case, the sin is particularly severe since the judges are *talmidei chachamim*.

✐ Measure for Measure

At the conclusion of the story involving Rabbi Akiva and Rabbi Eliezer ben Hurkanos, Rabbi Eliezer told his worker, "Just as you judged me favorably, so too should Hashem judge you favorably." The Talmud actually introduces this story with the statement: "Whoever judges others favorably will be judged favorably [by Heaven]."[9]

What does the Talmud mean by saying that Hashem will judge us favorably? Certainly it *does not* mean that Hashem will ignore our sins.

It means that in the merit of our having judged others generously, Hashem will judge us with an abundance of mercy. If our *mitzvos* are less than perfect or if we are guilty of wrongdoing, Hashem will take into account any possible factor in our favor. But if we fail to give others the benefit of the doubt and instead we choose to judge them strictly, then in Heaven, we will be judged accordingly.

On the other hand, R' Avraham Pam points out[10] that when a person does *not* give others the benefit of the doubt, he actually gives Satan power to testify against them in Heaven. When one Jew says of another, "He did something terrible — a real disgrace. He should not be allowed to get away with it..." he is like a prosecutor against the person and his words have a powerful impact in Heaven.

The Chofetz Chaim observed: No G-d-fearing Jew would dream of voluntarily offering incriminating information before the authorities about another Jew. A person who would do such a thing would be scorned and despised by everyone. How, then, can a person "inform" against his fellow Jew before the Heavenly Court by judging him critically and speaking badly of him?

Giving others the benefit of the doubt is good for others and good for ourselves. And it is a crucial *midah* for anyone who seeks to acquire the precious quality of *shemiras halashon*.

Chapter Five

A Shameful Mistake

"Shlomo has the worst voice of anyone in the choir."

"You know, Yaakov, you really shouldn't have said that. It's *lashon hara.*"

"Why is it *lashon hara?* I would have said it even if Shlomo were standing right here. He knows that he has no business being in the choir!"

Yaakov is absolutely wrong. The fact that he would have uttered his derogatory statement in Shlomo's presence does not remove it from the category of *lashon hara.* In fact, had he said it to others in Shlomo's presence, he would have been guilty not only of *lashon hara,* but also of shaming his fellow Jew, a most serious sin. And had he uttered the statement *to a group of three* in Shlomo's presence, he would have been guilty of shaming a Jew in public. "One who humiliates his fellow in public...though he may have Torah and good deeds, he has no share in the World to Come."[1]

In *Parashas Vayeishev,* the Torah tells the story of Yehudah and Tamar. Tamar was willing to die rather than cause Yehudah embarrassment. Our Sages derive from this, "It is preferable that a person allow himself to be cast into a fiery furnace, rather than embarrass his friend in public."[2] *Rabbeinu Yonah* writes[3] that embarrassing someone, which causes a person's face to become drained of its blood,[4] is actually related to the cardinal sin of murder. *Rabbeinu Yonah* adds: "*The pain of embarrassment is more bitter than death.*" The reason for this may be that the shame of embarrassment can last for a very long time — in some instances, it can last forever.

✢ A Reason to Weep

Someone once found R' Yisrael Chaim Kaplan, who served as *Mashgiach* in Bais Medrash Elyon, weeping uncontrollably. The person asked R' Yisrael Chaim what was wrong, but for a long time, the *Mashgiach* was unable to respond. Finally, R' Yisrael Chaim wiped the tears from his eyes and said:

"Wouldn't you cry if you saw a Jew commit murder? Well, the *Gemara* likens embarrassing someone to murdering him — and I just witnessed how one Jew embarrassed another. Is that not reason to cry?"

The Chofetz Chaim writes that children should be taught from their early youth about the terrible severity of the sin of *lashon hara.* "The reason why the bitter sin of *lashon hara* is so widespread is that children become accustomed to saying whatever they want [concerning others] without a word of protest [by their parents and teachers]. It never enters the children's minds that they are doing anything wrong. When they get older and are told that such talk is forbidden, they find it hard to change their bad habits.

"This would not be the case if their parents would train them when they are young not to speak against *any* Jew. Then, this *mitzvah* would become implanted in them and they would find it easy to be careful about *lashon hara* as they grow older. And through this, they would merit blessing in this world and the Next."[5]

The Manchester Rosh Yeshivah maintained that the same applies to embarrassing others. If, from their early youth, children would be taught the severity of embarrassing someone, and that our Sages liken this to murder, they would grow up with the firm resolve never to embarrass another Jew.

ꙮ *Tea, Anyone?*

It was the custom of R' Yehoshua Leib Diskin to deliver a *shiur* in his Jerusalem home on *Motzaei Shabbos* to a small circle of *talmidim*. *Rebbetzin* Diskin would serve tea before the *shiur* began.

Once, on a *Motzaei Shabbos* shortly after Pesach, a student brought out a pitcher of tea and served everyone. Then he returned to the kitchen, came out carrying a sugar bowl, and placed a few teaspoons of the white, granular substance into R' Yehoshua Leib's tea. R' Yehoshua Leib suffered from low blood sugar and it was important that he have a generous serving of sugar with his nightly drink.

In the middle of the *shiur*, the *Rebbetzin* rushed into the room and gasped upon seeing that her husband's glass was more than half empty. R' Yehoshua Leib, however, calmed her by saying, "Everything is fine."

After the *shiur* ended, a *talmid* entered the kitchen and inquired about the *Rebbetzin's* dismay. She explained:

"I had put on the counter a white bag of coarse Passover salt. That bag looks very much like the sugar bags that we use all year. I had thought that the *talmid* who did the serving tonight had mistakenly filled the sugar bowl with salt. When I saw that the *Rav* had already drunk half of his tea, I became alarmed. However, he told me that 'everything is fine,' meaning that the tea did, in fact, contain sugar and not salt."

Hearing this explanation, the *talmid* went into the dining room and picked up R' Yehoshua Leib's glass, which had only a few droplets of tea remaining. The *talmid* tasted the droplets and spat them out — they tasted heavily of salt. The *Rebbetzin's* fear had been correct after all.

Later, R' Yehoshua Leib was asked why he had drunk the tea when it had tasted so awful and was actually quite unhealthy. The *tzaddik* replied simply, "Because had I not drunk the tea, the mistake would have been discovered and my *talmid* would have been embarrassed — '*It is preferable that a person allow himself to be cast into a fiery furnace, rather than embarrass his friend in public.*'"

✍ *A Time to be Silent*

As we all know, being a *ba'al kriah* (one who reads from the Torah at the public reading) can be a very daunting task. The *ba'al kriah* must be fluent in the correct pronunciation of the words as well as the *trop* (cantillations). Even the most experienced and well-prepared *ba'alei kriah* occasionally make mistakes.

What is the *halachah* regarding what to do when a *ba'al kriah* makes a mistake? In situations where the pronunciation is slightly changed, but the word is essentially unchanged (such as reading אֶת for אֵת), the *ba'al kriah* should not be corrected. Where the mistake has changed the meaning of the word, the *ba'al kriah* should be corrected. However, this does not mean that everyone in the *shul* has to shout the correction. This can cause unnecessary embarrassment to the *ba'al kriah*. It is sufficient for the *rav* or *gabbai* to correct the mistake. Of course, if someone thinks that he heard a serious mistake which has not been corrected, he can approach the *bimah* and bring the matter to the *ba'al kriah's* attention.

In a certain *shul* one Shabbos, the *ba'al kriah* made a mistake — and from all sides of the room people shouted their correction. The *ba'al kriah* became flustered and made the same mistake again. Again, people shouted the correct word, and one person laughed loud enough for everyone —including the *ba'al kriah* — to hear.

By now, the mistake is long forgotten. But in Heaven, that man's laughter cannot be forgotten, unless he seeks the *ba'al kriah's* forgiveness and is granted it.

Tur[6] cites the opinion of *Sefer HaManhig* (an early commentator) that one should *never* correct a *ba'al kriah* because this will cause him embarrassment. While this is not the accepted *halachah*, *Sefer HaManhig's* opinion shows us how careful we must be not to cause a *ba'al kriah* — or anyone else — unnecessary embarrassment.

ℒ *Reb Yaakov's Concern*

R' Yaakov Kamenetsky, a leader of Torah Jewry until his passing in 5746 (1986), once attended a Shabbos bar mitzvah where the bar mitzvah boy had a difficult time with the Torah reading. In the middle of the reading, R' Yaakov had to briefly leave the *shul*. When he returned, he was asked if he wanted the portion to be read again from the point where he had left. R' Yaakov declined this offer, out of concern that the bar mitzvah boy would think that he was being asked to read the portion again because he had read it poorly the first time. *Krias HaTorah* (the public Torah reading) is a Rabbinic *mitzvah,* but the requirement that we not cause hurt or embarrassment to our fellow Jew is mandated by the Torah.

ℒ *No Strength to Shame*

A Torah scholar living in Eretz Yisrael related a story from his youth:

> Once, my study partner and I found a difficulty in a *Tosafos,* based on a *Gemara* which we had studied together. After discussing the difficulty and being unable to

resolve it, we decided to present our question to the Chazon Ish.[7] My partner remained in the *beis midrash* while I hurried to the Chazon Ish's home.

Soon, I found myself in his room. The Chazon Ish appeared weak; he was lying in bed engrossed in Torah study. I told him my name, the yeshivah in which I was studying, and I presented our question. The Chazon Ish looked at me, then sat himself up and finally, stood up. He lifted his frail hand and rested it upon my shoulder and together, we proceeded to 'stroll' across the room.

He asked me: "Suppose *Tosafos* would have used the two words _____ and _____ instead of the words which you have quoted — would your difficulty remain?" And he continued to walk with me, despite his obvious weakness.

I mulled over his response and said, "True, if *Tosafos* had used those words, there would be no difficulty at all — but this itself is perplexing! Why didn't *Tosafos* express itself in this way?"

I had the audacity to ask if I could withdraw a *gemara* from the bookcase, to confirm that I had quoted *Tosafos* correctly. But the Chazon Ish stopped me. "I have no more strength..." he explained.

I thanked him and with a parting "*Shalom,*" took leave of him.

As I walked home, I thought how unfortunate it was that the Chazon Ish's weakened condition prevented him from answering my question...

Later, when I examined the *Tosafos* again, I found that its wording was *exactly* as the Chazon Ish had suggested — I had misquoted it! I then realized that when the Chazon Ish said, "I have no strength," he really meant that he had no strength to cause me embarrassment.

Chapter Six

Painful Words

I n the previous chapter, we learned that not only is saying *lashon hara* in the subject's presence forbidden, it also involves an additional sin of causing the person embarrassment.

There is another serious sin which comes into play when the subject of one's *lashon hara* is present. The Torah warns us: וְלֹא תוֹנוּ אִישׁ אֶת עֲמִיתוֹ, *A man shall not cause hurt to his fellow,*[1] which is referring to *ona'as devarim,* pain caused by hurtful words. Any time we tell someone something that hurts his feelings, we have transgressed a *mitzvah* of the Torah.

The Chofetz Chaim[2] offers the following examples of *ona'as devarim:* mentioning someone's past sins or mistakes; mentioning an embarrassing fact of his family history; saying that he "hardly knows how to learn [Torah];" or that he is inept at his work. In fact, the list of examples is endless. Telling someone,

"You can't hit a baseball to save your life"; "No one values your opinion"; "Your new coat looks like a 'hand-me-down'"; and countless other hurtful comments, all fall within the category of *ona'as devarim*.

One point about *ona'as devarim* cannot be stressed enough. It is a sin to hurt someone's feelings with words *even in private, when only the speaker and the subject are present*. In such a case, the words would not be considered *lashon hara*, but they would be in the category of *ona'as devarim*.

Consider this: It is suppertime in yeshivah and the cook is dishing out that night's main course — breaded turkey roll. As he offers one boy his portion, the student pulls his tray back and says, "No, thank you. I can't eat 'hockey pucks' — they're too hard to chew." This student has undoubtedly hurt the cook's feelings and is guilty of *ona'as devarim*. If there were other students on line who heard the comment and smiled, then the speaker was also guilty of speaking *lashon hara* and of causing embarrassment.

In the Manchester Yeshivah, a few *talmidim* complained to their *rebbi*, R' Yehudah Zev Segal, about the quality of the food. R' Segal responded that the cook was a widow and it is a severe sin to cause a widow any sort of pain or distress.[3] He implored the boys not to say another word about the matter, and they heeded his request.

In that incident, the students had not said a word to the cook. They understood on their own that any comment which they would have made could have hurt her feelings — and they wanted to avoid this. They had brought the matter to R' Segal in the hope that he would speak to her, in his kind and gentle way. Because she was a widow, R' Segal refused to do this.

❧ *"I Didn't Mean it"*

In *All for the Boss*,[4] Ruchoma Shain's inspiring biography of her father, R' Yaakov Yosef Herman, a story teaches us how serious a matter is *ona'as devarim*.

For a time after R' Yaakov Yosef's wife passed away, a relative lived with him in his Jerusalem apartment. One night, R' Yaakov Yosef had difficulty falling asleep, which for him was most unusual. He was a person who weighed his every action and word, and he was sure that if he could not fall asleep, then something wrong must have happened that day. He lay in bed thinking, trying to discover the source of the problem, but he came up with nothing. Finally, he saw no choice but to awaken his companion.

"What happened here today?" he asked his sleepy relative.

"Nothing, nothing at all."

"Did anyone visit today?"

"Yes, your grandson Avremal."

"Did anything happen during his visit?"

"Not really."

"Tell me the truth," R' Yaakov Yosef pressed. "Did anything at all happen while Avremal was here?"

"Well, nothing really terrible. Avremal and I had a bit of an argument, and I told him that he should not come here any more — but I didn't mean it; it was just a joke!"

R' Yaakov Yosef was extremely disturbed by this. "Get dressed," he instructed. "Though Avremal is already married, we must not forget that he is an orphan. [His mother died when he was a boy.] You may have hurt his feelings. We will go to his house now and you will ask him forgiveness."

"But it's the middle of the night!" the relative protested. "Avremal is surely asleep — I will go to speak with him first thing in the morning. I'm sure that he did not take me seriously."

But R' Yaakov Yosef was adamant. "When a wrong is committed it must be corrected immediately. We are going now."

They walked through the quiet Jerusalem streets until they arrived at the apartment complex where Avremal lived. Looking up at the windows of his third-floor apartment, they saw that a light was on in his dining room.

They climbed the stairs and R' Yaakov Yosef knocked softly on the door. Avremal opened the door and exclaimed, "*Zeidy* (Grandfather), what are you doing here in the middle of the night?"

"And what are *you* doing up in the middle of the night?" R' Yaakov Yosef responded.

"I could not sleep; something was troubling me," said Avremal.

R' Yaakov Yosef then motioned to his relative, who had been standing in the hallway, out of view. The man rushed in to the apartment and exclaimed, "Avremal, surely you did not take me seriously when I said that you were not welcome any longer in your *zeidy's* apartment. If you did take me seriously, please forgive me." Avremal forgave him.

Turning to his grandfather, Avremal said with deep emotion, "*Zeidy,* you have lifted a heavy weight from my heart. I could not imagine that I would not be welcome in your house, where I grew up."

R' Yaakov Yosef and his companion returned home. As soon as R' Yaakov Yosef returned to his bed, he fell asleep.

✒ *Practical Jokes*

"Devorah, there is a spider crawling up your sleeve!"

"Aaaaah! Get it off of me!"

"April Fools! Just kidding."

"April Fools' Day" may be an American custom, but it has no place in Torah life. Jokes are fine, as long as no one is hurt by them.

In *Teshuvos Chasam Sofer*[5], written by the nineteenth-century Torah giant, R' Moshe Sofer of Pressberg (Hungary), we find an unfortunate case involving a practical joke:

A man who happened to be a *shochet* (ritual slaughterer) approached a distinguished person who was renowned as a *mohel* (one who performs circumcisions) and said, "*Mazal tov*! My wife had a baby boy!"

The other man wished the *shochet* "*Mazal tov*" and was then told, "Well, it is my honor to ask you to serve as *mohel* at my son's *bris*." The invitation was accepted and the man was told the time and place of the *bris*.

On the appointed day, the *mohel* headed for his destination. The wagon ride took over an hour. When he reached the neighborhood where the *shochet* lived, he asked for directions to the *bris* — but the townspeople did not know what he was talking about. The *shochet's* wife, they insisted, had given birth to a girl, not a boy!

The *mohel* found his way to the *shochet's* house and demanded an explanation. The *shochet's* response was quite shocking: "Wasn't that a good joke?!" The *rav* of the city didn't think so, and he wasted no time in writing to the *Chasam Sofer* to ask how to deal with the *shochet*.

The *Chasam Sofer* responded: According to the letter of the law, the *shochet* should be liable to pay for hiring the man as a *mohel* and for the *mohel's* traveling expenses. He also should have been severely penalized in other ways, but the Austro-Hungarian empire did not allow Jewish courts that degree of power.

However, the *Chasam Sofer* concluded, there was one thing that the *rav* could and should do: because the *shochet* brazenly transgressed the sin of *ona'as devarim*, he should be removed from his position as *shochet* until he sought forgiveness of the *mohel* and was granted it.

To become a *shochet*, he had surely achieved an impressive level of Torah knowledge. Nevertheless, he was not fit to provide his fellow Jews with kosher meat as long as his *neshamah* was stained by the hurt and humiliation which he had caused his fellow Jew.

❦ Sensitive Souls

Remarks that are fine when said to one individual may be in the realm of *ona'as devarim* when said to someone else.

For example: There is nothing wrong with a boy letting his bunkmates know how much he looks forward to seeing his father and mother on Visiting Day. But if one of his bunkmates is an orphan, such remarks can be very painful to him. To make such a remark in his presence might be *ona'as devarim*, along with the additional serious sin of causing pain to an orphan.[6]

Similarly, a woman can excitedly tell everyone about the new baby clothes she purchased for her daughter, without taking into account that one of the women listening to her has been married for many years and does not have children. Or, a man can be discussing the "problem" of having more business than he can handle, without considering that one of his listeners is currently unemployed. Such remarks can cause enormous pain to those who are sensitive to them.

Some might argue that it is hard to be so careful in conversation. "I forgot that he doesn't have a father," the camper in our first example might argue. "I didn't think that my remark would offend her," the woman in our second example might contend. "I had forgotten that he was unemployed," the man in the third example might say. True, we are only human and we do make mistakes, especially in conversation. Nevertheless, we should always be on the alert for situations such as the ones which we have described.

The great people among us *are* on the alert. In their lifelong striving to follow in the ways of Hashem, Who is All-Merciful, they are careful not to say anything which might, inadvertently, cause someone emotional pain.

Once, R' Yehudah Zev Segal was attending a *sheva berachos* meal when he was asked to come to the phone. On the other end was a young woman who had been trying unsuccessfully for many years to find her *zivug* (marriage partner). R' Segal was asked if he would offer the woman his blessings. "Certainly," he replied, "but please direct me to an extension in another room. There is lively singing going on in this room, and I am afraid that if the woman will hear these sounds of joy in the background, it will make her feel worse about her own situation."

R' Yitzchak Hutner, late *Rosh Yeshivah* of Mesivta Rabbi Chaim Berlin, developed a close relationship with scores of his *talmidim*, many of whom would call to share good news with their *rebbi*. R' Hutner would rejoice with them like a father.

Once, a *talmid* called with the news that his wife had just given birth to a baby girl. To the *talmid's* surprise, R' Hutner did not respond with the customary *"Mazal tov"* wish. "Yes, call me back in fifteen minutes," was all he said.

When the *talmid* called back, R' Hutner explained: "When you called before, I had a visitor with me who is childless after many years of marriage. Had I rejoiced with you in his presence, he might have felt bad about his own situation. Now, however, I am alone. *Mazal tov!*"

ℒ *Thoughtful Silence*

I once saw firsthand that a "plain person" is capable of great sensitivity in conversation.

It was during a summer in Camp Agudah when a staff member approached me and asked, "How recently have you seen your brother?" "I last saw him in the city before camp opened," I replied. "Why do you ask?" I queried.

"Oh, no particular reason," was the fellow's reply.

Later that day, another staff member met me and exclaimed, "I saw your brother in Shop-Rite today — did he stop by to visit?" I replied that he had not stopped by.

The first staff member had overheard this exchange. He approached me after the second fellow had left and said, "I also met your brother in Shop-Rite and I was curious to know whether he had stopped by in camp. But I didn't tell you, on the chance that he had not visited you and you might feel bad about it. So I simply asked you when you had seen him last." I thanked him for being so considerate and assured him that my brother was almost certainly limited by time, and this is why he had not stopped by to visit.

The next time my brother and I met, I related the episode to him. My explanation as to why he had not stopped by had been correct. He agreed, as did everyone to whom I have told this story, that the sensitivity which the staff member showed is something from which we all can learn.

R' Yisrael Salanter pointed out that certain *midos* (character traits) are only good when directed toward oneself, but not towards others. For example, we should "be happy with our lot" and not run after materialism, but if we see that a formerly rich man is distressed over his loss of previous honor and comfort, we should provide him with this to the best of our ability. We should flee from honor, but we should honor others at every opportunity.

Similarly, we should exercise great caution when speaking to others, and be careful not to say things which might hurt their feelings. However, if someone says something hurtful to us, we should overlook it and not bear a grudge.

R' Avraham Pam explains[7] how this can be done. "Love covers over all offenses."[8] A sign of love for one's fellow Jew is the overlooking of his wrongs, to the point where they seem to be non-existent. When there is love among people, it is easy to find merit for others and it is difficult to find fault.

At times, one is offended by his friend's words though his friend meant no harm; rather, he is quick-lipped and he talks without thinking. Amid his torrent of speech are words which hurt and insult, though he does not realize it.

Sometimes a person becomes enraged and yells, and you wonder: "What happened to this person that he pounces upon people over nothing?" It is quite possible, says R' Pam, that he is immersed in pain or worry and out of bitterness of heart, he is not in control of his emotions. Our Sages have taught, "A person cannot be held accountable when he is in pain."[9]

In our day, many people are, unfortunately, preoccupied with personal worry and pain which weigh heavily upon their hearts. Because of this, they are liable, from time to time, to do things which should not be done or to say things which should not be said. Very often, when they calm down, they regret their conduct and are pained by what they did or said.

R' Pam concludes that whoever gives serious thought to this will find it within himself to overlook harsh words which are directed his way.

Chapter Seven

Put-downs

There was a time not too long ago in America when an election race for public office was a dignified battle, in which each candidate tried his best to convince the people that his ideas and vision would lead them to a glorious future. Unfortunately, this is rarely the case today. Instead, candidates regularly engage in "mudslinging," hurling insults and finding every opportunity to ridicule and criticize one another.

Why must they do this? Why do they find it necessary to resort to such tactics, which cause the average citizen to view politics with little more than disgust? One reason is that many of these politicians are people of low character; no trick or gimmick is too low to employ, if it can get them elected.

But there is another reason for this sad state of affairs. If a candidate really has "a product to sell," meaning that he is a man of impeccable character and his ideas are exciting and original, then he should not have to resort to put-downs. It is when he actually has very little to offer the people that he will find it necessary to resort to mudslinging.

The same applies to the world of business. If a salesman has a product of genuinely high quality, then to sell it, he merely has to explain its true value. But if his product is actually cheap and flawed, then he may resort to "knocking" whatever the competition has to offer.

✒ Trust in Hashem

The Chofetz Chaim informs us that just as it is forbidden to speak badly of a person, so too, it is forbidden to speak badly of his merchandise. He adds, "To our misfortune, it is very common for a storekeeper to degrade the merchandise of his competitor or to engage in similar practices out of jealousy — and this is full-fledged *lashon hara* which the Torah prohibits."[1]

While the Chofetz Chaim identifies jealousy as the root cause of this bad business practice, it is certainly not the only factor. Quite often, it is the merchant's fear that the competition will deprive him of business and cause him a loss of income.

As we have mentioned, if a merchant is suffering a loss of business, it may be because his own product is inferior. If that is the case, then the proper course of action is to improve his product, and *not* to degrade his competition's item.

If his product is not inferior, then he should place his trust in Hashem, Who decrees on Rosh Hashanah exactly how much we will earn in the coming year. A Jew who has true *bitachon* (trust) knows that spreading bad information about one's competition will not earn him one additional cent.[2]

✒ The Right Approach

R' Yitzchak Silberstein, distinguished *Rav* of Ramat Elchonon in Bnei Brak, related the following story:

In the days when Bnei Brak was still a small, developing community, a G-d-fearing man opened a publishing company there for the publication of *sefarim*. There was little competition in those days and his business prospered. After a few years, a second publishing firm opened only a block or two away. The children of the first publisher were incensed by this — but the publisher himself was not incensed at all. In fact, he made his way to the new publishing house, greeted the owner warmly and said:

"You are new in the neighborhood and you do not have any knowledge of whom to seek as customers. Let me share my customer list with you." And he proceeded to name a long list of customers.

"Are you familiar with the printing machinery?" he then asked. "If not, I will be more than happy to show you how everything works." The other man was new to the publishing business and he gratefully accepted the man's offer. For the next hour, the experienced publisher taught the tools of the trade to his competitor.

Later, the man's children asked him, "We can well understand why you did not take any action *against* him — but why did you have to help him?"

Their father replied, "You agree, of course, that whatever we are to earn is decreed in Heaven. One person cannot deprive another of *one cent* that has been decreed for him. Therefore, whatever I did today to assist that man will not cause me any loss of income.

"We all know that this true — but the trick is to *feel* that it is true and to live by it."[3]

ℒ The Ravages of Jealousy

The Chofetz Chaim stated that jealousy is a primary cause of maligning a competitor's merchandise. Jealousy can cause a person to do horrible things. This lesson is taught at the very beginning of the Torah: Kayin was jealous that the offering of his brother Hevel was accepted by Hashem while his own offering was rejected.[4] This led to Kayin's murder of Hevel.

Jealously can lead to a different type of murder, that of "*character* assassination*,*" where a person seeks to destroy the reputation of the person of whom he is jealous.

There is a well-known story involving the author of *Sdei Chemed*, R' Chizkiyahu Medini. As a young man, he was falsely accused of having physically attacked someone. Ultimately, the accusations were silenced and R' Chizkiyahu gained renown as one of the greatest *tzaddikim* of his day. According to one version of the story, the man who was responsible for the slander was motivated by jealousy, for R' Chizkiyahu was the most respected and beloved young scholar in his community. The slanderer died suddenly at a young age soon after the accusations against R' Chizkiyahu were publicized.

R' Elazar HaKapar said: Jealousy, physical desires and [a passion for] honor can take a person out of this world.[5]

Of course, such cases are extreme. Nevertheless, jealousy is certainly a major cause of *lashon hara*, one of the most severe sins of all. People who are jealous of others will often look for every opportunity to point out their mistakes and weaknesses.

If they will not gloat openly over the mistakes of their "enemies," they will at least rejoice inwardly when they stumble. This, too, is a sin.

ℒ *The Prayer of R' Nechunia*

The Talmud relates that R' Nechunia ben HaKanah would recite a short *tefillah* upon entering the *beis midrash* to study Torah, and upon exiting it at day's end.[6] In the first *tefillah*, he asked Hashem, "...may I not stumble in matters of *halachah* and cause my colleagues to rejoice over me." As *Rashi* explains, R' Nechunia was concerned not only that he might make a mistake in *halachah*, but also that his fellow students might rejoice inwardly over his mistake and be liable for Heavenly punishment — and he prayed that this should not happen.

The *mitzvah* of וְאָהַבְתָּ לְרֵעֲךָ כָּמוֹךָ, *Love your neighbor as yourself*,[7] instructs us to rejoice over our fellow Jew's successes and to feel his distress when he fails. To rejoice when someone else stumbles is a contradiction to this *mitzvah*.

Color War is usually the highlight of a camp season. Staff and campers engage in a variety of competitions and use all their skills and energies to do their very best. It is wonderful to win and disheartening to lose. Therefore, there is often a natural tendency to rejoice over the errors and poor performances of the other team.

But there are those who can rise above the fray and bear in mind that, after all, it is only a game. In doing so, they can behave in a way that is a true *kiddush Hashem*.

In Camp Torah Vodaath, one of the main competitions involved woodcuts, which were judged on quality and how they related to theme. One year, one of the Color War generals happened to be highly skilled in carpentry, which gave him the edge in woodcuts. During Color War, he was seen helping the other general with woodcutting work! When someone asked him about this, he replied simply, "He's my friend — why shouldn't I help him?"

✌ *Bad Humor*

What do Color War and Purim have in common? — *grammen*, amusing rhymes which are sung to a particular tune. Getting people to laugh is a wonderful thing. In fact, the Talmud relates[8] that Eliyahu *HaNavi* identified as "people of the World to Come" two jesters who made it their practice to cheer up people who were sad.

But there is no excuse for rhymes which are insulting and hurt people's feelings.

The Chofetz Chaim states:

> Consider how severe is the sin of *lashon hara*: Even if the speaker does not talk out of hatred and does not intend to belittle the person, rather, he talks in a joking, light-headed way, he has nevertheless done something forbidden by the Torah...[9]

Just as a storekeeper may not degrade his competitor's product, so too, a Color War participant may not sing *grammen* which ridicule the plays, paintings or projects of the opposing team. Similarly, comedy skits may not ridicule members of camp (or anyone else).

R' Avraham Pam writes the following regarding Purim:[10]

> The singing of *grammen* can be a beautiful thing, if it is not mixed with lightheadedness and ridicule, for then it is "frivolity" rather than "joy." Obviously, one should be careful in matters *bein adam l'chaveiro* (between man and his fellow) when singing *grammen* — Heaven forfend to embarrass or insult someone!
>
> There are those who think that one can say whatever he pleases on Purim; they reason that surely everyone is forgiving and does not mind being ridiculed on Purim. But who can say that this is actually so? Perhaps in his heart the person is upset over what is said, but he is ashamed to admit it. Even if he is not upset, to ridicule others is not [the way of Torah which is] the way of pleasantness[11] and [it contradicts] the respect which we must show others...
>
> The Chofetz Chaim would often quote a saying: "A fool turns gold into dirt, a wise man turns dirt into gold." So it is with joy. There is an uplifting type of joy which brings a person to love and awe of Hashem, and there is frivolity which brings to lightheadedness and lowliness. Therefore, one should be very careful that his celebration of Purim is a *simchah shel mitzvah* (joy which derives from a *mitzvah*)...

Chapter Eight

Not-So-Innocent Remarks

*I*t is a cool summer night and some women in a bungalow colony are sitting outdoors enjoying the fresh air. The conversation turns to their daughters' friends. "Miriam is a wonderful girl," one woman remarks, "although as a high school senior she was slapped with a two-day suspension for cutting class to go on a picnic...I know, because my daughter was in her class!"

It sounds like a fairly complimentary statement. After all, the speaker did refer to Miriam as a "wonderful girl." As for her cutting class, we all make mistakes. And cutting class one time certainly does not reflect on her personality or capabilities.

It would seem, then, that such a statement would not be considered *lashon hara*. But it is.

Suppose that one of the women taking part in that group discussion happens to work as a secretary in a yeshivah office. One day after returning home at summer's end, she looks up from her desk and is surprised to see Miriam entering the office.

She greets Miriam and is later addressed by the principal. "I noticed that you greeted that young woman warmly when she came in. She has applied for a first grade teaching position. What do you know about her?"

"Well, I know who she is, but I don't really know her well," the woman replies truthfully. Then, she suddenly recalls that bungalow colony conversation. Happy that she has some information to share with the principal, she tells him of the comment regarding Miriam.

That is all the principal needs to hear. He wants teachers who are responsible and hardworking. If this young woman could cut class to go picnicking, then it might indicate that she is either irresponsible or lazy. In either case, she is probably not what the principal is looking for in a teacher.

The secretary was wrong for sharing this information with the principal. Firstly, she does not know this information firsthand. The woman who made the remark based it on something which *she* heard from her daughter — which may have been misinformation.

Even if the secretary had known the information firsthand, she would have been wrong to share it with the principal. A one-time incident proves nothing. If that was the only stain on Miriam's high school record, then there is no reason to think that she would not make a fine teacher. By sharing this information, the secretary caused a negative impression of Miriam to form in the principal's mind. The principal's attitude is, "Why should I hire this girl when I have so many other applicants about whom I have heard nothing negative?"

The remark could hurt Miriam in other ways as well.

The main culprit in this episode is the woman in the bungalow colony who made the comment about Miriam — for no reason other than to make conversation.

ℒ Negative Comments

The Chofetz Chaim informs us[1] that it is forbidden to say that someone is lacking intelligence, that he is a "weakling," or to make any other negative remark which can cause him physical, financial or emotional harm — though the information may be true. If the information is *false*, it is deemed *hotza'as shem ra* (slander) and the sin is even greater.

How can saying that someone is a "weakling" cause him harm? Suppose, for example, that this fellow were to one day apply for a position as a cook. The kitchen manager, who decides which applicants to hire, learns of this remark. He says to himself, "Why should I hire someone who is going to have a hard time 'shlepping' heavy sacks of flour or bags of potatoes? I might as well look for a cook who can handle such items without a problem. Besides, if he is a weakling, that might mean that he gets sick often. I don't want to be busy looking for substitutes every time the cook calls in sick."

Of course, the kitchen manager is wrong. A person does not have to be blessed with strength to be healthy. There are plenty of thin, frail "weaklings" who are excellent specimens of health and do not miss work. And not being able to 'shlep' a large sack of flour is not a reason to disqualify someone as a cook. His skills as a chef may far outweigh his inability to carry heavy loads.

But the labeling of this candidate as a "weakling" is enough to convince the kitchen manager to select someone else for the job.

✒ Loose Tongues

The following is a true story:

A group of yeshivah students were discussing their *rebbi*, whom they liked very much. Then, the conversation turned to the *rebbi's* family. One boy remarked, "I heard that *rebbi's* younger sister has a heart condition."

One day, someone suggested a *shidduch* (marriage match) between a brother of one these boys and the *rebbi's* sister. The boy remembered the conversation and told his parents what he had heard about the girl's health. The parents were unable to determine whether or not the information was correct.

Concerned that it might be true, they would not consider the *shidduch*.

Later, it was learned that in fact the girl was healthy. She suffered from allergies, and one day her breathing had been a bit labored due to congestion in her lungs. A woman who noticed this thought that perhaps the girl had a heart condition which affected her breathing. She mentioned this to others and the "news" was out.

Thankfully, this girl eventually found her match and is happily married. But the careless remark about her health could have hurt her for the rest of her life.

There are times when the *halachah* permits and may even *require* us to tell others negative information. The Chofetz Chaim lists seven conditions which must be met before we are permitted to speak *lashon hara l'toeles* (for a constructive purpose). These will be discussed in a forthcoming chapter.[2]

Chapter Nine

"In My Opinion..."

W ho doesn't like a good meal? Even better is a *seudas mitzvah*, a festive meal tendered in connection with a *mitzvah*. A *seudah* held in honor of a *bris*, *pidyon haben*, wedding or bar mitzvah all fall under this category.

What many do not realize is that such "*mitzvah* meals" can be breeding grounds for sin, namely, the sin of *lashon hara*.

"This meat is awful."

"Yes, hard as a rock."

"Where did they dig up this caterer, anyway?"

"Most probably he offered them a 'good deal.' Considering how lousy the food is, he had *better* give them a good deal!"

Yes, we live in a democracy where freedom of speech allows one to express his opinion about almost anything. But the Torah's laws of *lashon hara* do not allow us to express opinions which are negative, unless we have a definite constructive purpose in mind. Letting your friends know that you don't like the food serves no constructive purpose. What such statements *may* accomplish is damage to the caterer's business — especially if the guests go home and spread their opinions to others.

In other words: I don't have to like the food, but I do have to live by the laws of *shemiras halashon* and keep my opinion to myself.[1]

℘ *The Chofetz Chaim and the Cook*

There is a famous story about the Chofetz Chaim and another *rav*, who were traveling together. They stopped at an inn, where the innkeeper recognized the two prominent *rabbanim* and ushered them to a table reserved for distinguished guests. At the conclusion of their meal, the innkeeper returned to their table and inquired, "Was the food to your satisfaction?"

The Chofetz Chaim replied that it was, but his companion mentioned that the soup needed more salt.

The Chofetz Chaim was greatly distressed by this remark. "Woe to me, that I should hear such words!" he exclaimed. The *rav*, however, said that the Chofetz Chaim was overreacting. "I didn't say the food was bad; I just said that it could have used a bit more salt."

The Chofetz Chaim was not convinced. "The innkeeper came over to our table hoping to hear a compliment, and instead he heard a criticism. No doubt, he has reported your comment to the cook, who may be a widow and is especially sensitive to criticism."

Now it was the *rav* who remained unconvinced. The Chofetz Chaim invited the *rav* to come with him to the kitchen to see if his concern was well-founded.

They opened the kitchen door and saw the innkeeper speaking to the cook, an older woman, as tears streamed down her cheeks.

The *rav* hurried to tell the innkeeper that the food had really been quite good and he apologized to the cook for causing her distress.

Let us return to our "*mitzvah* meal" illustration:

The main course has been served and everyone has already voiced his opinion about the quality of the food. Some people groan as the first speaker of the evening takes his place at the lectern.

"Oh, no — not him! He never speaks for less than half an hour!"

"And he's positively boring!"

The speech lasts only fifteen minutes. "Well, I guess he decided to cut it short for a change," one person says. "He probably couldn't think of anything more to say."

"Yes," another man comments, "a lot of these professional speakers say the same thing at fifty different *bar mitzvahs*."

"I'll tell you something else," another man chimes in. "I went to yeshivah with that fellow. I can't believe that he's the *rav* of a *shul*! He was not among the better students in the class, as I recall."

Every one of the comments mentioned here is *lashon hara*.[2] The entire discussion about the speaker is pointless. A person has a right to dislike a speaker's style — but such opinions are *not* to be expressed. The last comment, about the speaker's poor performance in yeshivah, is a most serious form of *lashon hara*, because this could harm the speaker's influence as a *rav*. Hearing this remark, some of the members of his *shul* might reason, "If it's true that he did poorly in yeshivah, then he probably isn't that smart. And if that's the case, then maybe we should look around for a new *rav*. In the meantime, if I have any *halachic* questions, I'll find someone else to ask."

ℒ Watch Your Praise

Let us return to the discussion about the caterer and his catering. Suppose the conversation were to open this way:

"Wow! These cutlets are great! Best I've ever tasted! Does

anyone know who the caterer is?"

"Yes, it's *'Gershon's Gourmet'* on Forest Road."

"I knew it! They're the best. Their food is outstanding and the people who work behind the counter are quick and very polite. It's the best 'take-out' store in the neighborhood."

"Oh, and I happen to know Gershon, the owner, very well. He's a very fine person and a great chef. He's also head chef at Camp Achdus where I spent many summers. It was like eating at a wedding every night."

What could possibly be wrong with such a conversation? After all, thus far, everything that has been said is highly complimentary. Gershon would surely be pleased to learn of all the nice comments offered about him and his cooking.

This introduces us to the subject of *avak lashon hara* (literally, the dust of *lashon hara*), statements which are not actual *lashon hara*, but which are forbidden nonetheless. We are forbidden to praise someone excessively, says the Chofetz Chaim.[3] To understand why, let us proceed with a possible continuation of the 'Gershon Gourmet' conversation:

"Yes, I agree with you that Gershon's food is quite good — that is, most of it. But have you ever tasted his chicken soup with *kneidlach* (matzah balls)? I think my son's baseball is softer than those matzah-meal rocks!"

"And as far as the service behind the counter — have you ever been served by the tall guy with the tinted glasses? It takes him so long to dish out each portion that sometimes I wonder if he's cooking it on the spot!"

Praising someone a lot often leads to comments like "...Yes, he is a good fellow, except for..." In other words, excessive praise often leads to *lashon hara*. Therefore, the praise itself falls within the category of '*avak lashon hara*.'

The Chofetz Chaim gives us the following rules about praising others:

Never praise someone in front of his enemies, for they are bound to criticize him.

Never praise someone in front of a crowd, because there is bound to be someone there who has something negative to say.

Never praise someone *excessively* to anyone.

An exception to these rules is when someone praises a famous *tzaddik*. For example, there would be nothing wrong with singing the praises of R' Moshe Feinstein or the Steipler *Gaon*, for only a fool would say anything critical of these *tzaddikim*.

Chapter Ten

Common Misconceptions

"And there we were, Naftali and I, safely inside the camp kitchen, about to open the cake closet and help ourselves to some of the next day's snacks. Suddenly, we heard footsteps and then the director's voice growling, 'What's that noise in the kitchen?' At that point, Naftali and I quickly hoisted ourselves on top of the huge walk-in refrigerator...

"The director turned on the lights in the kitchen and investigated, while Naftali and I lay flat on our stomachs barely breathing. After about ten minutes, the director gave up his search and left.

"We breathed a sigh of relief, but as a precaution, we remained on top of the refrigerator for another ten minutes. Then, we climbed down and headed once again for the cake closet.

"It was easy to get the closet open. In those days, they locked it with one of those old-fashioned locks that you could pick with a popsicle stick. Naftali and I decided that since we had endured so much strain and stress, we had to eat more than we had originally planned. We each took five small chocolate danishes. Quickly and quietly, we scampered back to our bunk, and enjoyed our treasures under the covers.

"It's hard to believe that twenty years have passed since then. Today, Naftali is a prosperous real-estate investor. You know, he's one of the most generous people I know. Why, just the other day, I met a poor man from Eretz Yisrael who is here trying to raise money to marry off his daughter. He told me that Naftali gave him a check for *eighteen hundred dollars!*

"Yes, he and I have stayed close all these years. In fact, I often stop by his house for a short, fifteen-minute visit. It's not just that I enjoy his company. His wife is a superb cook and whenever I'm there, no matter what time of day or night, I always find food on the table.

"Now Naftali's brother, Chaninah — he's altogether different. But we're best off not talking about him..."

It is quite possible that the speaker will walk away confident that he has avoided any trace of *lashon hara.*

He is wrong on many counts.

Let us identify his mistakes, one by one.

℘ *"And There We Were..."*

The story about the bakery raid is filled with negative information. Two boys snuck into a camp kitchen, picked the lock on a closet, and stole some of its contents. The speaker might have two reasons why, according to his erroneous thinking, he is allowed to relate this story:

He unashamedly made it clear that he was one of the two boys in the story. Since he includes himself, it could not possibly be *lashon hara* — or so he thinks.

The Chofetz Chaim states: "You should know that even if the speaker includes himself in the derogatory report about his friend — and even if he degrades himself before mentioning his friend — he has, nevertheless, been guilty of speaking *lashon hara*."[1] The fact that someone speaks badly of himself does not permit him to speak badly of others.

The speaker may also reason that the story is not *lashon hara* because it occurred twenty years earlier, when he and Naftali were youths.

This is also incorrect. The fact that the speaker is not ashamed of the incident does not mean that Naftali is not ashamed of it. It is quite possible that Naftali does not want people to know that he was involved in something which, according to *halachah*, was surely an act of theft and was forbidden.[2]

✌ "...Eighteen Hundred Dollars!"

The speaker praised his friend Naftali by telling of his eighteen-hundred dollar donation to a poor man. But does Naftali want people to know about that gift? If the news spreads, chances are that Naftali will soon find himself swamped with *tzedakah* requests, some of them from dishonest people who claim to be in need.

The Chofetz Chaim states:[3]

> A person should be careful not to praise someone in a way that will cause him loss, such as a visitor who publicizes the fact that his host exerted himself very much on his behalf and also provided him with much food and drink. This may cause low-class people to descend upon that house, where they will ravage the host's food and other possessions. It is concerning such matters that it is written:[4] "If one blesses his friend loudly from early in the morning, it will be considered a curse to him."
>
> The same would apply to someone who obtains a loan from his friend and publicizes his friend's goodness. Through this, dishonest people will flock to him and he will not be able to be rid of them.

By mentioning the eighteen-hundred dollar donation, the speaker has been guilty of *avak lashon hara*.

✒ *"...I Always Find Food on the Table"*

Saying that "there is always food on the table" could mean that Naftali and his family are always eating, which is not at all complimentary. On the other hand, it could mean that they are very hospitable and always have food prepared in case a surprise visitor knocks on their door. Thus, such statements may or may not be *lashon hara*, depending on how they are said and the impression which they convey.

The Chofetz Chaim offers the following example:[5]

> Someone asks: "Where can I find a fire [to warm up some food]?" The other person replies, "Go to So-and-so — they're always cooking meat and fish over there." Whether or not this statement is forbidden depends on how it is said. The speaker could say this in a way that is not derogatory, for sometimes, it does not indicate anything negative. For example, the person [in whose house is the fire] may be the head of a large family and Hashem may have blessed him with wealth [so that he can afford to regularly feed his family meat and fish]; or, he may have an open house for guests... it all depends on how it is said.
>
> If the speaker's voice and motions indicate that the person is always feasting... then this would be *avak lashon hara*.[6]

✒ *"Now, Naftali's Brother..."*

The Chofetz Chaim writes: "There are some statements which are forbidden because of *avak lashon hara*. For example: someone says, 'Who would have believed that he would have come this far,' or, 'Let's not talk about _____, I'd rather not discuss what happened...'; or similar remarks [which hint at something negative]."[7]

When the speaker said of Naftali's brother Chaninah, "We're best off not talking about him..." he clearly implied something negative.

But what if he did not mean anything negative? Perhaps he meant the following: "We're best off not discussing Chaninah, because Chaninah happens to be a very sensitive person and is not happy when he becomes a topic of discussion. Though he is really a wonderful fellow and he is not present, I would rather not discuss him, because if he finds out that I spoke about him, he will be upset."

The Chofetz Chaim says that even if this was the speaker's intention, he is still guilty of speaking *avak lashon hara*, because his words implied something negative.[8] If the speaker really has good intentions, he should explain himself.

ℒ *Double Identity*

The above is illustrated by a story told about the Chofetz Chaim:

Once, the Chofetz Chaim traveled to a certain town to address his fellow Jews on issues of the day. He took the train to the stop nearest to the town, and from there hired a wagon to take him to his destination.

The wagon driver, a Jew who happened to live in the town to which they were heading, struck up a conversation with his elderly passenger whom he did not recognize.

"It's a big day in our town, you know."

"A big day?" the Chofetz Chaim responded. "And why is that?"

"Haven't you heard?" the driver asked incredulously. "The Chofetz Chaim is coming to town!"

"Oh, the Chofetz Chaim," said the passenger, "yes, I am aware that he is coming today. But that is not a reason to call this a 'big day!'"

"What are you talking about?" the driver demanded angrily. "Don't you know who the Chofetz Chaim is? He is a great *tzaddik* and the author of some wonderful *sefarim*. They say that he is one of the thirty-six *tzaddikim* in whose merit the world exists!"

The Chofetz Chaim's face took on a pained expression. He responded, "Do not believe everything you hear. Much of what people say about the Chofetz Chaim is exaggerated. He is really just a plain person like everyone else."

"How dare you talk like that, you *mechutzaf* (brazen person)! One more word from you and I'll leave you off right in the middle of nowhere!"

They traveled the rest of the way in silence. They arrived at the town and the driver directed his horses toward the main *shul*, where his passenger had asked to be left off.

They found a large crowd waiting. The driver jumped off his wagon and asked someone what the commotion was all about.

"You must be kidding," the man replied. "You mean you didn't know that your passenger was none other than the Chofetz Chaim? We are all here to greet him!"

The wagon driver almost fainted. Before he had a chance to recover, he saw the Chofetz Chaim coming toward him.

"Please, *rebbi*," the driver cried, "forgive me for speaking to you so disrespectfully. I had no idea..."

"No," replied the Chofetz Chaim, "it is I who must ask *you* for forgiveness. You see, I am so worried that all the praise that I hear will cause me to become arrogant. That is why when you said those praises of me I immediately protested. But I was wrong, for you had no idea that I was speaking about myself. To your mind, I was speaking *lashon hara*. I am sorry for misleading you."

✒ Silent *Lashon Hara*

It is possible to be guilty of *lashon hara* without saying a word.

In *Mishlei*, Shlomo *HaMelech* describes a *baal* (frequent speaker of) *lashon hara*: "He winks with his eyes, shuffles with his feet, points with his fingers... he plots evil all the time, stirs up strife."[9] *Rashi*, in explaining the primary verse which forbids us to speak *lashon hara*, writes: "It is the way of all who gossip to wink with their eyes, and gesture their intentions so that the other listeners will not understand [their wicked intentions]."[10]

Therefore, using body language to communicate something derogatory about someone is considered actual *lashon hara* (in contrast to *avak lashon hara*).[11]

It is also forbidden to show others a letter which someone wrote, if the letter reflects badly on the writer in any way.[12] It would be forbidden to pass around the following letter, if its author was old enough to do better:

> Dear Chaim:
> It was grate seeing you at the jim the other knight. I forgetted how wunderfall you play basketball. It ain't the same since you mooved to Tchicargo. Plees cum viset agen.

Similarly, it is forbidden to ridicule someone by passing around a photograph in which that person looks silly or is doing something wrong.

ℒ *Hidden Lashon Hara*

"Someone was looking at your homework during recess. I'm not going to tell who you it was, but you can figure it out for yourself — there's only one kid in the class who remained in the room during recess today!"

The Chofetz Chaim informs us: "The sin of *lashon hara* includes a situation where one does not mention the name of the one he is talking about, in a case where the listener will know the person's identity."[13]

There is another type of "hidden *lashon hara*." *Talmud Yerushalmi*[14] tells the following story:

> Once, a group of Jews were called for government service. One man, whose name was *Bar Chovetz*, did not show up on the appointed day, but his absence was not noticed

by the officers in charge. A few of the people in the group did not like the fact that *Bar Chovetz* was "getting away with it" while they had to work hard. So they hit upon a plan. Within earshot of the commanding officer, one man called to another, "What's for lunch today?" "*Chuvtza* (a type of lentil)," the other one replied. Hearing the word *chuvtza* made the officer think of *Bar Chovetz* who, he suddenly realized, did not report for duty that day.

Said R' Yochanan, "This is 'hidden *lashon hara*.'"

The Chofetz Chaim sets forth this rule as follows: "If one's words contain nothing derogatory at all, but through his words some sort of harm or disgrace will be brought upon the subject — and this was the speaker's devious intent — it is considered *lashon hara*. This is what our Sages call 'hidden *lashon hara*.' "[15]

Chapter Eleven

Bad News

*T*he front page of one of the world's most widely read newspapers bears the slogan "All the news that's fit to print." This statement is false. That newspaper, like its competitors, regularly carries articles and illustrations which depict violence and immorality.

But that is not the only problem with newspapers. Often, they contain articles which are patently false, especially when the topic under discussion is Judaism and the Jews. Such pieces are often filled with distortions and misinformation.

✷ The Big Lie

In the fall of 1997, the media was fed the "Big Lie" and wasted no time in spreading the "news" throughout the world.

According to this report, Orthodox Jews believe that in order to be Jewish, you have to be Orthodox. According to this slanderous report the millions of Jews in America and elsewhere who do not observe *mitzvos* are, in the eyes of Torah Jewry, not Jewish.

Of course, nothing could be further from the truth. One who is born Jewish is a Jew forever. Even a Jew who, G-d forbid, would renounce his Jewishness and embrace another religion is still considered a Jew according to *halachah.*

My friend related:

> I was riding in a taxi cab in Jerusalem and struck up a conversation with the *chiloni* (secular) driver. At one point, the driver turned to me and said, "Why do you people hate us?" I replied: "I give you my word that I consider you my brother; in fact, if, G-d forbid, you were drowning, I would risk my life to save you."
>
> The driver was taken aback by my response. He said to me, "You have changed my entire outlook."

Unfortunately, when the international news media was informed of the "Big Lie," they were quick to accept it as fact. This terrible slander of Orthodox Jewry became front page news. Major newspapers not only carried the story, they also used the opportunity to ridicule religious Jews. The West Coast's most respected newspaper, *The Los Angeles Times*, carried a cartoon on its editorial page, showing a broken *menorah* on top of which sat the head of a religious Jew, with black hat and *peyos*. The caption had the religious Jew declaring: "Only I am a Jew!"

Orthodox Jews were forced to spend hundreds of thousands of dollars to try to set the record straight. A full-page ad by the *Am Echad* coalition appeared in many secular newspapers. The ad chose the lighting of the Chanukah *menorah* as a means of depicting Jews of varying levels of religious observance. In one window, there was a *menorah* of candles; in a second window, an electric *menorah*; and in a third, nothing at all. The caption read, "No matter how we celebrate Chanukah, we are all

Jews...Don't believe anyone who tells you otherwise. However we choose to label ourselves, all Jews are Jews."

We have used this episode as an example of how the media distorts the truth, particularly when Orthodox Jews are concerned. We are not permitted to believe negative information about Jews appearing in newspapers — including Jewish newspapers — and certainly we may not repeat such information.

As we have learned previously, even if we were to confirm that the story *is* true, it would be forbidden to discuss it without a constructive purpose.[1] The Torah considers it improper to focus on the negative behavior of others.[2]

ℒ *Disparaging Torah Scholars*

While it is certainly a sin to speak *lashon hara* against any Jew, it is a particularly severe sin to speak against a *talmid chacham* (Torah scholar). *Shulchan Aruch* states that to disgrace a *talmid chacham* is to disgrace the Torah itself.[3] Certainly if a newspaper were to write something critical of a *talmid chacham*, it would be forbidden to believe it or repeat it.

Our Sages tell us that the sin of shaming Torah scholars was a major cause for the destruction of Jerusalem.[4]

The Chofetz Chaim informs us of a common mistake which can lead a person to speak disrespectfully of a Torah scholar. "Why must I respect that *Rosh Yeshivah*?" a person might contend. "Had he been living in the days of the Chofetz Chaim, he would not have been considered anything special!"

Our Sages taught us that this sort of thinking is wrong. "Yiftach [*HaGiladi*] in his generation is like Shmuel [*HaNavi*] in his generation. You must treat him with respect."[5] Hashem, in His infinite wisdom, sees to it that each generation has Torah leaders who are qualified to lead and guide that particular generation.

Similarly, says the Chofetz Chaim, we should not make the mistake of using earlier generations as a measuring rod to decide if a certain individual should be considered a "*talmid chacham.*" Rather, we should show honor and respect for all those who dedicate themselves to the study and teaching of Torah.[6]

❧ A Thoughtless Remark

In his great humility, the Chofetz Chaim authored *Sefer Chofetz Chaim* anonymously; his name did not appear on the *sefer's* title page. He would travel from town to town selling his new work and would usually address the people with a heartfelt plea that they should study the *sefer* and live by its teachings. He tried very hard to give the impression that he was nothing more than a "salesman" who considered it his sacred duty to make this *sefer* available to the public. In many cities, the local *rav* and others eventually realized that this humble man was actually the *sefer's* author, and as time went on, people began to refer to him as "the Chofetz Chaim."

The first time the Chofetz Chaim came to Kiev, he arrived at the main *shul* around noon, and found it almost empty. One of the few people there was R' Baruch, a wealthy individual who studied Torah regularly. He greeted the stranger and asked, "Where are you from?"

"From a small province near Vilna," came the reply.

"And what is your occupation?" asked R' Baruch. "Are you, perhaps, a *rav* or a fund-raiser for a yeshivah?"

"I am neither," said the stranger.

Trying to be witty, R' Baruch countered, "If you are not a rabbi or a fund raiser, then what are you — a dogcatcher?"

The Chofetz Chaim replied, "I am a plain Jew."

No sooner had R' Baruch arrived home than his head began to hurt, and his limbs felt like heavy weights. He climbed into bed and a doctor was summoned, but he could not find any cause for R' Baruch's symptoms.

The next day, R' Baruch was visited by some friends who told him that the Chofetz Chaim was visiting their city. From their description of the *tzaddik*, R' Baruch realized that the man whom he had suggested might be a "dogcatcher" was none other than the renowned author of *Sefer Chofetz Chaim*. R' Baruch was certain that the mysterious illness which had suddenly befallen him was a punishment for his having insulted this *tzaddik*.

As soon as he was well enough to leave his bed, R' Baruch hastened to visit the Chofetz Chaim at his lodging. With tears in his eyes, he begged forgiveness for his thoughtless words, which should not have been said even in jest. The Chofetz Chaim replied sincerely that he had not felt the least bit insulted and there was no need to ask forgiveness. Nevertheless, R' Baruch imposed upon himself a fine of $5,000, which he distributed to various yeshivos.

✷ When Great Men Disagree

In the Mishnah, we find many disputes between Beis Hillel and Beis Shamai. Nevertheless, these arguments in *halachah* did not have any ill effect on the relationships between the students of these schools. They loved peace and truth, and even married into each other's families.[7] Like their great teachers, Hillel and Shamai, their disagreements were purely for the sake of Heaven.[8]

And so it has been with Torah leaders in every generation. They may disagree, at times vehemently, over major issues, but their disagreements are never personal. They respect one another, as people and as *talmidei chachamim*.

Once, the great *gaon* and *tzaddik* R' Moshe Feinstein issued a halachic ruling which aroused opposition in many circles. Most prominent among those who disagreed was the saintly Satmar *Rav*, R' Yoel Teitelbaum. A distinguished delegation of *rabbanim* volunteered to visit R' Moshe to convince him to retract his decision. Before going, they conferred with the Satmar *Rav* to seek his guidance and blessing. The *Rav*, who was famous for his sparkling sense of humor, responded, "But what will you do if he speaks with you in learning?"

The group failed to sway R' Moshe. R' Moshe, in turn, sent an emissary to the Satmar *Rav*, declaring his readiness to retract his *psak* (halachic ruling) if someone could offer what R' Moshe considered to be a solid refutation. This did not happen.

Another famous Lithuanian Torah giant with whom the Satmar *Rav* sometimes disagreed was R' Aharon Kotler. R' Aharon once remarked, "The Satmar *Rav* and I do not have the same approach — neither in Torah study nor in other matters — but I must say, he is a giant in Torah and a giant in *midos*."

At R' Aharon's funeral, the Satmar *Rav* asked permission to deliver a eulogy and praised the great Lakewood *Rosh Yeshivah* as a leader who never strayed an iota from the path of Torah truth.[9]

Yes, our *gedolei Yisrael* (Torah leaders) often disagree on important issues, but always with respect and never with *lashon hara*. How unfortunate it is when their followers take matters into their own hands and turn a respectful disagreement into a bitter feud. Even worse is when the followers speak disrespectfully of the "other *rav*," and transgress the very serious sin of disgracing a *talmid chacham*.

_____

ℒ *Living* Scrolls

The Book of *Shmuel* tells of King Shaul's pursuit of David, who was to succeed him as king. At one point, Shaul entered a cave in which David and his men were concealed. David's men urged him to kill Shaul, but instead, David merely cut off a corner from Shaul's garment as he relieved himself.[10] The Talmud states, "Whoever dishonors clothing will in the end not have use of them," for at the end of King David's life, his garments could not warm him.[11]

R' Aharon Kotler points out: David was being wrongfully pursued by Shaul and acted righteously in doing nothing more than cutting the corner of Shaul's garment. He did it as a gesture of peace and later regretted what he had done.[12] Nevertheless, he could not be warmed by his clothing, because he had cut Shaul's garment. This was not as much a punishment, says R'

Aharon, as it was a natural consequence of David's action. A natural consequence of disrespect towards something is being unable to derive benefit from that thing.

Surely, says R' Aharon, this is true of Torah. The Torah's wisdom is revealed only to those who show respect for Torah. And only they will be transformed into greater individuals through the Torah's awesome light.[13]

The Talmudic Sage Rava declared: "How foolish are some people who stand up in respect for a Torah scroll, but they do not stand up in respect for a Torah sage."[14]

Torah scholars are living Torah scrolls. Anyone who hopes to be influenced by the Torah's holy light must treat every *talmid chacham* with proper respect.

❧ Highway Robbery

The following was related by the *Mashgiach* of Beth Medrash Govoha, R' Matisyahu Salomon:

Some years ago, a former *talmid* of the Chofetz Chaim in Radin became *rav* in a small Jewish community in England. His *kehillah* (congregation) was not very learned; its president was a man who was ignorant of Torah and who did not treat the *rav* with the respect which he richly deserved. This was apparent in the manner in which the president would speak to the *rav* as well as how he spoke about him.

One day, the president came to discuss a potentially tragic matter: his daughter was on the verge of becoming engaged to a gentile. The president asked the *rav* to meet with his daughter and prevail upon her to change her mind.

The meeting took place shortly thereafter and lasted over an hour. The *rav* tried his best to explain to the young woman the severity of what she was considering, but unfortunately, his efforts failed. She left the meeting unmoved.

When her father learned of this, he remarked to the *rav* in his typically disrespectful way, "So even this you can't do for me?"

Throughout the years, the *rav*, a quiet and unassuming man, had borne every insult in silence. This, time, however, he felt that a response was in order. He told the president a parable which he had heard from the Chofetz Chaim:

In a certain province, a terrible epidemic broke out afflicting scores of children. Doctors tried every remedy, to no avail. Many children succumbed to the disease, while hundreds were in danger of dying.

Then, one day, a doctor appeared who claimed to have a cure. Anxious parents stood on line with their children waiting their turn to see the doctor. He began to administer his potion... and it worked! Each child whom the doctor treated recovered from the illness. The doctor proceeded to make his way from town to town, and everywhere he went, long lines of people waited anxiously to see him.

One day, as he was traveling alone between towns, he was held up by highwaymen. They searched him and found little money, so they took his suitcases and told him to move onward if he valued his life. He fled down the road, bereft of his potions and potion-making equipment.

Meanwhile, the bandits opened the suitcases and found nothing but clothing, some jars of what appeared to be medicine, and equipment which did not look very valuable. Frustrated, they cast the suitcases and their contents into the ocean.

The doctor arrived at his destination, shaken and exhausted. He made his way to a hotel where the town had already set up an office for him to see patients. A long line of parents and their children were already waiting. The doctor called in the first man and said:

"I will tell you something which you should pass on to everyone else on line. I am terribly sorry, but I cannot see anyone. On my way here, I was attacked by armed bandits who took my belongings from me — including my potions and the tools with which I make them. It will take me about five weeks to procure new equipment and then to produce a new supply of potion. Unfortunately, by that time, it will be too late to help anyone who is now suffering from the disease."

The father paled and grasped onto something to keep himself from collapsing. He knew all about those highwaymen... he was their leader! Unwittingly, he had thrown into the ocean the very materials which could have saved his child's life.

Said the Chofetz Chaim: *Talmidei chachamim* are treasuries of Torah wisdom; therefore, they have the ability to correct any sort of situation through their teaching, wise counsel and inspiration. But that is only if they are accorded the respect which is due them. However, when people treat a *talmid chacham* with disrespect, they rob him of his "tools and potions," as they cause others to disregard his words.

"You have only yourself to blame," the *rav* told the president, "for the fact that I was unable to convince your daughter not to marry that man. All these years, you have treated me with utter disrespect. This is no secret — I'm sure that your daughter is well aware of how you speak of me. Is it any wonder, then, that my words are meaningless to her?"

Chapter Twelve

Wholesale Destruction

O ne *Succos*, I found myself sitting in a *succah* many hundreds of miles from the New York area. Sitting opposite me was a nice Orthodox fellow, who had lived all his life in this suburban, all-American community. We were enjoying a very pleasant *yom tov* conversation — until he said something which disturbed me very much.

"You know," he remarked, "I never eat chicken or meat that is from _____ *shechitah*" (he named a well-known brand of kosher meat and poultry).

"And why is that?" I asked.

"Well," he replied, "the *chassidim* who are behind that *kashrus* symbol have no *ahavas Yisrael* (love of a fellow Jew)."

I would have liked to voice my disagreement and set the record straight, but it was obvious to me that had I attempted to do this, he would have launched into a tirade filled with more *lashon hara*.

Had he been interested in listening, I would have explained that he was grossly mistaken.

Those *chassidim* have no *ahavas Yisrael?* He would be hard-pressed to explain the fact that *every single weekday* of the year, rain or shine, winter or summer, the women of this chassidic sect travel by bus to hospitals throughout New York city, delivering delicious hot meals to Jewish patients. These women do not differentiate between *chassidim* and non-*chassidim*, between what is known as modern Orthodox and ultra-Orthodox. In fact, they do not differentiate between religious and non-religious; if you are Jewish, they will provide you with delicious, home-cooked kosher food.

Once, I witnessed the amazing *chesed* of these women first-hand. It was an *erev Shabbos*, and I was visiting a relative who was hospitalized. One of these women entered the room to bring the patient whatever she would need for Shabbos: *challah*, grape juice, gefilte fish, liver, a thermos with chicken soup, and even some cake. The patient thanked the woman, but explained that because of her condition, she did not have much of an appetite and would not be able to eat most of the food. The kindhearted woman responded, "That's okay. Whoever will spend Shabbos with you here in the hospital is welcome to enjoy it."

✑ *"The Shopping Bag Ladies"*

After I had written the above, I came across an article[1] entitled, *"The Shopping Bag Ladies,"* all about this wonderful group of chassidic women. The article informs us that:

Each day, the volunteers distribute one hundred and fifty hot and wholesome meals, to Jewish patients of all types, both religious and non-religious, at fifteen metropolitan area hospitals. For some of the recipients of these hot meals, it is the first kosher food that they have ever tasted.

The meals are cooked by another team of women (from the same chassidic sect), at a large *Bikur Cholim* kitchen in Williamsburg (Brooklyn). They happily fill "special requests," such as sugarless foods for diabetics.

All the women are volunteers; some do their volunteer work as often as three times a week.

The women make their hospital rounds via a special bus which was purchased with charity donations. Their lists of Jewish patients are provided by hospital chaplains and sometimes by the patients or their families.

The women go about their special *mitzvah* with heart. They get to know many of the patients and their families, and even stay in touch with some after they are discharged from the hospital. The article describes how one of these women approached a bare-headed man in a hospital waiting room, and spoke with the man for a while about his wife's condition. She then offered the man a food package which he gratefully accepted. He explained that his wife was unable to eat, but that he was very hungry and would enjoy the food for lunch. The woman told him, "By tomorrow, your wife will probably be able to eat jello and clear broth. I'll order it for you."

When the *Bikur Cholim* bus headed back to Brooklyn, this woman remained at the hospital. "I like to stay here a bit longer," she explained, "and spend some extra time with the children."

If this is not *ahavas Yisrael*, then what is?

That fellow in the *succah*, who had never met any members of this chassidic sect personally, had been fed misinformation which unfortunately he was very quick to accept as fact.

Perhaps he would have spoken differently had he digested the following poem,[2] which sums up what our attitude should be toward Jews whose customs and way of dress may differ from our own:

One *shtreimel*,[3]
One (hat) bent down,
One bent up,

One straw,
One wide-rimmed
One with a feather,
One *kipah*,[4]
One Hamburg,
One cap,
One *spudik*,[5]

Each one an individual,
Yet joined together.
Ten men ready for one purpose,
To *daven* to their One Creator.

❧ *His Second Mistake*

With his claim that this particular group "has no *ahavas Yisrael*," the fellow in the *succah* was guilty of a very severe strain of *lashon hara*. The Chofetz Chaim writes:[6]

> "If...he has disgraced an entire community, he has committed a dreadful sin... Certainly, it is forbidden to speak against an entire community of Jews, who are steadfast in their belief in Hashem — surely this is a great sin."

In fact, the man was actually guilty of *hotza'as shem ra* (slander) of an entire community, which makes his sin even worse.

Unfortunately, this man's mistake is not uncommon. Sometimes, people have a bad experience with one individual and because of it, they label the person's entire community as "bad."

Sometimes, a boy or girl has an unpleasant encounter with a student of another school and as a result, he or she labels that school as "bad" or its students as "no good." This, too, is the severe type of *lashon hara* of which the Chofetz Chaim speaks.

Remember: *Do not label groups — communities, shul congregations, chassidic sects, yeshivos, or any other group — in a negative way.*

And let us not label another group: our non-religious brothers and sisters in Eretz Yisrael.

Yes, there are major problems which religious Jews in Eretz Yisrael face. There are government officials and Knesset members who feel threatened by the thriving religious community in our Holy Land, and therefore try to make life difficult for religious Israelis. We should view these people not with hatred, but with pity. What a pity that they are so sunk in their sinful way of life that they are totally out of touch with the Jewish soul within themselves. What a pity that while living in our holy and precious Land, they feel no attachment to the Land.

At the same time, let us be aware of a crucial fact: *Not all secular Israelis dislike religious Jews.*

✌ A First-hand Lesson

When I visited Eretz Yisrael for the first time in sixteen years, I was expecting to be shown nasty looks and outright unfriendliness by the non-religious. I am happy to report that my experience was not this way.

In the taxi from the airport to Jerusalem, the non-religious driver initiated a friendly conversation:

"So how often do you visit Israel?"

"This is my first visit in sixteen years."

"Sixteen years? That is much too long to wait between visits! You must come more often."

"I'll tell you what," I replied jokingly, "you buy me a ticket and I will be happy to return here, G-d willing, in the near future."

"Fine," replied the driver, "I will buy you a ticket — a bus ticket!" and he laughed.

The remainder of the trip was equally pleasant.

The last day of my trip was a Sunday. I decided to arise early and *daven Shacharis* at the *Kosel* at sunrise. I called for a cab and headed for the *Kosel* in the stillness of night. I said to the bareheaded driver: "I'm sure that we will pass some people walking to the *Kosel*. Please stop to pick them up. I will pay you extra for the stops."

The driver seemed a bit upset. "What?" he responded. "You want to pay me extra for the stops? Why can't I begin the new week with a good deed? I will stop for the people and I will not charge extra!" He kept to his word.

Many, perhaps most, non-religious Israelis have no quarrel with us. If we bear this in mind and treat them with love and respect, we may be pleasantly surprised to find them coming closer to the truth and beauty of Torah.

Chapter Thirteen

Playing with Fire

One Chanukah, the yeshivah which I was attending invited a respected *talmid chacham* to address us at the annual Chanukah *mesibah* (festive gathering). How surprised I was to hear this *talmid chacham* quote, of all people, a professional football coach!

The coach's name was Vince Lombardi and his statement was, "Winning isn't everything — *it's the only thing.*"

The speaker mentioned this not to compliment Vince Lombardi, but to contrast the way a Torah Jew views the world, and the way society at large looks at things. In the gentile world, power and strength are measured by one's ability to dominate over others. If you and I engage in competition and I come out ahead, then I am a "success" and you are a "failure."

The Torah, however, has a very different view of things. True strength is not measured by who wins the game or who wins the argument. The Torah teaches that what is *truly* important is inner strength, how well *I can control myself.* "Who is truly strong? One who controls his *yetzer hara.*"[1]

If I win the game and I ridicule the loser, then *I* am the real loser. If I lose the game and I tell my teammate whose error let the winning run score, "Forget about it; it could have happened to anyone," then I am truly a winner.

So, Mr. Lombardi was more than a bit mistaken. The correct motto is:

"Winning isn't everything — *doing what is right is everything.*"

✌ *The Real Enemy*

Our Sages teach that "there is no vessel that can contain blessing like [the vessel] of peace."[2] On the other hand, there is nothing as destructive as *machlokes* (dispute and strife). The Chofetz Chaim writes:[3]

> For Jews to feud with each other is a dreadful sin that is often accompanied by other sins: *lashon hara, sinas chinam* (senseless hatred), *ona'as devarim* (causing hurt through words), embarrassing someone, seeking revenge, bearing a grudge... At times, strife leads to *chillul Hashem* (desecration of Hashem's Name), a very severe sin.

A great *Rosh Yeshivah* once discussed the *yetzer hara* which some people seem to have for taking sides in an argument. What is it, this *rosh yeshivah* wondered, that pulls these people into the quicksand of dispute, which can destroy friendships, family peace and sometimes, whole communities?

To answer this question, he drew an analogy to America's preoccupation with professional sports. What is it that drives millions of people to spend countless hours listening to or viewing "their team" perform? What do they stand to gain from seeing their team win? If their favorites go on to win the world championship, will they show appreciation to their loyal fans and share their championship paycheck with them?

The source of "sports-mania," explained this *talmid chacham*, is an urge to emerge triumphant from competition. If Mr. Jones roots for the Carolina Southerns and the Southerns win, then in Mr. Jones' mind, *he* has won.

This very same urge is what drives people to take sides in disputes and engage in mudslinging, protesting and all the other shameful activities that dispute brings with it. When a person takes a side in a feud and his side prevails, then he sees himself as a winner.

But as we have explained, this is contrary to a very basic quality which every Jew should possess: *self-control.* We should seek to conquer the real enemy — our own *yetzer hara* — and bend over backwards to make peace even when we know that the other side is at fault.

Eight days before he passed away, R' Moshe Sherer shared his very last Torah thought on this earth with a young man who entered his hospital room to wish him "*Good Shabbos*":

As we all know, three times a day, every Jew takes three steps back at the conclusion of *Shemoneh Esrei* and says, "*Oseh Shalom* (May He who makes peace)..." We bow to the left, to the right and then forward as we say these words. Why must we step back and bow?

This, explained R' Sherer, is to teach us that there is really only one way for a person to truly achieve peace among people. He must "step back," meaning, he must drop his personal interests and not cling stubbornly to his personal viewpoint. Instead, he must concern himself with what is truly good for everyone and he must strive to understand the viewpoint of his adversary.

But merely stepping back is not sufficient. After he has convinced himself to think openly and objectively, he must take action for the sake of peace. He must turn to the left, to the right and to the center, each time "bending," that is, compromising a little.

Humble yourself and compromise, for only then can you achieve true peace.

From the great *gaon* and *tzaddik* R' Moshe Feinstein, we can learn the meaning of true inner strength.

Once, R' Moshe issued a *psak* (halachic ruling) which caused somewhat of a stir in the Torah world. There were great *poskim* of that time who disagreed with R' Moshe's ruling, but they were careful to do so in a manner which showed their tremendous awe and respect of R' Moshe. One *rav*, however, attacked R' Moshe's decision in a manner which bordered on disrespect. R' Moshe knew of this, but did not respond.

The following summer, R' Moshe and this *rav* vacationed in the same area in the Catskill Mountains. A new *mikveh* was built in the neighborhood and before it was used, R' Moshe was asked to inspect it to make sure that it was built according to *halachah*. R' Moshe agreed — on one condition. Since the other *rav* was also in the neighborhood and it would be beneficial to have his endorsement as well, it was only right, said R' Moshe, that he should be asked to accompany him on the inspection.

Someone present could not believe his ears. "*That rav...?*" he asked incredulously. "But he had the nerve..."

R' Moshe interrupted him. "I *must* have the *rav* accompany me." And he did accompany R' Moshe.

Someone without the *midos* (character traits) of R' Moshe might have been happy to see the *rav* excluded from the *mikveh* inspection. "Wonderful," he might have thought, "now, that *rav* will be put in his place. Everyone knows that both of us are staying in this neighborhood. When the announcements of the *mikveh's* opening are posted, bearing *only my endorsement*, people will realize whose opinion is *really* valued! I will emerge from this dispute victorious!"

Of course, such thoughts never entered R' Moshe's mind. To the contrary, as a *tzaddik* who loved peace and pursued it, he insisted on according honor to a person who had acted improperly towards him.

R' Moshe was a man of true inner strength.

In fact, the lesson of how to act when we are wronged can be learned from none other than Moshe *Rabbeinu*. The Torah relates, in great detail, the shameful rebellion led by Korach, Dasan and Aviram.[4] That rebellion was not the first time that Dasan and Aviram had opposed Moshe. In Egypt, they informed on Moshe to Pharaoh, causing Moshe to flee the land and remain separate from his people for many years.[5] In the Wilderness, it was Dasan and Aviram who left over manna from one day to the next after Moshe had instructed the people, in Hashem's Name, that nothing was to be left over[6] (except for the extra portion which fell on Friday in honor of Shabbos).

Yet when Korach rejected Moshe's plea for peace, Moshe sent a message to Dasan and Aviram in the hope of convincing them to abandon their dispute before it was too late. From here, our Sages derive the lesson, "One should not keep up a dispute, for Moshe went after them to restore harmony with words of peace."[7]

In his introduction to *Sefer Chofetz Chaim*, the Chofetz Chaim writes that a person who is involved in a dispute and speaks *lashon hara* about his opponent has also transgressed the commandment "*that he not be like Korach and his assembly.*"[8]

Our Sages compare strife to fire. A fire that rages out of control can cause untold destruction. And so it is with strife. When a dispute is not settled quickly and with the two sides showing respect for one another, the situation is likely to get out of hand. Outsiders join the argument and *lashon hara* spills over into the streets. Ultimately, the dispute can engulf an entire community and permanently shatter the peace and harmony that once reigned.

✌ The Only Solution

"Altman's Appliances"* was busier than ever. Mr. Altman was a fine gentleman with a sterling reputation, and for the most

---

*Names and circumstances in this story have been changed. The basic idea is true.

part he had surrounded himself with workers who had helped him to build his business.

One day Eli, a salesperson who had been with the store for two years, became involved in an argument with a customer. It was not the first time that the hot-tempered young man had argued with a customer, but this was by far the worst. The two had come close to blows when a quick-thinking worker, who decided to escort the customer out of the store, saved the day.

After closing time, Mr. Altman called Eli in. "You know, I've spoken to you many times about controlling your temper. What happened today is inexcusable. Had the argument continued any longer, the police might have been called in. The *chillul Hashem* was horrible. I'm sorry, but you cannot work here any longer. I will provide you with up to a half-year's pay until you find another job."

Eli wasted no time in informing his close friend, Shlomo, of the news. Shlomo had been with the store since its opening and Mr. Altman relied on him for many things. Shlomo knocked on his boss' office door and entered to plead Eli's case. But Mr. Altman would not budge. "His behavior with the customers is shameful and I've spoken to him about it many times. He has six months to find a new job; I'll pay him his full salary all that time should he remain unemployed.

"The matter is closed."

Shlomo was upset. He felt that his loyalty and excellent performance of many years entitled him — and his friend — to special consideration. And he was not afraid to speak his mind — he knew that Mr. Altman needed him.

"You may be the captain of this ship, Mr. Altman, but you'd be nowhere without your crew. And frankly, I feel like jumping ship right now." Shlomo turned and left.

Tzvi, another longtime employee, happened to be outside the office, and since the door was ajar, he had overheard the conversation. He was shocked by Shlomo's words and attitude and he told him this in no uncertain terms.

"I cannot believe that you spoke to Mr. Altman like that! First of all, he is considerably older than you. Secondly, you and I both know what a wonderful boss he's been all these years. I understand that Eli is your friend, but..."

Shlomo cut him off in mid-sentence. "I didn't ask you for your opinion, Mr. Know-It-All. Stay out of my business!"

The next day, after he had calmed down, Shlomo apologized to Mr. Altman. But he steadfastly refused to speak to Tzvi. When Tzvi wished him "Good morning," Shlomo simply ignored him. When their paths crossed on a business matter, Shlomo spoke only the absolute minimum. This situation continued for a few days.

Tzvi was extremely upset. It is very unpleasant working side by side with someone who refuses to speak with you. A few other workers who were friends of Shlomo were acting cooly towards Tzvi, though they were speaking to him. Tzvi felt that he could not continue this way indefinitely. And he did not want to quit and search for a new job.

He knew that he had done nothing wrong. If anything, Shlomo should have apologized to him. But that was not going to happen. Knowing Shlomo, he might very well ignore him for the next forty years.

Tzvi decided that there was only one solution to the problem. He approached Shlomo privately and said, "I'm sorry for what I said the other day. I was only trying to be helpful."

It seemed that Shlomo had been waiting for an apology. "That's okay," he quickly replied. "Let bygones be bygones." And that was the end of the matter.

Once, a middle-aged man fell ill and underwent tests. The diagnosis was not good; the man had a life-threatening growth which required immediate surgery. The man told his family members, "I'm not going through with this surgery. I suffered enough under the Nazis; I will not subject myself to this sort of surgery and its aftermath." The man agreed to consult R' Avraham Yitzchak Kohen, the late Toldos Aharon *Rebbe* of Jerusalem, whose guidance he often sought.

The *Rebbe* listened patiently as the man expressed his anguish and fears. When he finished, the *Rebbe* asked, "Am I not correct that it is now many months that you and R' ____ are embroiled in a bitter feud?" The man replied affirmatively. "Well," continued the *Rebbe*, "the time has come for you to make peace. I realize that you feel that you have been wronged and it will be very hard for you to humble yourself and approach him in a gesture of peace. Nevertheless, you must do it. In this merit, you will be fine and will not require surgery."

The man did find the *Rebbe's* instructions extremely difficult to carry out. Nevertheless, he approached his adversary, apologized, and was successful in bringing the feud to an end. Later, he returned to the doctor and had the tests repeated. To the doctor's amazement, there was no trace of a growth. The man received a clean bill of health.

✒ Sign of True Love

Machlokes (strife) is so dreadful that the Chofetz Chaim found it necessary[9] to caution children that if their parents are involved in a dispute, they should not take their parents' side and join the fray. For example, even if a son is certain that his father is right, he should not take his side. It is quite possible that his love for his father will blind him so that he will not recognize the truth, for a parent and child are like a single soul.[10] Even if a father orders his son to join him in the dispute, the son must respectfully refrain from doing so. Our Sages derive from a Torah verse[11] that a parent should not be obeyed when he or she instructs a child to sin.

In a situation where a father has a high regard for his son's opinion, it is a *mitzvah* for the son to seek to make peace between his father and the other party. In fact, there is really no greater help that a child can offer a parent than to extricate him or her from the flames of dispute.

In the Chofetz Chaim's yeshivah in Radin, a major dispute concerning curriculum arose among the *talmidim*, which threatened to permanently destroy the peace and harmony that had existed in the yeshivah until that point. The yeshivah administration attempted to hide the matter from the aged Chofetz Chaim, out of fear that the news might affect his health. However, the Chofetz Chaim learned of the dispute and he felt broken over it. Despite his frailty, he made his way to the yeshivah where he delivered a two-hour address on the destructiveness of strife. At one point he cried out, "What do you think, that I too will join the fray? I would sooner close down seventy yeshivos than join a group of *baalei lashon hara.*"

The Chofetz Chaim succeeded in resolving the dispute.

❧ Sound Advice

R' Yitzchak Koledetsky writes of his father's *rebbi*, R' Shabsi Varnikovsky:

R' Shabsi was taught by his *rebbeim* that at a time when a dispute erupts in the community, even a dispute *l'shem Shamayim* (for the sake of Heaven), there is great danger of speaking the forbidden. The only solution, then, is to refrain from becoming involved in the dispute, to flee from it as far as can be, for the danger is great.

At such times, one should be especially careful to avoid taking part in group conversations, for there is a strong *yetzer hara* (evil inclination) to speak out against the other side. Every day there will be new developments which involve *lashon hara* and *rechilus,* and it is virtually impossible to avoid transgression.

It happened that a dispute erupted in a certain city to which a *talmid* of the Chofetz Chaim was preparing to travel. The Chofetz Chaim warned his *talmid* in strong terms not to spend the night there, for he would very likely become entangled in *lashon hara* and *rechilus.*

My father, R' Shachna Koledetsky, of blessed memory, would add that experience has shown: Those who become entangled in *machlokes* (strife), though their intentions were *l'shem Shamayim*, ultimately crossed the bounds of what is correct and proper, may Hashem save us from this.

My father would caution us to stay far away from strife. He would forbid discussion of such matters in our home, in keeping with the verse,[12] "One who guards his mouth and tongue guards his soul from troubles."[13]

ᦂ Seek Peace

David *HaMelech* declared, "Seek peace and pursue it,"[14] to which our Sages comment, "Seek peace today and pursue it tomorrow."[15]

The Chofetz Chaim explains this with the analogy of a wagon which is pulled by thick ropes. No matter how thick the ropes are, if they are strained day after day, year after year, they will eventually tear. Similarly, if a peacemaker does not succeed in his first attempt to settle a dispute, he should not give up. Ultimately, his words will accomplish something. Even if he does not settle the quarrel completely, he may succeed in making it a more civilized disagreement, or he may convince some of the "minor players" in the feud to make peace among themselves. In this way, he will have saved them from the bitter results of strife and will be worthy of the great reward for those who make peace, of which our Sages say, "The fruits are enjoyed in this world, while the primary reward remains intact for the World to Come."[16]

Chapter Fourteen

When Bad is Good

A shochet (ritual slaughterer) once mentioned to R' Yisrael Salanter that he was planning to change professions and become a businessman. "And why?" asked R' Yisrael. The man explained that he found the responsibility of being a *shochet* too difficult. After all, there are so many laws that a *shochet* needs to know and bear in mind each time he slaughters an animal. Business, on the other hand, is relatively simple, as far as Torah law is concerned, or so the man claimed.

R' Yisrael, however, disagreed. "You are mistaken," he told the man. "There is much more to know for one who seeks to conduct his business dealings according to Torah law. Open up the *Choshen Mishpat* section of *Shulchan Aruch* and see how many chapters deal with business laws.

"Take my advice and remain a *shochet*. It is easier to slaughter animals correctly than to run your business properly."

A person cannot do anything in life in full accordance with *Halachah* unless he studies the laws related to that activity. A *shochet* needs to know the laws of *shechitah*, a businessman needs to know the laws of lending, interest, etc. A Jew who hopes to keep Shabbos correctly needs to study the laws of Shabbos. And any Jew who hopes to avoid the sin of *lashon hara* needs to study the laws of *shemiras halashon*.

But there is another reason to study the laws of *shemiras halashon*. There are actually times when we are permitted and *even required* to speak what would normally be considered *lashon hara*. Without study of the laws, a person cannot possibly know which situations permit such words to be spoken. The Chofetz Chaim refers to negative statements which are permitted (and often required) as *lashon hara l'toeles*, *lashon hara* for a constructive purpose.

✑ *Risky Partnerships*

Mr. Stern is shopping in the local supermarket, where he overhears a conversation concerning some "big news." His friend Chaim is on the verge of embarking on a new business venture with David, a fellow whom Mr. Stern has known since childhood.

Mr. Stern is dismayed by this information. Chaim is a very rich man and is surely the one who will be supplying the money for this venture. David has very little money, but he is known to have a keen business sense.

It sounds like a perfect match. But there is something that Chaim obviously does not know. David does have exceptional business sense, but he can be extremely reckless — especially with someone else's money. Mr. Stern knows first-hand that in recent years, David has convinced others to give him some of their money for investment, only to risk the money on some "get-rich-quick" ventures which failed miserably.

Without a doubt, says the Chofetz Chaim, Mr. Stern *must* warn Chaim not to enter into such a partnership.[1]

Yosef is starting a computer software business and he is looking for a partner. He sets his eyes upon Daniel, who has been working with computers for fifteen years. Daniel has recently been laid off from a computer firm which has decided to streamline its operations.

Yosef's good friend Asher happens to be a close friend of Daniel. Yosef phones Asher to ask whether or not it would be a good idea for him to take Daniel as a partner.

There is silence on the other end. Asher is not sure how to respond, for he knows something that few people know. *Daniel was not "laid off" from his position, as he went around telling everyone — he was fired!* And for good reason. He tampered with a few of his company's programs in the hope of improving them, and succeeded in ruining them. Asher knows this to be the truth, because Daniel told it to him. What concerns Asher the most is that Daniel does not regret his having tampered with the programs without authorization. When Asher had tried to explain to him that he had no right to tamper with company property, without permission of the company president, Daniel had answered arrogantly, "I have more brains in my toes than that president has in his head."

Asher has become convinced of two things: Daniel knows less about computer software than he claims to know, and he has little regard for anyone's opinion other than his own.

Asher is *obligated* to tell Yosef that he does not recommend this partnership. His response falls under the category of *lashon hara l'toeles*.

Actually, such statements are not *lashon hara*, which means *evil speech*. Words which we are *permitted* to say are not *evil*. In labeling such statements *lashon hara l'toeles*, the Chofetz Yosef means that were it not for the fact that the statement is being made *l'toeles*, for a constructive purpose, it would considered *lashon hara*. For example, if Asher were to tell others what he knows about Daniel when there is no pressing reason to say it, he would certainly be committing the grave sin of speaking *lashon hara.*

♪ *Two Sides of a Coin*

The very same verse which prohibits us from speaking *lashon hara*[2] concludes with the words לֹא תַעֲמֹד עַל דַּם רֵעֶךָ, *Do not stand aside while your brother's blood is shed.* In its plain meaning, this teaches that if someone's life is in danger, we must do whatever we can to save him. The Chofetz Chaim sees another message in these words, which explains why the Torah placed this commandment in the same verse as *"Do not go as a peddler of gossip among your people"*: In most situations, speaking *lashon hara* is a terrible sin. However, when we know vital negative information that can save someone from harm, then we *must not stand aside while our brother's blood is shed, or while his money is lost, or he is hurt in some other way.* Rather, we should convey this information to those who need to know it.

But before relating such information, we must be certain that we are acting correctly. Consider the following case:

Shimon is an honest, responsible and successful business-man of many years. Two weeks ago, a company in which Shimon was a primary shareholder had a major setback and its investors suffered huge losses. Overnight, Shimon lost much of his wealth.

Yesterday, Shimon received a phone call from his friend Levi, asking him to become a partner in what seems to be a very profitable venture. Levi knows nothing about Shimon's recent losses — but Levi's friend Ari knows all about it. Should Ari warn Levi that to include Shimon in this partnership might be taking a risk?

Here, the Chofetz Chaim says that Ari is *not permitted* to say anything to Levi concerning Shimon's losses. Before we are permitted to speak *lashon hara l'toeles* (for a constructive purpose), we must fulfill seven conditions.[3] As we shall see, in this case, at least one of the conditions has not been met.

ℒ An Innocent Victim

Three of the seven conditions of "to'eles" are
- **Be absolutely certain that your information is true.**
- **Do not exaggerate.**
- **Be certain that the person has actually done something wrong.**

In our case, the information concerning Shimon's losses are true and are not exaggerated. But has Shimon done anything wrong? It does not seem so. For ten years, his investments earned him great profits. The sudden failure of a particular company is often unpredictable. There is no evidence that Shimon's losses had anything to do with recklessness or poor judgment.

There is every reason to believe, says the Chofetz Chaim, that Hashem will take pity on him so that he can succeed as he did in the past. And there is another factor to consider. To assist someone so that he can earn a living and not have to live off charity is actually the highest form of *tzedakah* — and no one ever loses from an act of *tzedakah*.[4]

ℒ A "Sticky" Situation

Chaim, Yaakov and Yeruchom are classmates. Yaakov brought a new hockey stick to school to use during recess. While Yaakov was in the school dining room eating lunch, Yeruchom "borrowed" the stick without permission — and accidentally cracked it.

Chaim was present when the hockey stick cracked. He and Yeruchom do not get along and he is actually quite happy to see his nemesis get himself into trouble. He tells Yeruchom, "You know, you're a *ganav* (thief) and a *shlemazal* (ne'er-do-well) and you're gonna have to pay for that! And you had better watch your stuff — Yaakov is liable to destroy everything in your locker!"

Yeruchom does not take too kindly to Chaim's insults and warnings. He retorts, "You stay out of this! You know that Yaakov has a ferocious temper, and you *want to see* him destroy my things! So just keep quiet about what happened. Besides, it wasn't my fault that the stick is cheap stuff — I'm not paying a cent for it!"

Of course Yeruchom is wrong. He had no right to borrow the hockey stick without permission and he is obligated to pay for it.

On the other hand, Chaim is not allowed to tell Yaakov about what happened.

Two more conditions for speaking *lashon hara l'toeles* are:
- **His intentions must be solely to help the victim. If he has any ulterior motives, then he must first eradicate them or remain silent.**
- **He must be certain that his words will not cause the wrongdoer to suffer more harm than the halachah permits.**

In our case, Chaim *does* have ulterior motives in telling Yaakov of what happened; he wants to see Yeruchom in trouble. Furthermore, the *halachah* would allow Yaakov to demand payment for the hockey stick, but he certainly has no right to exact revenge by destroying Yeruchom's possessions. For both of these reasons, Chaim must remain silent.

⚬ The Way to Criticize

In our example, Chaim ridiculed Yeruchom after he broke the hockey stick. One of the seven conditions of *lashon hara l'toeles* is:
- **Before speaking negatively about the person, approach him privately and attempt to convince him to correct the wrong he has committed. Only if this fails are you per-**

mitted to tell others of his wrongdoing (provided that the other six conditions have been fulfilled).

Chaim did attempt to convince Yeruchom to pay for the stick, but his attempt was doomed from the start. Calling someone a *ganav* and a *shlemazal* is not going to inspire him to mend his ways. To the contrary, such talk will only serve to enrage him and make him determined *not* to change his ways.

The Chofetz Chaim would tell his own *talmidim* who were appointed as *rabbanim* that they should be careful how they criticize their congregations. As Shlomo *HaMelech* said: "The words of the wise when spoken gently are heard."[5] A person who has done wrong is likely to accept criticism when he is spoken to with love and respect. However, if he is reprimanded harshly and is made to feel like a *rasha* (wicked person), he will probably ignore the criticism. Certainly, to embarrass a person for his wrongdoing is a severe sin and can only cause harm.

The Chofetz Chaim taught by example how to speak to a sinner. Once, the Chofetz Chaim was informed that a student in his yeshivah had intentionally desecrated the Shabbos. The Chofetz Chaim summoned the boy to his room and took his right hand in both his own. The Chofetz Chaim began to weep and with a mixture of pain and love, he uttered one word — "Shabbos...!" His hot tears dripped from his cheeks and fell upon the boy's hand.

The boy was so moved by this display of love and emotion for the sake of Shabbos that he resolved to mend his ways.

℘ The Seventh Condition

Devorah's food processor is broken and she wants to buy a new one. She mentions that she is planning to visit "Edward's Electronics" that afternoon. She has never been to that store, but she has seen its advertisements and its prices seem reasonable.

Chaya has shopped at "Edward's" many times. The store's manager, who happens to be an Orthodox Jew, is a very persuasive salesman and is an expert at recognizing an "easy" customer. Sometimes, in his desire to make a sale, he will convince the customer to purchase an item which may be of inferior quality; Chaya has seen this firsthand. She also knows that Devorah is very impressionable and will easily be persuaded to make a purchase.

Can Chaya warn Devorah not to shop at "Edward's"?

Not if she has an alternative. The seventh condition for speaking *lashon hara l'toeles* is:

- **He may relate it if the result can be accomplished only by saying the negative information. If there is a way to accomplish the same result without lashon hara, then that method must be employed.**

In our example, Chaya does have an alternative. Since Devorah is very impressionable, Chaya can convince her to shop at another appliance store without her having to mention anything about "Edward's." For example, she can tell her about a store where she has shopped often, where the prices are competitive and the salespeople are very helpful. If this plan does not work, she would be permitted to mention her concerns about "Edward's."

✌ *A Quick Review*

Let us briefly review the seven requirements which permit us to speak *lashon hara* for a constructive purpose:

1. **Be absolutely certain that the information is accurate.**
2. **Do not exaggerate.**
3. **Be sure that the information indicates that the person has actually done something wrong.**
4. **Be certain that you have no ulterior motives. Your sole intention must be that the wrong should be corrected.**
5. **Be certain that relating the information will not cause the wrongdoer to suffer more harm than that which the halachah permits.**

6. Before relating the information, first approach the wrong-doer (if possible) and try to convince him to correct the wrong. Be sure to treat him with dignity and respect.
7. Be certain that there is no way to correct the wrong other than to speak lashon hara.

"Its ways are ways of pleasantness."[6] The Torah, the wisdom of Hashem, teaches us proper *midos* and how to apply them. We are taught to stay far away from falsehood,[7] but we are permitted to alter the truth to maintain peace.[8] Similarly, it is permissible and sometimes *required* that we speak what would otherwise be *lashon hara*, if something constructive will be accomplished.

Chapter Fifteen

Family Talk

*A*s we have mentioned, the Chofetz Chaim states that it is virtually impossible to avoid speaking *lashon hara* without studying the laws of *shemiras halashon.*[1]

This is especially true within the family. Consider the following situations:

Case One: Chaim and Sholom are brothers who attend the same yeshivah. Chaim is present at recess when Sholom loses his temper during a basketball game and intentionally throws the ball the length of the gym. At supper that night, with the entire family gathered around the table, Chaim relates the incident to his family and adds, "Sholom, if you do that one more time, I'm sure that you'll get yourself into hot water."

Case Two: Chaya is baking a cake while her parents are out shopping. Chaya loses her balance and drops two eggs on the kitchen floor. She cleans up the mess and then bakes the cake. Her mother comes home and exclaims, "Oh, Chaya, that cake smells delicious! I see that you've been very busy while I was out." Chaya's younger sister Yaffa says, "Yes, she's been busy cleaning egg yolks off the kitchen floor!"

Case Three: It is the height of tax season and the accounting firm of Goldberg and Sanders is working overtime. Mr. Goldberg leaves the office at 9:00 P.M. after a twelve-hour work day. "So how was your day?" Mrs. Goldberg asks. "You really want to know?" her irate husband replies. "You know that Langer fellow who sits behind me in *shul*? Well, he decided that he'd like me to do his tax returns. So he showed up today at my office with three shoe-boxes full of papers and he expected *me* to organize them for him — the nerve of that fellow! He wasted two hours of my time. Next year, I'll be sure to tell him to find someone else to do his return!"

Let us examine these cases.

ℒ *Chaim's Mistakes*

"Regarding *lashon hara*, there is no difference between man or woman, relative or stranger... though when relatives speak about one another, it is usually not to disparage each other, but simply to state the truth, that the relative acted incorrectly."[2] In our first example, Chaim tells the family of Sholom's outburst with his brother's best interests in mind. He wants his parents to know what happened and he closes with his own personal warning to his brother that for his own good, he had better learn to control his temper.

Nevertheless, Chaim is wrong. Relating the incident to his parents would seem to be in the category of *toeles* (constructive purpose),[3] for it is the responsibility of parents to train their children in proper *midos*. And Sholom's father and mother are surely in a better position to correct their son's behavior than is his brother. However, Chaim should have spoken to his parents in private, not at the supper table in the presence of his brothers and sisters.

Furthermore, as we have learned, seven conditions must be fulfilled before we can speak *lashon hara l'toeles*. One condition is:

Before relating the information, first approach the wrongdoer (if possible) and try to convince him to correct the wrong. Be sure to treat him with dignity and respect.

If Sholom is prone to losing his temper, then Chaim probably has little to gain by speaking to him privately. He then would be correct to go directly to his parents. However, if such behavior is out of character for Sholom, then Chaim should either make no mention of the incident, or he should speak to him directly and in private.

Another condition of *lashon hara l'toeles* is:

Be certain that you have no ulterior motives. Your sole intention must be that the wrong should be corrected.

If Chaim and Sholom have been getting along, then this condition would probably not be a factor. However, if Chaim is upset at Sholom about something and he does derive a certain satisfaction from telling his parents of Sholom's outburst, then he would have to remain silent — unless he can work on himself to overcome his ill feelings towards his brother and truly have only his benefit in mind.

✌ *Yaffa's Humor*

"Yes, she's been busy cleaning egg yolks off the kitchen floor!" This was Yaffa's exclamation when her mother complimented Chaya on having surprised her with a cake.

Even the most careful people can drop things every now and then; Chaya's mishap was certainly not something that had to be reported to her parents. Yaffa may have only intended her comment as a joke. Nevertheless, as we have already learned,[4] *lashon hara* is forbidden even when said in jest. Yaffa may try to convince herself that Chaya knew she was only joking and "didn't mind." However, quite often a person is ashamed to admit that he has been hurt by a joke which was directed at him.

♫ Between Husband and Wife

As we all know, Chavah (Eve), the wife of Adam, was fashioned from a part of Adam's body. This teaches us that in a marriage, a husband and wife should be like a single person, living in harmony with one another and caring for one another as one would care for his very own self.

But this does *not* mean that husband and wife should share *lashon hara* with one another. When there is no constructive purpose in speaking *lashon hara*, it is a sin to relate it to *anyone*.

R' Shlomo Zalman Auerbach could never have become a world-renowned *posek* and *tzaddik* without the help and encouragement of his devoted Rebbetzin. In later years, when asked questions about raising small children, R' Shlomo Zalman would say humbly, "I'm not sure what was done in that case with my children, because I entrusted such matters to my Rebbetzin, who was a wise and pious woman and the daughter of great people."

They lived in accordance with *halachah*, at every instance and in every situation.

Once, a sister of R' Shlomo Zalman came to him to inquire about a prospective *shidduch* (marriage match) for her daughter. She waited until all visitors had left and then with no one in the room but R' Shlomo Zalman, his rebbetzin and herself, the sister mentioned the boy's name and asked if he would be a suitable mate for her daughter. R' Shlomo Zalman nodded in apparent approval.

In the same neighborhood lived another sister of R' Shlomo

Zalman, who had been a widow for many years. R' Shlomo Zalman asked his visiting sister, "Surely you will not return home without visiting our sister?" She replied that, of course, she would call on their sibling. How surprised she was when, upon leaving her sister's home, she found her brother waiting outside for her!

"About that boy of whom you inquired before... No, you should not pursue the *shidduch*; it is not an appropriate match for your daughter. You see, by telling you this, I am conveying a negative impression of this boy. To have uttered such words in the presence of my wife — for whom the matter is not relevant — would have been *lashon hara*. I could only tell you this in absolute privacy."

In the fictitious story below, we learn how tragic it can be when husband and wife do not live by the laws of *shemiras halashon*.

ℒ One Small Spark

"How was your day?" Mrs. Golden asked her husband.

"How was my day?" he retorted. "Well, it would have been fine if Mr. Rothman would have decided to stay home! You know who he is — the fellow who is always grabbing opportunities away from me.

"This morning, our boss mentioned that he needed someone to travel to Los Angeles for the company. I was all excited at the thought of escaping this frigid weather for a few days, but before I had a chance to even open my mouth, Rothman already had it wrapped up for himself! That's the second time he did that! And I *know* that I'm more qualified to represent the company than he is.

`You know why he got the assignment? I'll tell you why — because he has a way of making the boss think that he's an expert on things. He's got charisma, though I'm really the better businessman."

Mrs. Golden seethed with rage over the injustice to her husband. She was determined to do something about it. The next time she met Mrs. Rothman, she got straight to the point.

"So I hear your husband is going to Los Angeles!"

"Why, yes, he is, but how do you know?"

"Well, actually, my husband was supposed to be the one going, but your husband stole the opportunity right out from under him."

"Oh, he did, did he?" Mrs. Rothman replied angrily. "In other words, your husband is jealous that *my* husband was given this assignment. Well, did it ever enter your husband's mind that he might not be as qualified for the job as my husband? Does he have as many years of experience as my husband? I highly doubt it. So don't go accusing my husband of depriving your husband of an opportunity!"

Now Mrs. Rothman was quite upset over all this. At the supper table that night, she told her thirteen-year-old daughter, "You know that girl named Golden whom you spent time with last Sunday? I met her mother today while shopping and we had a very interesting conversation. What we discussed is not important for you to know — but I do wish you would find someone else to be friendly with. The Goldens are not exactly the nicest people, if you know what I mean."

Does this scenario seem far-fetched? Not according to the Chofetz Chaim.

> Many make this mistake: they tell their wives all that transpired between themselves and others at work and in *shul*. Besides speaking *lashon hara*, they also bring about *machlokes* (strife). Surely his wife will harbor a grudge over what happened and she will quarrel with the other person or with his wife... Therefore, any G-d-fearing person will be extremely careful not to relate such information.[5]

As we have learned, there are times when *lashon hara* may be spoken for a constructive purpose. If a woman is about to call a repairman who her husband knows is dishonest, he should stop her from placing the call. If possible, he should do this without resorting to *lashon hara*. "Why don't you call Mr. _____? I've known him for years and we've used him many times." However, if the wife were to respond, "Yes, he's okay, but my friends tell me that the fellow I'm calling is the best repairman around," the husband would be allowed to say, "That may be true, but unfortunately, I know from personal experience that he is dishonest."

ૐ Another Exception

Rachel (a fictitious character) was the top student in her class and was liked by almost everyone. Devorah was one of the few who disliked Rachel. Devorah burned with envy every time Rachel received an award or a compliment from her teacher.

Rachel invited the class to her house for her birthday party, but few girls came. The next day, Rachel discovered that Devorah had invited the classmates to her house for a free concert given by her cousin, a famous singer and musician. Though the girls liked Rachel, they did not want to miss this opportunity. When Rachel asked Devorah why she had scheduled her cousin's performance at the time of her party, she replied bluntly, "Because I don't like you."

Rachel was crushed. She had no idea that Devorah's dislike for her was so strong. She was terribly hurt that her friends opted to attend a performance instead of participating in her birthday party. And she was fearful that Devorah had other tricks up her sleeve.

Would Rachel be permitted to discuss her problem with her parents even though this would mean speaking *lashon hara* about Devorah?

Certainly, for this is *lashon hara l'toeles*, for a constructive purpose. Sharing her problem with her parents would help to ease Rachel's inner pain. And it is quite possible that her father and mother would come up with a solution to her problem.

The same applies to husband and wife. If a wife is finding it difficult to cope because she is suffering at work from her employer's unfair demands or from a co-worker's hostility, it is correct for her to unburden herself to her husband so that he can share her pain and perhaps offer suggestions to help the situation.[6]*

ℒ A Place for the Shechinah

A *shul* or *beis midrash* is not the only place which our Sages refer to as a *mikdash me'at*, a miniature *Beis HaMikdash*. A Jewish home is also a *mikdash me'at*, a place in which Hashem rests His Presence. It is a Jew's responsibility to make sure that his or her home is a place where the *Shechinah* will "feel at home." First and foremost, our homes needs to be places of peace and harmony. As Rabbi Akiva taught, when a husband and wife live together in peace, then the *Shechinah* dwells in their midst.[7]

Our homes need to be fortresses of *kedushah* (sanctity), free of the terrible influences of today's world at large.

There is another crucial ingredient which a Jewish home needs to qualify as a miniature *Beis HaMikdash*.

Think for a moment. What was the primary factor which caused the *Shechinah* to depart from the Second *Beis HaMikdash* at the time of the Destruction?

...*The Second Beis HaMikdash — we know that they*

---

*In *The Man of Truth and Peace — Rabbi Shlomo Zalman Auerbach* by Rabbi Yoel Schwartz (Feldheim Publishers), the following quote from R' Yitzchok Y. Borodiansky (a son-in-law of R' Shlomo Zalman) appears:

"My father-in-law taught that for a marriage to function properly — and he gave me permission to publicize this — a husband and wife must share their feelings. If some aspect of a woman's interpersonal relationships has disturbed her, and she feels that she must unburden herself, her husband should not thrust her aside by saying, 'It's *lashon hara*.' If the problem is too difficult for her to bear alone, he must share her packets of *tzaros* and help her overcome them. Of course, their purpose must be to reach a viable solution for the problem and to ease the pain of the aggravated party, and not to gossip or malign one's fellow. Yet even while 'letting off steam,' both parties must be very careful to abide by all the laws of *lashon hara*.

"Certain halachic authorities express doubts about the permissibility of repeating *lashon hara* to strangers in order to unburden oneself. However, because of the uniqueness of the marriage relationship, a husband and wife have a special obligation to listen to each other's problems."

*studied Torah, performed the mitzvos, and did kind deeds
— why was it destroyed? Because there was sinas chinam
(senseless hatred) among them.*[8]

And *lashon hara* is the primary cause of *sinas chinam*.

If we want our homes to be dwelling places for the *Shechinah*, then we must ensure that our families and guests are careful in matters of *shemiras halashon*.

It is not surprising that the Chofetz Chaim writes of a parent's obligation to teach his or her children about *shemiras halashon*. When a parent hears a child speaking *lashon hara*, he or she must rebuke the child. Above all, parents must set a proper example by avoiding *lashon hara* in their own conversation.[9]

The Chofetz Chaim also writes that children have an obligation not to remain silent when they hear their parents speaking *lashon hara*.[10] Of course, a child must be careful to be respectful when pointing out his parent's mistake, in keeping with the laws of *kibud av v'em* (honoring father and mother). Surely, parents will appreciate their child's concern and will be proud that he or she is striving to live by the laws of proper speech.

At the funeral of his *rebbetzin*, R' Shlomo Zalman Auerbach said, "Though it is customary to ask forgiveness of the deceased, I will not do so. My wife and I lived by the laws of *Shulchan Aruch*; we never offended each other or hurt each other in any way."

And they never offended *anyone else* or spoke *lashon hara* about anyone else as well. Theirs was a home where the *Shechinah* (Hashem's Presence) felt welcome at every instant.

Chapter Sixteen

Rechilus

Eliyahu is a pleasant, respectable, kindhearted fellow. His day is filled with learning, *davening*, work and *chesed*. He does not have a moment to spare.

Because he is so pressed for time, he has developed the bad habit of double-parking in front of every store in which he shops. On the busiest street, at the busiest time of day, you can see Eliyahu's blue sedan double-parked.

One Friday, the traffic was particularly congested. Two city buses, heading in opposite directions, were inching along — when the blue sedan blocked their paths and brought traffic to a standstill.

Horns began to honk. Drivers got out of their cars and yelled. About five minutes passed before Eliyahu emerged from a bakery with his bag of *challos*.

Shlomo, a friend of Eliyahu, had watched the entire scene.

Deeply distressed, he muttered, "He'd be better off eating *matzah* rather than cause this jam for a bag of *challos* — what a *chillul Hashem* (desecration of Hashem's Name)..."

Two days later, Eliyahu meets his friend Mendy, who also witnessed the scene when the traffic jam occurred. "I was standing right next to Shlomo," he tells Eliyahu, "and I can tell you that he was not pleased by the traffic snarl you caused. In fact, he said that you would have been better off eating *matzah* instead of buying those *challos*..."

Mendy is guilty of speaking *rechilus*, *lashon hara* which causes ill feelings between people. This applies even if Shlomo would readily admit to having made the remark. It is natural to feel hurt upon learning that someone criticized you when you were not present. The fact that Shlomo's comment was correct does not erase the animosity caused by Mendy's remark to Eliyahu. Mendy has caused a strain in the relationship between Eliyahu and Shlomo, and for this he must do *teshuvah*.[1]

The term *rechilus* comes from the word רָכִיל, *peddler (of gossip)* in the verse לֹא תֵלֵךְ רָכִיל בְּעַמֶּיךָ, *Do not go as a peddler of gossip among your people*.[2] A person who speaks *rechilus* "peddles" his gossip as he goes from person to person saying, "So-and-so said this about you..." Regarding *rechilus*, the Chofetz Chaim states:

> It is a great sin and it destroys many souls. This is why this sin is placed in the very same verse as "Do not stand idly by as your brother's blood is shed..."

Rechilus is forbidden even if the speaker has no intention of causing ill will.

✒ Third-party Support

Have you ever tried to enlist "third-party support" after offering a friend corrective criticism only to find your words falling on deaf ears?

"I'm telling you, David, you really blew it when you spoke up at today's office meeting. All you succeeded in doing was to put the boss into a bad mood."

"Well, I think I did the right thing, Ben. Sometimes you have to stand up for what's right even if the boss doesn't like hearing it."

"I couldn't disagree with you more, David. And as a matter-of-fact, Zev also thinks that you blew it — he told me so after the meeting."

Though Ben is well-meaning, he is guilty of speaking *rechilus*.[3] He may feel that it is important for David to know that he erred, and that he will appreciate being told Zev's comment. However, David's reaction may very likely be the opposite. He may be upset to learn that his friends have been discussing him in a critical light. Ben may have caused ill will between David and Zev.

Instead, Ben should have approached Zalman and suggested that he speak to David privately, without letting him know that they had conferred. Perhaps hearing the same message at different times from two close friends would be enough to convince David that indeed, he should not have upset their boss.

✌ In All Circumstances

In the unfortunate event that two Jews are bitter enemies, it would seem that it would be permissible to tell one of them concerning the other one, "Do you know what he said about you yesterday at the *kiddush*...?" After all, they are already enemies; certainly, one should be allowed to tell them what they already know!

Wrong, says the Chofetz Chaim. Each additional report strengthens the animosity between the warring parties. Therefore, it is forbidden to relate such information.[4]

It is also forbidden to relate *rechilus* under pressure. The Chofetz Chaim finds it necessary to point out that even if a parent were to say to a child, "Tell me what Mr. Katz said about me!" or if a teacher were to order a student, "Find out which parents complained about the assignment!" — the child or student would have to explain in a respectful manner that the *halachah* does not permit this.[5]

✒ When the Stakes Are High

A Jew has to be prepared to sacrifice any amount of money rather than transgress a single לֹא תַעֲשֶׂה (negative commandment). For example, a boss might tell his worker, "I understand that there were some complaints about the new rules for taking vacation. Would you mind telling me who had a problem with it?" The worker would have to politely refuse to divulge such information — even at the risk of losing his job.[6]

It is at such times that a Jew must strengthen his faith in Hashem, Who provides every person and every creature with its needs. Surely Hashem will provide for someone who makes a monetary sacrifice for the sake of a *mitzvah.*

R' Yaakov Yosef Herman and his wife emigrated to Eretz Yisrael in August of 1939. Their sea voyage from America was prolonged due to the threat of war. On Friday, September 1, 1939, the Second World War erupted and it was on that day that the boat carrying the Hermans docked at Haifa.

One hour before Shabbos, the passengers were ordered to disembark and claim their baggage at the pier.

All of the Hermans' possessions were on board, packed into sixteen crates and nine suitcases. They knew that it would be impossible to transport everything to their lodging before sundown. Mr. Herman (as he referred to himself) grabbed the suitcase containing his personal *sefer Torah, tallis,* and *tefillin,* while his wife took only her pocketbook. Mr. Herman then attempted to explain to the officer in charge that the Sabbath would soon begin and therefore, he could not possibly remove the rest of his belongings. Tears rolled down his cheeks as he said, "I have never desecrated the Sabbath in my life. To dese-crate it here in the Holy Land is unthinkable."

The officer responded curtly, "Rabbi, this is *war*. You must make allowances. If you leave your baggage here, it will be left unattended. Arabs will surely come along and take everything away. You will return tomorrow night to find nothing left."

"I don't care about the baggage," Mr. Herman replied. "Please stamp our passports and let us go."

It was then that the officer asked how much baggage the Hermans would be leaving behind. Amazed by their response, he called to another officer, "Stamp their passports and let them through! This rabbi is willing to lose all his belongings so that he can get to the city in time for their Sabbath."

The entire Shabbos, Mr. Herman was in a state of heightened ecstasy. Again and again he exclaimed, "The Boss [i.e. Hashem] does everything for me. What could I ever do for him? Now, at last, I have the privilege of giving all for the Boss, for the sake of Shabbos and to sanctify His Name."

After Shabbos ended, the Hermans returned to the pier to see if anything at all remained of their possessions. They spotted a small light in the darkness. "Who goes there?" a British-accented voice called out.

Mr. Herman identified himself.

"So you've finally returned! I've been waiting for you! My su-perior, with whom you spoke yesterday, was deeply impressed by your faith in G-d and by the strength of your convictions. That's why he ordered me to guard your possessions until you would return to claim them. Kindly check that all your belong-ings are here — my superior will have my head if anything is missing!"[7]

ℒ *For the Sake of Peace*

Mr. Sanders is an important man in his company. His job is secure. At a corporate meeting one afternoon, his boss turns to him and says, "Sanders, I understand that you are a next-door neighbor of our biggest competitor. Does he ever comment about us?"

"He sure does," Mr. Sanders is thinking to himself. "And he does not speak very kindly about your business tactics."

"Well," Sanders tells his boss, "he has mentioned our company in conversation, but it's never been anything important."

"I'll be the judge of that," the boss retorts. "Tell me what he said!"

Mr. Sanders is in a quandary. His neighbor has, on various occasions, told him that "the company you work for makes shoddy merchandise," and, "I've heard your boss is a real tyrant." He has also offered Mr. Sanders a position in his company, an offer which Sanders declined.

If he tells all this to his boss, a very tough businessman and a hot-tempered fellow, it could lead to a war between the two companies. It could also damage the friendly relationship between the Sanders family and their neighbors. What should Mr. Sanders do? The Chofetz Chaim leaves no room for doubt:

> If he can formulate a reply which will not be *rechilus* and will also not be an outright lie, then he should reply in this way. However, if he knows that his friend will not accept such a reply, then he is permitted to say an outright lie for the sake of maintaining peace.[8]

This law is derived from the episode in the Torah where the angels (disguised as wayfarers) informed Avraham and Sarah that they would be blessed with a child. Sarah laughed incredulously, for how could a couple so old be granted a child? Hashem was displeased with Sarah's laughter and He confronted Avraham, asking, "Why did Sarah laugh, saying, 'Can it be true that I will give birth when I am old?'"[9] Actually, Sarah had said that both she *and Avraham* were old. For the sake of peace, Hashem only related half of her statement to Avraham, for Avraham might have felt hurt that his wife referred to him as "old."[10]

Elsewhere,[11] the Chofetz Chaim derives another important law from this episode. It is forbidden to tell someone a remark which was made about him, if that remark will cause him to be even slightly upset — even if the remark is not actually derogatory.

At the time of this incident, Avraham was ninety-nine years old. Certainly it was correct to say that he was old. But the relationship between husband and wife is a very delicate one. Hashem, in His infinite wisdom, determined that even someone as great as Avraham *Avinu* (our Forefather) might feel slightly hurt upon learning that his wife referred to him as "old." Therefore, Hashem omitted this portion of Sarah's remark when relating it to Avraham.

✒ *Shame of Honor*

Let us return to our case of Mr. Sanders and his difficult boss.

Suppose that Mr. Sanders decides that altering the truth will not work; he is not very good at "spinning yarns" and his boss, a very sharp fellow, is sure to know whether or not he is being truthful. Therefore Mr. Sanders says, "I'm sorry, but I cannot repeat my private conversations with my neighbor."

His boss flies into a rage. In front of everyone, he ridicules his worker. "So, Sanders, you're being Mr. Goody-goody! If I didn't need your expertise, I'd fire you right now, you ungrateful, disloyal fool! You don't care about the company, right? It doesn't bother you if our competition hurts us behind our backs...

"Sir," Mr. Sanders interrupts, "I honestly do not believe that a few comments told to me privately by our competitor will hurt us in any..."

"Don't contradict me!" his boss bellows, and he proceeds to hurl insults at Mr. Sanders, embarrassing him in front of his co-employees.

Suffering embarrassment can be very difficult, but it does not permit us to speak *lashon hara* or *rechilus*.[12] The Chofetz Chaim assures us that the reward for suffering such shame in silence is very great. Our Sages teach:[13]

Those who are insulted but do not insult [in response], who hear disgrace but do not reply, who perform [Hashem's will] out of love and are happy in suffering, to them we apply the verse,[14] "But they who love Him [Hashem] shall be as the sun going forth in its might."

In *Sefer Shemiras HaLashon*,[15] the Chofetz Chaim relates the following story:

R' Chaim and R' Zalman of Volozhin were brothers and famed disciples of the Vilna *Gaon*. Once, while traveling, they stopped off at an inn. The Jewish innkeeper, who had no idea who they were, was extremely nasty. Hurling insults and abuse at them, he refused them a room for the night. They had no choice but to continue on their way in the darkness.

To his surprise, R' Chaim heard his brother weeping. "Why are you weeping?" he asked R' Zalman. "Why should those foolish insults and abuses bother you? I paid no attention to them."

His righteous brother replied, "No, my dear brother, I am not weeping because the innkeeper insulted me. What upsets me is that when the insults were hurled at me, I felt some resentment in my heart. This means that I have not yet reached the level of 'Those who suffer insult... to them we apply the verse...'

"It is for this that I weep..."

Chapter Seventeen

Shades of Ill Will

*I*t was a very unpleasant experience.

The Brechers and the Finestones lived in the same neighborhood for fifteen years. They belonged to the same *shul* and their children attended the same schools. A bad word never passed between them — until the crash.

It happened when Mr. Brecher backed his Cadillac out of his driveway as Mr. Finestone was heading down the street behind the wheel of his Lexus. Brecher claims that he honked loudly and looked to make sure that no one was coming. He insists that Finestone must have swerved around the corner at top speed, as he often does. Mr. Finestone says that there was no honk and that he could not have been going more than twenty miles per hour.

Thankfully, it was nothing serious. Neither party was even slightly injured. But the driver's side of the Cadillac was badly dented. There was a sharp exchange of words between the two drivers, as each blamed the other for the mishap. For three weeks, they did not speak to one another. All matters pertaining to the crash went through a third party.

But time helped to heal their wounds. Neither man was happy about the situation and when someone suggested a compromise solution to end the dispute, both Mr. Brecher and Mr. Finestone quickly accepted it. After Mr. Finestone paid the amount which had been agreed upon, the two shook hands and resumed speaking to one another. After that, they would greet each other cordially; both were careful never to make mention of the crash.

Everyone was happy — except for a neighbor of the Brechers, Mr. Rosen. Rosen had a long-standing feud with Mr. Finestone. When he learned of the crash and the resultant dispute, he was quite pleased that now he was not the only one who was not on speaking terms with Finestone.

He was genuinely disappointed to learn that the matter had been resolved.

One day, he and Mr. Brecher were having a conversation about car insurance. "I just took out a new policy that gives me excellent coverage for collision, " Mr. Brecher remarked.

"Here's my chance to bring back old memories!" Mr. Rosen thought.

"Yes," he countered, "and you *had better* have good coverage for collision! After all, you might pull out of your driveway one day, to find someone crashing into you — if you know what I mean!"

The Chofetz Chaim states:

> It is forbidden to relate *rechilus* in a deceitful way. [For example], a person might know that someone suffered a loss or was degraded on account of someone else, and that this led to a quarrel between the two. Now, this person wants to reignite the old dispute in a way that will disguise his true intentions. So with his sly lips, he makes mention of what had happened as if he is just talking casually and does not even know who was the culprit in that incident. By

doing this, he causes his listener to remember who had wronged him.[1]

ℒ Causing Distress

In the above example, Mr. Rosen's deviousness could stir up bad feelings and possibly reignite an old feud. *Rambam* teaches that even a statement which might frighten someone unnecessarily or cause him unnecessary heartache is forbidden.[2] For example:

The law firm of Bruk and Bornfeld was established fifteen years ago and is highly successful. But unknown to Mr. Bornfeld, Mr. Bruk was negotiating secretly with Mr. Ross in the hope of breaking up the partnership and opening a new firm. However, the negotiations fell through and the old partnership remained. Anyone who tells Mr. Bornfeld about the failed negotiations is guilty of *rechilus*; such a report would probably cause ill will between the partners and could ultimately lead to the breakup of the partnership. At the very least, it would case Mr. Bornfeld distress.[3]

ℒ Avak Rechilus

In an earlier chapter, we learned that certain statements, while not overt *lashon hara*, are forbidden under the category of "*avak lashon hara*" ("the dust of *lashon hara*"). For example, it is forbidden to reveal that someone gave a poor man a very large donation, because it is possible that the man wants this to remain a secret, so that he will not be swamped with *tzedakah* requests.

Other statements are forbidden as *avak rechilus*. For example: it is forbidden to say to a person who has turned down your request for a donation, "Why are you refusing me? So-and-so told me that just the other day, you gave him a very generous contribution." Obviously, this will cause the donor to become upset at his beneficiary for having revealed that he received a generous donation.[4]

It is forbidden to tell a businessman that in his absence his partner showed great generosity — if this might make the man upset at his partner. For example, to say, "It was really nice of your partner to have one of your workers fix the leak in my roof," would be *avak rechilus*. Perhaps this man is not as generous as his partner and will be upset to learn that his worker was used to provide a repair free of charge.[5]

We have learned that it is forbidden to say, "I'd rather not talk about So-and-so," because it implies something negative. Similarly, to say, "I asked him about you and he said, 'I'd rather not talk about him,'" would be *avak rechilus*, for it can cause ill will.[6]

We have learned that it is forbidden to criticize someone's merchandise without any constructive purpose. Similarly, to *tell someone* that someone else spoke badly of his merchandise would be speaking *rechilus*.

"Mr. Altman said that the last car he bought from you was a real lemon!" Obviously, the car dealer will not be too pleased to hear of this; the statement is sure to cause ill will between him and Mr. Altman.[7]

ℒ *Unfortunate and Avoidable*

The Chofetz Chaim bemoans an all-too-common occurrence:

Reuven tells Shimon: "Do you know what Levi said about you...?" Shimon walks away furious at Levi. Of course, Reuven is guilty of speaking *rechilus*.

But the story is not over.

Later, Shimon confronts Levi, "So I hear that you've been talking about me...?"

Even if Shimon does not mention Reuven by name, he is guilty of *rechilus*, if Levi will be able to deduce that Reuven told Shimon about his remarks. By confronting Levi, Shimon has caused ill will between Levi and Reuven.[8]

Of course, this could have been avoided if Shimon would have simply chosen not to believe Reuven's report. Elsewhere,[9] the Chofetz Chaim elaborates on this idea with a powerful illustration:

A buyer negotiates a price with Baruch the wine merchant for the purchase of several barrels of wine. They agree on a price and the buyer brings his barrels to Baruch, who will have them filled by the next day. But that evening, the buyer meets Chaim the wine merchant and without telling him that he has already concluded a deal with Baruch, asks the price of his wine. Chaim is anxious for some business, so he quotes a very low price. The buyer places an order with Chaim, then returns to Baruch and cancels his order.

Baruch is astounded. "But we had a deal, and your barrels are sitting in my cellar! How can you break the agreement?" The buyer, trying to save face, replies, "I'll tell you the truth. I met Chaim on the street and in conversation, I happened to mention that I had made a wine order. He asked me, 'Why don't you buy from me? My wine is far better than Baruch's and my price is cheaper!'"

Baruch is ready to explode. "How could Chaim do such a thing? He literally took the bread right out of my mouth! That's it — if he could do such a thing, then I declare war!" Baruch makes his way around the neigborhood telling everyone what Chaim did and assuring them that it is a *mitzvah* to spread the word of Chaim's wickedness.

It does not take long for Chaim to catch wind of what is happening. He responds in kind, vilifying his competitor and "enemy" and making sure that the news spreads.

And how did it all begin? With Baruch accepting the buyer's slanderous report about Chaim. "*He asked me, 'Why don't you buy from me? My wine is far better than Baruch's and my price is cheaper!'*"

As we will learn in forthcoming chapters, the Torah prohibits us from accepting *lashon hara* or *rechilus* as fact. Listening to evil speech and accepting it is as much a sin as speaking it. By following the Torah's commandments and refraining from both speaking and believing all forms of *lashon hara*, we avoid dispute and pave the way for a pleasant, peaceful life — in this world and in the World to Come.

Chapter Eighteen

Repairing the Damage

*I*t is told that a yeshivah student once came to R' Yisrael Alter of Ger to request his blessing. "Where do you study?" the *Beis Yisrael* asked the young man.

The student named a well-known yeshivah where most students are *baalei teshuvah*, those who have returned to the path of Torah and *mitzvos*. "However," the student quickly added, "I am not a *baal teshuvah*."

"And why not?" asked the *tzaddik*.

The *Beis Yisrael* meant that a Jew should repent his sins at every opportunity, all through the year. Three times a day, we beseech Hashem, "Bring us back, our Father, to Your Torah...Forgive us, our Father, for we have erred." Every Jew, whether or not he is religious from birth, should consider himself a "*baal teshuvah*."

As the Chofetz Chaim stresses, speaking *lashon hara* usually involves a number of sins. To be forgiven by Hashem for speaking *lashon hara*, a person must engage in the three basic steps of *teshuvah*: חֲרָטָה, *regret for his sin*; עֲזִיבַת הַחֵטְא, *acceptance upon oneself never to repeat this sin*; and וִדּוּי, *confession of one's sin before Hashem*.[1]

חֲרָטָה means to sincerely regret the sin. For example: Raphael spoke *lashon hara* about a classmate named Yosef. Raphael later regrets his words; he tells himself, "I wish that I had never spoken those awful words about Yosef. In making those remarks, I transgressed a number of commandments. I lowered Yosef's stature in the eyes of my listeners and I lowered my own stature before Hashem. I deeply regret my words."

That is חֲרָטָה.

עֲזִיבַת הַחֵטְא is to firmly decide in one's mind to do everything possible to avoid repeating the sin. *Rambam* writes that this means that Hashem, Who knows our innermost thoughts, can bear witness that if we were to be in the same situation as before, we would not repeat our past sin.[2]

It is late at night, and the counselor has left the bunk. Everyone is wide awake, exchanging funny stories that happened at school during the year. Yosef's name is mentioned. "He's the most absent-minded fellow I've ever seen!" Daniel exclaims. "He once opened up his lunch bag — or so he thought. It was actually a bag of garbage that his mother had asked him to throw out on the way to school!"

Raphael is lying quietly in his bed, tingling with excitement. Just wait until they hear about the time when Yosef wore his sister's coat to school! It wasn't until the rebbi noticed everyone laughing during recess that he whispered to Yosef to take off the coat and come with him to the office to call home.

It's on the tip of his tongue. But then he remembers. Before the summer, he made up his mind to "Say 'No!' to lashon hara." This is Rapahel's first real test.

Is he going to fail?

No. Instead of telling his story about Yosef, he deftly changes the topic of conversation, steering clear of any lashon hara.

That is עֲזִיבַת הַחֵטְא.

Which comes first, חֲרָטָה or עֲזִיבַת הַחֵטְא? It depends, writes *Rabbeinu Yonah*.[3] When a person commits a sin which for him is out of character, his first step should be חֲרָטָה, *regret*. However, when he seeks to do *teshuvah* for a sin which he commits often, then his first step should be עֲזִיבַת הַחֵטְא, where he demonstrates the reality of his change of heart by refraining from the sin when the opportunity presents itself.

Rabbeinu Yonah offers the well-known parable of a person who immerses himself in a *mikveh* to purify himself, while holding onto a dead *sheretz* (crawling creature) which contaminates him! His immersion in the *mikveh* accomplishes nothing. Similarly, when a person commits the same sin again and again, the first step of *teshuvah* must be to abandon that sin.

Therefore, a *baal lashon hara* (one who speaks *lashon hara* regularly) should begin the *teshuvah* process by resolving not to speak *lashon hara* and not to associate with those who speak it — and he should demonstrate his change of heart by carefully avoiding *lashon hara* at every instance.

✒ "I Have Sinned"

Viduy, confession, is a basic component of *teshuvah*. In fact, the requirement to confess before Hashem is the only component of *teshuvah* which is explicitly mentioned in the Torah.[4]

Why is it necessary to tell Hashem, "I have sinned..." Why isn't it sufficient to feel regret in one's heart and resolve to change?

R' Samson Raphael Hirsch explains:[5] Through the course of the day, literally thousands of thoughts flow through the human mind. How often are we suddenly possessed by an idea to perform some wonderful deed — only to forget it moments later! However, when we pause for a moment and express our thoughts verbally, it is an entirely different matter. By saying, "I have sinned," the person takes what might have otherwise been just a passing emotion and makes it something concrete. This is why *viduy* is essential to *teshuvah*.

Another reason has been suggested as to why *viduy* is crucial: When a person hurts himself badly, it is natural to cry out in pain. Suppressing one's cries actually makes it more difficult to bear the pain. In a famous incident, R' Moshe Feinstein restrained himself from crying out when someone accidentally closed a car door on his fingers. R' Moshe did this so that the person, who had been his driver, would not realize what had happened. This certainly took great effort on R' Moshe's part. Without a doubt, it made his injury more difficult to bear.

When a person engages in sincere *teshuvah*, he feels pained over the wrongs which he committed. *Viduy* is a way of crying out, a means through which to ease the pain.[6]

But even חֲרָטָה, עֲזִיבַת הַחֵטְא, and וִדּוּי are not sufficient for the sin of *lashon hara* to be forgiven. There is still one more vital step which must be carried out.

ℒ *Between Man and Man*

The Mishnah teaches: "This did Rabbi Elazar ben Azariah expound: ...Regarding sins between man and his fellow man, [even] Yom Kippur does not atone, until he appeases that man."[7] One who has spoken *lashon hara* must seek forgiveness, if the listeners accepted his evil words as truth. If they rejected the *lashon hara*, then the sin is only between man and Hashem and one need not seek forgiveness from the person of whom he spoke.[8]

In *Mishnah Berurah*,[9] the Choftez Chaim writes that when seeking forgiveness, one should specify exactly what it was he said or did, unless this will cause embarrassment to the person.

R' Yehudah Zev Segal would remind his *talmidim* that although the requirement to seek forgiveness is stated in the Mishnah and *Shulchan Aruch* regarding Yom Kippur, it is a requirement *all year long*. As the Chofetz Chaim himself points out, this *halachah* is stated regarding Yom Kippur because the special cleansing powers of Yom Kippur will not erase a sin between man and his fellow man unless forgiveness has been sought and granted.[10]

One should be sincere in *seeking* forgiveness and one should be sincere in *granting* forgiveness, as the following stories demonstrate.

✒ R' Elyah Lopian

A stranger once approached the legendary *mashgiach* R' Elyah Lopian and asked forgiveness for having spoken *lashon hara* about him. R' Elyah replied that he could not forgive the man with a whole heart unless the man told him what it was he had said. At first the man was very reluctant to comply, but since he wanted to be forgiven, he finally did tell R' Elyah what he had said. His words shocked R' Elyah.

The *tzaddik* said, "It would be easy for me to *tell you* that I forgive you, but I want to forgive you with my whole heart. What you have done to me is very serious and if I am honest with my-self, I know that my forgiveness at this time will not be wholehearted. I suggest that you return to me in about two weeks. In the meantime, I will do my best to learn a great deal of *mussar* on the subject, with the goal of granting you complete forgiveness."

True to his word, R' Elyah worked on himself, and by the time the man returned, he was able to grant him the forgiveness he sought.

The above incident took place in London. Years later, when R' Elyah was *Mashgiach* of the Kaminetz Yeshivah in Jerusalem, a student approached him to beg forgiveness for having spoken *lashon hara* about him.

"I would forgive you," R' Elyah responded, "but according to the *halachah*, once I forgive, I would not be allowed to hold any grievance against you should I later find out what it is that you said about me.

"But what if I *do* find out one day? What if I find your words offensive and as a result, feel ill will towards you? I would then be guilty of hatred towards a fellow Jew.

"What should I do? I want to forgive you! I'll tell you what: Tell me the *lashon hara*, and I will see if I can forgive you."

The student told R' Elyah what he had said, and R' Elyah responded, "It's a good thing that you told me — I don't feel that I can forgive you with my whole heart! Come back in two hours. I will spend those two hours learning *mussar*, and then I will be able to erase any ill will from my heart."

Two hours later the student returned and R' Elyah told him, "Now I can forgive you wholeheartedly."[11]

❧ A Child's Regret

Seeking forgiveness for having wronged someone can be difficult, but it must be done nonetheless. This is illustrated by a beautiful story involving the famed *maggid* R' Sholom Schwadron when he was but a child.

The head of the *chevra kaddisha* (burial society) in Jerusalem's Meah Shearim neighborhood was a very tall man who had an unusual walk. His height and way of walking gave him a strange appearance as he strode down the street.

One day, Sholom and some friends were playing in a schoolyard when the man climbed the stairs of a *shul* next door. Young Sholom imitated the man's walk, as his friends doubled over with laughter.

At first, the man tried to ignore the laughter coming from behind him. But as it grew louder, he spun around and shouted, "Who is making fun of me?" The man quickly descended the stairs as the children fled in all directions. After a while, the man gave up the chase and, frustrated, made his way to *shul.*

Sholom, though only a boy, was very bothered by the man's humiliation. Filled with regret, he could not rid himself of the thought, "A Jew's feelings were hurt because of my wildness..."

The next morning, Sholom made a daring decision. He would ask the man for forgiveness. The problem was, he did not know where the man lived.

He searched the length and breadth of Meah Shearim until finally he found the man standing at the center of another neighborhood *shul*. Sholom's first reaction was to turn and flee in panic. He was small for his age and the man appeared to him like a giant. What if the man would decide to "give him what he deserved"? But as terrified as he was, his feeling of regret was stronger.

Heart pounding, he stepped back into the *shul*, cupped his hands around his mouth and called out in Yiddish, "I am the boy who made fun of you yesterday. Forgive me!" With that, he turned and fled.

But the man was much faster. With his giant strides, he quickly overtook Sholom and caught him in his two hands. Sholom tried to struggle free, but he could not loosen the man's grip.

The man, a goodhearted soul, patted Sholom vigorously as he brought him back into the *shul*. Then, he lifted the boy up, kissed him on the forehead and called out for all to hear, "Look! Have you ever seen a mere child ask forgiveness?" Lovingly, he brought Sholom back down and let go of him.

Sholom then left the *shul*, with a great burden lifted from his young heart.[12]

Chapter Nineteen

The Art of Not Listening

As a young man, the Chofetz Chaim published his first work, *Sefer Chofetz Chaim*, anonymously. He would travel from town to town in the guise of a *sefarim* peddler selling a new *sefer* on the laws of proper speech. It would be some time before word spread that this "peddler" was none other than the author himself, and that he was an outstanding *gaon* and *tzaddik*.

On one of his incognito travels, the Chofetz Chaim found himself on a horse-drawn carriage, in the company of butchers and horse traders who were on their way to a fair. For a long time, the men discussed business — the quality of oxen, cows and horses. The Chofetz Chaim sat deep in thought, seemingly unaware of the conversation all around him. Then one of the dealers mentioned another dealer by name, mocking and ridiculing him. Suddenly, the Chofetz Chaim came to life and spoke up:

"Dear brothers," he said, "until now, you have spent your time well, talking of matters connected with your occupation. Why turn your conversation to discussing people? This pulls everyone into a web of gossip — a most serious sin!"

The traders looked scornfully at this plainly dressed stranger who dared to criticize them. Ignoring his reproof, they continued their conversation.

The Chofetz Chaim, however, could not sit silently in the presence of such shameful talk. He began to plead with them, imploring them that, for their own sake, they change their topic. A few of them responded by hurling insults at him. "Beggar, who needs your fine moral lecture? If you don't like it, get out of the carriage!" And they continued their conversation.

The Chofetz Chaim bore these insults in silence. After a few moments, he moved closer to the driver and asked him to please stop the carriage so that he could descend from it. He preferred to remain alone on the road and search for another means of transportation, rather than continue to ride with a group of *baalei lashon hara*.

The Chofetz Chaim was *not* acting *lifnim mishuras hadin*, beyond the letter of the law. He was doing what is required of every Jew in such a situation.

ל *A Time to Leave*

The Torah states: לֹא תִשָּׂא שֵׁמַע שָׁוְא, *Do not accept a false report*,[1] to which *Rashi* comments: "It is a command against accepting *lashon hara*."

This means that if I happen to overhear a conversation spiced — or better said, poisoned — with *lashon hara*, I am not allowed to believe what I hear. What is the reason for this? "Because by accepting the report as fact," explains the Chofetz Chaim, "we will look scornfully upon the person who was the subject of the *lashon hara*."[2] It is lowly to *think* badly of other Jews, just as it is lowly to *speak* badly of them.

The Chofetz Chaim teaches us that there is another aspect to this negative commandment: "The Torah also prohibits us from listening to *lashon hara*, even though we have no intention of believing it — merely turning one's attention to listen [is forbidden]."[3]

The Chofetz Chaim elaborates upon this *halachah*:[4]

> What if someone finds himself among people who turn their conversation to *lashon hara* and he is reasonably sure that they will ignore all reproof?
>
> If it is possible for him to leave the group or to stick his fingers into his ears, then it is a great *mitzvah* to do this. However, if he finds it impossible to leave the group and he is very reluctant to stick his fingers in his ears because they will laugh at him,[5] then at the very least, he must garner his inner strength at this time of distress and wage spiritual war with his *yetzer hara* so that he will not be guilty of the Torah prohibition against listening to and accepting *lashon hara*. This requires a three-point plan:
>
> 1) He must decide in his mind that he absolutely will not believe the *lashon hara* that is being spoken.
> 2) He should not derive pleasure from what is being said.
> 3) He should ensure that his facial expressions do not convey any hint of approval of what is being said. At the very least, he should sit stone-faced; if possible, his facial expression should convey strong *disapproval*.

This applies if one innocently sat down, unaware that those around him were going to speak *lashon hara*. However, if someone overhears a *lashon hara* conversation and stops to listen, or if he joins a group of known gossipers, then he has sinned by listening to their conversations, even if he disapproves of what is being said.

The Chofetz Chaim adds that someone who associates with a group of gossipers will be inscribed in Heaven as a *baal lashon hara* and "his sin is too great to bear."[6]

The Chofetz Chaim concludes by quoting from the ethical will which the *Tanna* (Mishnaic Sage) R' Eliezer *HaGadol* wrote to his son Hyrkanos:

My son, do not sit among groups who speak badly of others, for when their words ascend to Heaven they are recorded, and whoever is present is inscribed as being part of a wicked group of *baalei lashon hara*.[7]

ℒ Of Fingers and Ear Lobes

The Torah teaches us that even when in the midst of battle, a Jewish soldier must maintain his human dignity and keep his camp holy. He should take care of his bodily needs outside the camp and take with him a spike so that he can cover over his waste:

וְיָד תִּהְיֶ׳ לְךָ מִחוּץ לַמַּחֲנֶה, וְיָצָאתָ שָׁמָּה חוּץ וְיָתֵד תִּהְיֶ׳ לְךָ עַל אֲזֵנֶךָ...
You shall have a place outside the camp, and to it you shall go out. You shall have a spike in addition to your weapons [to use for this purpose...][8]

This is the plain meaning of these verses. Our Sages, however, offered another interpretation:

Bar Kappara taught: Why is it written: "You shall have a spike in addition to your weapons [אֲזֵנֶךָ]?" Do not read it אֲזֵנֶךָ, *your weapons*, but rather [as if it were pronounced] אָזְנֶךָ, *your ear*. For if a person hears something that is not proper, he should place his fingers [which narrow at the tip like a spike] in his ears [to block out the sound].

...It was taught in the academy of R' Yishmael: Why is the entire ear hard while the lobe of the ear is soft? So that if a person hears something that is not proper, he is able to bend the lobe into [the ear and block out the sound].[9]

Did you ever wonder why the fingers of our hands are so different from the toes of our feet? The toes are rather square-shaped, while the fingers are thinner and are tapered. Bar Kappara tells us why this is so. Our fingers serve a crucial function. They can protect our ears from whatever we are not supposed to hear. The academy of R' Yishamel informs us that Hashem made the ear lobe soft for this same reason.

The human body is undoubtedly the most incredible and complex creation. We recognize the wondrous way in which our bodies function every time we recite the *Asher Yatzar* blessing: *"Blessed are You, Hashem... Who fashioned man with wisdom...Blessed are You, Hashem, Who heals all flesh and acts wondrously.*

Bar Kappara and the academy of R' Yishmael are teaching us that even seemingly minor details of the body — such as the shape of our fingers and the softness of our ear lobes — were fashioned that way with important purposes — spiritual purposes — in mind.

Is blocking out *lashon hara* really that important a purpose? Most certainly. We have learned that speaking *lashon hara* is among the most severe sins. Even worse, say our Sages, is the sin of accepting *lashon hara*.[10] Perhaps this is because by listening to the *lashon hara*, the listener is giving silent encouragment to the speaker to provide gossip on other occasions. In the Chofetz Chaim's words:

> We see this with our own eyes: When someone listens passively to *lashon hara*, he lends strength to the sinner. Once the speaker sees that his audience is paying attention, he will not refrain from speaking *lashon hara* all the time. This would not be the case if the listener would tell him [or show him by closing his ears], "I don't want to hear such things." Then, he would be more careful in the future, for he would see that by spreading his evil reports he brings shame upon himself and is viewed as a *baal lashon hara*.[11]

Rabbeinu Yonah quotes a verse in *Mishlei*: "As the north wind drives away rain, an angry face [holds back] hidden slander."[12] Just as a strong wind scatters rainclouds, so too does a listener's angry face send a message to the gossiper that his *lashon hara* makes him the object of scorn, not appreciation.

֍ On the Battlefront

In *Lieutenant Birnbaum: A Soldier's Story*,[13] Meyer Birnbaum vividly paints the picture of himself as a young, devoutly religious Jewish soldier, among an army of soldiers whose behavior off the battlefield was, for the most part, one of wild partying and sin. The soldiers were so upset with Lieutenant Birnbaum's refined and correct ways, with his refusal to join them in their drinking and merrymaking, that they considered him "weird," and at one point, even requested that he be replaced as their superior.

But this, and the many other tests that came his way, did not cause Meyer Birnbaum to weaken an iota in his strict observance of every *mitzvah*. Throughout the harrowing years of the Second World War, he ate only kosher food, put on *tefillin* and *davened* every day, and against official army rules wore his *yarmulka* whenever he ate. And at all times, his behavior and language were proper and praiseworthy. His years as a soldier were one continuous *kiddush Hashem*.

In passing his spiritual tests so successfully, Lieutenant Birnbaum lived up to the expectations which the Torah puts forth for a Jewish soldier. For as *Ramban* writes:

> It is known that [in the gentile world] when army camps go out to war, they do every disgusting thing, they rob and plunder, they are not ashamed to behave immorally and do anything despicable. Men who are proper by nature become wrapped in cruelty and rage when they go out against the enemy. Therefore, the Torah warns [the Jewish soldier]: *You shall guard yourself against anything evil.*[14]

There is another battlefront on which Jews fight against the enemy. In this struggle, every one of us is a soldier on the front lines. As *Mesilas Yesharim* writes:[15]

> Hashem has placed man [in this world] where many factors can draw him away from Him... Thus, man is actually

placed in the midst of a raging battle, because everything that he will encounter in the world, whether good or bad, is a test.

For example: It is nighttime in camp and a counselor goes to the canteen to purchase a snack. He finds a few friends seated around a table, and it does not take much to figure out what their discussion is about. Laughter rocks the porch as someone imitates the head waiter's "bossy" mannerisms.

So what does the counselor do? Does he sit down to listen and laugh? Does he try to put a stop to what is obviously *lashon hara*? Does he at least walk away so as not to be guilty of listening to *lashon hara*?

...Man is actually placed in the midst of a raging battle...

This, says *Maharal*, is the connection between Bar Kappara's teaching about sticking one's fingers in his ears and the plain meaning of the verse which talks of a soldier's behavior on the battlefront. The message is: When *lashon hara* comes your way, be strong in battle and use every "weapon" at your disposal to overcome its temptation.[16]

✒ Against the Current

Before entering the army, Meyer Birnbaum and his friends received words of inspiration and encouragement from R' Yitzchak Hutner, legendary *Rosh Yeshivah* of Mesivta Rabbi Chaim Berlin and one of the greatest Torah personalities of his day. In a letter to one of these soldiers, R' Hutner wrote the following *mashal* (parable):

A *treifah* (lit. one that is torn apart) is an animal that has suffered an injury which renders its meat unkosher even if the animal is slaughtered according to *halachah*. If an animal falls and breaks a limb it may or may not become a *treifah*, depending on whether or not the limb heals properly. The way to test this is by placing the animal in a stream where it will have to swim against the current. Only if it can do so can we be sure that the limb has healed properly.

Said R' Hutner: When a young man is taken away against his will from his Torah environment and forced to spend years in army service, he is faced with a major test: Can he "swim against the current"? Can he practice the *mitzvos* correctly in the face of ridicule and opposition?

Someone who finds himself among a group of *baalei lashon hara* is faced with a similar test. Does he have the spiritual strength to walk away from the discussion even though he may be looked at as an "outcast" or "weird"? If he cannot walk away, can he at least not particpate in the discussion and show through his facial expressions that he is not happy about the conversation?

Can he "swim against the current"?

One who understands the severity of *lashon hara* can pass this test.

℘ *Air Pollution*

The sounds of *lashon hara* are not the only ones that we need to block out. Unfortunately, the low state of today's world often makes walking down the street a nauseating experience. Vulgar language mixed with "boom box" noise which somehow got mislabeled as "music" make us cringe in disgust. Let us not kid ourselves; these sounds definitely pollute the spiritual air around us.

In 1938, R' Elchonon Wasserman, the great *Rosh Yeshivah* who was martyred in the Second World War, came to America to raise funds for his yeshivah in Baranovich. There was a Jew named Shraga Block who proudly referred to himself as *"dem Rebben's baal agalah,"* the *Rebbe's* wagon driver, for he chauffered R' Elchonon to his many daily appointments during his long stay in New York. Being the *tzaddik* that he was, it was R' Elchonon's practice to always look toward the ground when outside in the street, so that he would not see a forbidden sight. When he rode in a car, R' Elchonon kept his eyes fixed on the floor of the vehicle; he never looked out the window.

One day, R' Elchonon had an appointment in Manhattan. To get there, Mr. Block drove his car down a Manhattan street which was known as a place where low-class people would engage in improper behavior. Suddenly, R' Elchonon winced as if he had been stung. "Where are you taking me?" he demanded. "This place is filled with *tumah* (spiritual impurity)! How is it possible to study Torah in such a place?"[17]

R' Elchonon was affected by the sinful behavior of people who had no direct contact with him. Their sins created an atmosphere of spiritual "air pollution" which R' Elchonon's sensitized *neshamah* (soul) could feel. Surely, then, we are affected by the vulgar language or music that we hear.

So the next time you are walking down the street and hear language or music that is offensive, try your best to block it out. If you are a passenger in a taxi and the music is coarse, say politely, "Excuse me, sir; would it be possible to shut the radio or at least to switch stations?" (In fact, it is within a passenger's rights to *demand* this of the driver, since he is paying for the ride. Nevertheless, it is always preferable to request rather than to demand.)

✒ *Strategies*

Taking one's car to the mechanic can sometimes be a harrowing experience — not because of the price or the extensive repairs, but because of the atmosphere.

My regular mechanic is an honest, kindhearted observant Jew. Once, he was unavailable when I needed him, so I took my car to a nearby auto shop staffed by tough young gentiles. I was told to come back in about two hours for my car, but when I returned, it was far from ready.

I had brought a *sefer* with me, but the loud, vulgar conversation all around me made it difficult to concentrate. I was saved, however, by a man and his son who were waiting for their car and who were appalled, as was I, by the language that they were hearing. The man launched into a lively discussion with his son over a topic in *Gemara* which he had been studying. Their sweet, sacred words drowned out the noise and served as a holy shield against the *tumah* that was all around us.

One small repair shop; within it, two opposite worlds: One, a world of lowliness and profanity; the other, a world of *kedushah* (sanctity). In the worlds of the Steipler *Gaon*:

> Every word, every bit of logic of Torah is *kodesh kodashim* (holiest of holies)... When it becomes ingrained in one's mind, he becomes sanctified beyond measure with the sanctity of Torah; his body and mind become like a sacred Torah scroll.[18]

❧ Corrupted Speech

It is important to note that our Sages speak very severely about the sin of נִבּוּל פֶּה, speaking vulgar language.[19] It is apparent from their words that נִבּוּל פֶּה is even worse than *lashon hara*, which is among the worst sins in the Torah. *Maharal*[20] explains why this is so.

Lashon hara is a sin *bein adam lachaveiro*, between man and his fellow. When a person speaks *lashon hara*, the words in and of themselves are not bad; it is *their effect* that is bad. They cause harm to someone or lower his stature in the eyes of others. Vulgar language, on the other hand, is not bad only because it is harmful to those who hear it. *The very words themselves are sinful.*

The power of speech is the precious gift which distinguishes man from beast. A person who is guilty of נִבּוּל פֶּה has taken this precious gift and corrupted it in the worst way.

Chapter Twenty

Listening vs. Accepting

C haikel (a fictitious character) is a familiar sight in Boro Park *shuls*. His squashed hat perched on top of his head and his well-patched brown suede jacket stamp him as a needy individual. For years, he has made his rounds of the *shuls* month after month, collecting nickels, dimes and quarters. On Purim and during the days between Rosh Hashanah and Yom Kippur, many dollars come his way. At those times, he smiles broadly and pronounces his blessings upon his benefactor: "*Zeit gezunt!* (Be well!) May you be granted children, life and prosperity and may you live to see *Mashiach...*"

Nosson Stevens has a particular liking for the middle-aged collector. Chaikel never gets upset, even when a child runs past him and accidentally knocks the change out of his hand. "*Zol zein a kapparah* (It should be a source of atonement)" is his usual response to such mishaps. Nosson is a kindhearted fellow and often lends an ear as Chaikel tells whoever is interested in listening about the difficulties of poverty.

It therefore came as a shock to Nosson when after Chaikel left the *shul* one morning, his friend Aaron announced for all to hear, "How long will you people continue to give to that faker? A friend of mine told me that he knows for a fact that Chaikel is supported by a rich uncle and that all the money he collects is invested in the stock market!"

The following week, Chaikel arrives in *shul* and receives a cool welcome from the *minyan*. Some give him nothing at all, while people such as Nosson Stevens hand him a coin which is less than their usual donation.

Aaron is satisfied. Chaikel is hurt and mystified.

The Chofetz Chaim states:

> I will mention something in which many people unfortunately stumble. Suppose there are a number of people in a certain city who are assumed to be poor and in need of *tzedakah*. Then, someone issues a report about them: in fact, they are not poor, but they pretend to be poor in order to trick people. Because of this report, many people refrain from giving to these people the amount which they had given in the past.
>
> According to the Torah, this is a great injustice, for it is in the category of accepting actual *lashon hara*. If these people would follow the *halachah* that we are not permitted to believe *lashon hara* — though we are permitted to suspect that it might be true — then they would not excuse themselves from helping these poor people. *For they are still assumed to be poor until it has been proven otherwise, and the neighborhood people are obligated to support them.*[1]

ℒ *The Death of Gedaliah*

Tzom (The Fast of) *Gedaliah*, which we observe on the day after Rosh Hashanah, commemorates the murder of Gedaliah ben Achikam. Gedaliah was a *tzaddik* and the leader of the remaining Jewish settlement in Eretz Yisrael following the Destruction of the First *Beis HaMikdash*. His death brought that settlement to an end.

Our Sages teach that Gedaliah's death followed an error on his part. He was informed that a Jew named Yishmael ben Nesanyah, with the backing of the King of Aram, was intent on killing him. Gedaliah refused to accept the report of another Jew's evil intent. However, the report was accurate, as Yishmael ben Nesanyah did murder Gedaliah. From here we derive, "Regarding evil talk, though we are not permitted to believe it, we should suspect [that it might be true]."[2]

But suspicion means just that — to protect ourselves on the chance that the report *might* be true, and to investigate the matter to determine whether or not it is, in fact, true. The Chofetz Chaim cautions us:

> *Chas v'shalom* (Heaven forfend) to take any action against him, or to cause him any harm or embarrassment over this...Furthermore, the Torah forbids us to harbor any inner hatred towards him, and certainly we cannot free ourselves of any obligations towards him because of what we have heard.[3]

The Chofetz Chaim's comments regarding people who collect *tzedakah* for themselves are as relevant today as they were in his times — perhaps even more so. Today we are witness to an evergrowing community of Torah Jews in Eretz Yisrael, numbering in the hundreds of thousands. Anyone who has ever visited the Orthodox neighborhoods in Jerusalem knows that a vast number of our brothers and sisters there are poor. Scores of large families live in small, run-down apartments and were it not for the help of charity organizations, these families would go hungry.

I cannot forget the day when a director of a well-known organization came to the yeshivah which I attended, to encourage us to collect *tzedakah* to help the poor in Eretz Yisrael. He broke down and cried in front of us as he related the following:

On a recent trip to Eretz Yisrael, he had entered the home of a needy individual whom his organization helped. The father was sitting at his kitchen table, holding an egg in his hand — the only egg he could afford on that day. He was trying to decide: Should he eat the egg so that he would have strength to work, or should he give it to his child who needed it for his nourishment and growth?

A tragic story.

When children in such families reach marriageable age, their parents are at a loss as to how they will meet the projected expenses of the most simple wedding, clothing for the bride and groom, and other related expenses.

Often, parents who have managed to support their families without having to accept *tzedakah* cannot come up with the additional monies needed for a child's marriage.

This is why so many of our fine, upright brethren in Eretz Yisrael have no choice but to leave their families for extended periods of time and travel to Europe and America to raise funds for their childrens' weddings.

So when we see these people making the rounds of our *shuls* and homes, our attitude should not be, "Here they go again — another collector! Is there no end to this?" Rather, we should be grateful that we can be on the giving end and not on the receiving end. (Children, of course, should never open the front door to admit a stranger without their parent's authorization.)

And if we suspect that a particular collector may be dishonest, we may request letters of authorization or other identification. But let us not condemn someone as a "faker" without conclusive proof.

ℒ Exceptions

In Chapter Fourteen, we learned that it is permissible to speak what would otherwise be *lashon hara,* for a constructive purpose *(lashon hara l'toeles).* Similarly, we are permitted *to listen* to *lashon hara* for a constructive purpose.[4]

The Chofetz Chaim identifies three main areas of constructive listening. The first is where the listener is giving thought to entering into some sort of relationship with a certain person and he wants to find out information about that person.

For example: A certain young man has been suggested as a possible *shidduch* (marriage partner) for someone's daughter. The girl's father wants to inquire about the young man to determine if he is truly suitable for his daughter. This is permissible, provided that the man makes it clear that he is inquiring for a constructive purpose and not for mere curiosity. He does not have to say that he is inquiring *for his daughter,* but he should say, "It's for a possible *shidduch* for someone." Otherwise, he will be causing the speaker to sin, for the speaker has no right to relate negative information unless he knows that it is for a constructive purpose.

Furthermore, the speaker must speak only for constructive reasons; if, for example, he bears a grudge against the young man and is happy to harm his *shidduch* opportunities, he must remain silent even if he knows that the information is true.[5]

Some people like to be secretive when inquiring about a *shidduch,* out of concern that people who are not careful about *shemiras halashon* will begin spreading rumors about an engagement before it has actually taken place. So they take to inquiring in a very casual way:

> Mr. Unger has been trying to find out information about Yaakov S. but has come away empty-handed thus far. One night after *Maariv,* he notices Zev R. making his way out of the *shul.* He hurries over to him and strikes up an innocent conversation.
>
> "...So you left that yeshivah a year ago. They have a good bunch of *bachurim* in that place. I know that Yaakov S. learns there and they say that he's very diligent and a true *baal midos.* Am I correct?"

Mr. Unger has acted incorrectly, for he gave the impression that he is inquiring about Yaakov merely out of curiosity. If Zev has only good things to say about Yaakov, he may relate them. Otherwise, he should try to avoid answering the question.

Another situation where listening is permissible is where the listener hopes that by hearing something negative, he will be able to convince the person to do *teshuvah*.[6] For example, someone tells you, "Listen to what your cousin Baruch did yesterday." You are very close with Baruch; you know that he respects you and will take your words of corrective criticism to heart. In such a case, you would be allowed to listen to the report. However, here too, if it seems that the speaker is gossiping with no constructive purpose in mind, he should be stopped.

The following is another case where listening to *lashon hara* is permissible:

Avi, your best friend, is burning with rage. "Mr. Tessler is absolutely the worst teacher in the school! He gave me a 68% for the term. Plenty of boys did worse than me and got better grades. I hate him and I'm going to do my best to have him fired!"

You feel bad for Avi but, knowing him, you realize that his conduct may have had a lot to do with his poor grade. Though you are not in his class, you know that he has a very sharp wit and has a difficult time controlling his tongue. You would like to ask him to describe what went on in the classroom over the course of the year, but you know that it will probably lead to more *lashon hara* about Mr. Tessler.

If your intention is purely to help the situation and not to hear amusing stories about Mr. Tessler, then you would be permitted to say, "Avi, are you sure that you haven't been making remarks that upset Mr. Tessler? We all know that you have a great sense of humor!" By listening to Avi, you may be able to point out where he spoke incorrectly and why the grade was well deserved.[7]

In this case, as in the previous ones, it is permissible to listen to the report provided that you do not accept it as fact.

You may be wondering: How do I balance the prohibition against listening to *lashon hara* against the need to listen to *lashon hara* for a constructive purpose? For example, a neighbor approaches you: "Did you hear what happened in *shul* yesterday?" It sounds like he is about to relate an interesting story which quite possibly will involve *lashon hara*. Your reaction, then, should be, "No, I did not hear what happened in *shul* and if it involves *lashon hara*, I don't want to know about it!" On the other hand, what if it is important for you to know what happened? Perhaps a friend of yours became entangled in a dispute and you are in a position to serve as a peacemaker.

The Chofetz Chaim raises this question and provides the answer:

> Someone who seeks to do what is right in Hashem's eyes should conduct himself in the following manner: If he is approached by someone who wants to tell him something about his acquaintance which is derogatory, he should ask him: "Is what you wish to tell me relevant to me personally? Is it something that I can correct by speaking to the parties involved, or important for me to know for some other reason?" If the speaker responds that *it is* important for him to know, then he may listen to the information; he should suspect that it might be true, but he should not accept it as fact. However, if he understands from the speaker's response that there is no benefit in his listening to the information… then it is forbidden for him to listen.[8]

The Chofetz Chaim concludes with a point which we have already mentioned — which bears repetition. People who enjoy listening to *lashon hara* are guilty of additional sin because they lend encouragement to gossipers. When a gossiper recognizes a certain individual as a good audience, he looks for every opportunity to share new information with him. By contrast, when a person develops a reputation as someone who avoids *lashon hara*, then others think twice before speaking *lashon hara* in his presence.

Chapter Twenty-one

Squandering One's Wealth

"Some are [apparently] wealthy, but have nothing."[1] So said Shlomo *HaMelech,* the wisest of men. The Chofetz Chaim explained this with a parable:[2]

A man who loves to study Torah is considering the purchase of an exquisite set of *Shas* (Talmud), the best that money can buy. The cover of each volume is made of genuine leather, embossed with a beautiful gold design. The paper is specially treated for lifetime use and an heirloom binding ensures that the volumes will withstand the test of time.

The *sefarim* dealer must soon leave town. He shows the prospective buyer a sample volume — but only its cover and binding. When the customer asks to open the *gemara,* the dealer says, "What's the point of opening it? You can see from the outside that it's the best on the market. This is my last set — do you want it or not?" Afraid to lose the opportunity, the customer pays the expensive price and with great excitement takes his new purchase home, packed in boxes.

As soon as he has brought the last box inside, the man sits down to examine his precious purchase. Lovingly, he opens the first volume — and almost faints from shock. The pages are covered with thick grime! Obviously, something spilled on this volume and soiled the pages beyond repair.

Anxiously, the man reaches into the open box and takes out a second volume... and a third... All of them are the same: stunning on the outside and badly soiled on the inside.

But it is too late. The dealer has left town and has no plans of returning. The man has invested a fortune of money in a *Shas* that is damaged beyond repair.

Says the Chofetz Chaim:

> Picture a *baal lashon hara* (one who speaks *lashon hara* regularly) who studies *Tanach*, *Mishnah* and *Gemara* every day. At the time of judgment (after he dies), he expects that all this Torah study will be spread out before his eyes — oh, how he awaits this! He looks forward to the moment when these *sefarim* will come and intercede on his behalf (to earn for him great reward).
>
> But when these *sefarim* are brought out, he sees that every page is enveloped in a *ruach hatumah* (spirit of impurity) created by the forbidden words which he spoke either before or during his learning — and all his learning is worth nothing! His distress will be enormous when he contemplates how he has lost all his Torah study through his own doing!
>
> *...A person can study all six orders of the Mishnah and all of Shas many times, and yet, when he ascends to Heaven, he will not find even one volume to shield him, because each one will be enveloped in a ruach hatumah and will be repulsive to look at.*

It is now obvious what Shlomo *HaMelech* had in mind when he said, "Some are [apparently] wealthy, but [in reality] have nothing." A person who has amassed a wealth of Torah study through the course of a lifetime may be shocked to discover that he has been denied all this wealth because of the sin of *lashon hara*.

🍃 A Frightening Exchange

Sefer Chovos HaLevavos[3] writes:

On the Day of Judgment, many people will find themselves credited with good deeds which they did not do. "These are not mine!" they will declare. Each such person will be told, "These are the good deeds of those who spoke *lashon hara* against you." The one who spoke *lashon hara* will be told, "These deeds were taken from you when you spoke against So-and-so."

And some will find sins on their account which they did not commit. When each person will protest, "These are not mine!" he will be told, "These were taken from the account of So-and-so against whom you spoke."

The Chofetz Chaim, quoting *Sefer Marpei Lashon,*[4] concludes: A person may spend a day or two earning eternal reward for himself through Torah and *mitzvos,* only to exchange this reward for his neighbor's sins by speaking against him. A few more days might go by as he earns more reward, only to lose it all in the same way. This pattern might continue until the day of death, when he departs this world deprived of all the learning and good deeds in which he invested so much effort.

Therefore, David *HaMelech* urges us, "Guard your tongue from evil," and only then does he say, "Turn from evil and do good."[5] The way to ensure that we retain our eternal reward for all of our spiritual accomplishments is by refraining from speaking *lashon hara.*

🍃 A Jew's Craft

As we have learned,[6] the skin condition of *tzaraas* is a Heavenly punishment for the sin of *lashon hara.* The *metzora* must live in isolation[7] and he should call out: '[I am] contaminated, [I am] contaminated!' [8] Our Sages explain the purpose of the *metzora's* proclamation: "He should inform the public of his misfortune so that they will beg [Hashem] for mercy for him."[9]

This demands explanation, for there are other cases of *tumah* in the Torah[10] where the person needs Hashem's mercy so that he may be cleansed of his impurity. Yet in those cases, the Torah does not state that the person should announce that he is *tamei* (impure) so that others will pray for him.

The Chofetz Chaim[11] quotes *Zohar:* "The prayer of someone who speaks *lashon hara* will not come before Hashem, because a *ruach hatumah* (spirit of impurity) hovers over it." The *metzora's* own prayers will not do him much good, for his *lashon hara* will prevent his *tefillah* from being accepted Above. Therefore, he must beseech others to pray on his behalf. Only after he has engaged in sincere *teshuvah* and has resolved to be careful in matters of speech can the *metzora* hope that his *tefillah* will find favor before Hashem.

A Jew's Torah study and *tefillah* are his most potent weapons, for they have the power to break any evil decree and they can bring about miraculous salvation in any situation. "When the voice of Yaakov is found in the synagogues, then the hands [of victory] are not those of Eisav — but if not — then the hands [of victory] are those of Eisav."[12] But this is only if the mouth which utters the *tefillah* is uncontaminated by forbidden speech.

The Chofetz Chaim likens this to a king who seeks to have something hand-crafted for his personal use. He seeks the most expert craftsmen for the job and offers them great reward if they produce an object to his liking.

The craftsmen are hired and are eager to undertake the assignment, but they have one problem — their tools are damaged. Unless they can repair their tools, they cannot succeed at their task, despite their great skill. Only with the finest tools can they produce a work of true craftsmanship.

The power of speech is the אוּמָנוּת, *craft,* of the Jew. His mouth is the tool of his craft. Only a mouth that is undamaged by *lashon hara* and other forbidden talk can produce Torah study and prayers which will bring satisfaction to the King of kings and reward for the one who utters them.[13]

✒ Turning Point

During the days of Mordechai and Esther, the evil designs of Haman threatened the Jews with annihilation. *Midrash Rabbah*[14] identifies the turning point in the hidden miracle of that time:

> After Haman constructed the gallows on which he planned to hang Mordechai, he went and found Mordechai sitting in the *beis midrash* with young boys sitting before him, wearing sackcloth and toiling in Torah. They were crying out [in prayer] and weeping as Haman counted them. He counted twenty-two thousand children and threw upon them iron chains. He appointed guards to stand watch over them and said, "Tomorrow, I shall kill these children first and after that I will kill Mordechai [so as to cause Mordechai additional anguish]."
>
> The mothers of these children brought them bread and water [for they had already fasted more than forty-eight hours] and said to them, "Our children: eat and drink before you die tomorrow, so that you will not die from hunger [which is a particularly painful death]." Without hesitation, the children placed their hands upon their *sefarim* (holy books) and swore by the life of their teacher Mordechai that they would not break their fast.
>
> They cried out in prayer as they wept and their cries pierced the Heavens. Hashem took note of their cries at the second hour of the night[15] and arose from His seat of Judgment and sat upon His Throne of Mercy.
>
> ...At that time, Hashem took the documents containing the [Heavenly] decree against the Jews which had been sealed with clay, and destroyed them. He brought confusion upon King Achashveirosh that night, as it is written,[16] "That night, sleep eluded the king..."

The Torah study and prayers of young children have awesome power.

Reish Lakish said in the name of R' Yehudah Nesiah: "The world exists only in the merit of the Torah study of children." Said R' Pappa to Abaye: "And what of our Torah study?" Abaye replied: "There is no comparison between words that are tainted by sin and words that are untainted by sin."[17]

The Chofetz Chaim observes:[18] We cannot begin to fathom the greatness of R' Pappa, Abaye and the other sages of the Talmud. Surely their sins were few, and by our standards might not have been sins at all. Yet Abaye declared that this minute degree of sin could affect the power of their Torah study. By contrast, the *neshamah* (soul) of a child is pure and untainted by sin. This is why a child's Torah and *tefillah* are so powerful.

The Chofetz Chaim continues: If Abaye could state that the Sages' few sins could weaken the power of their learning, how much more so is this true of someone who habitually speaks *lashon hara*.

There is another form of talk which can destroy the power of our *tefillah*.

ໄ Prayer Bashing

"Grab him!" the people shouted.

Beis HaKnesses HaGadol was the largest and most beautiful *shul* in the city. The multi-million dollar structure had recently been completed and Jews from the surrounding communities would stop by to admire the magnificent architecture and breathtaking furnishings.

When the strange-looking fellow entered the building that morning, no one paid much attention to him. No one noticed him taking a sledgehammer out of the sack slung over his shoulder. When the banging started, though, all eyes turned to watch in horror as the man began smashing apart the marble walls, bit by bit.

But not for long. In a matter of moments, three men were holding the man down, while a fourth man summoned the police. The man was placed under arrest and was never heard from again.

Is the above story true? No. But we need to be aware that there are other ways to destroy a *shul*. In his *Mishnah Berurah*, the Chofetz Chaim cites the words of *Eliyahu Rabba* in the name of *Kol Bo*:

Woe to the people who speak [in *shul*] during *tefillah*, for we have seen many *battei knessios* destroyed because of this sin...[19]

The words of *Shulchan Aruch* regarding those who speak during *chazaras hashatz* (the *chazzan's* repetition of *Shemoneh Esrei*[20]) are extremely severe:

One should not engage in idle conversation while the chazzan is repeating the Shemoneh Esrei. One who does speak is a sinner; his sin is too great to bear and his behavior should not be tolerated.[21]

The term גָּדוֹל עֲוֹנִי מִנְּשֹׂא, *his sin is too great to bear*, appears nowhere else in all of *Shulchan Aruch*. It is the term used by Kayin after he murdered his brother Hevel.[22]

Why is speaking during *davening* such a serious matter?

The Lakewood *Mashgiach*, R' Matisyahu Salomon, explained: *Tefillah* is a most powerful weapon. *Even if a sharp sword is upon one's neck, he should not refrain from [seeking Hashem's] mercy.*[23] The *tefillos* of a *minyan* are especially potent. But a person who speaks at a point when *halachah* forbids it is causing irreparable damage to that *tefillah*. He has weakened its effect beyond description. Therefore, his sin is too great to bear.

✤ In Hashem's Palace

The *Kosel Maaravi* (Western Wall) is the place at which hundreds of thousands of Jews pour out their hearts in prayer year after year. The *Kosel* is the western section of the wall which surrounded the *Har HaBayis* (Temple Mount) when the *Beis HaMikdash* stood. It is the place from which the *Shechinah* (Divine Presence) has never departed.[24]

If you have ever had the privilege of praying at the *Kosel,* ask yourself this question: Did you ever see people *there* engaged in conversation during *chazaras hashatz*? Probably not. The awe of this sacred place does not allow for such behavior.

Let us ponder another scene. *Mashiach* has arrived and the Courtyard of the *Beis HaMikdash* is filled with thousands of Jews who are praying fervently. Two old friends who have not seen each other for years meet in the Courtyard. Can we imagine them interrupting their *davening* to "catch up on the latest news"? Certainly not! The Torah commands us: וּמִקְדָּשִׁי תִּירָאוּ, *And you shall revere My Sanctuary.*[25] This means that our behavior in the *Beis HaMikdash* must reflect our deep reverence for Hashem's Palace.

The prophet Yechezkel referred to a *beis haknesses* or *beis hamidrash* (synagogue or study hall) as a מִקְדָּשׁ מְעַט, *miniature sanctuary.*[26] The Novominsker *Rebbe* sees this as the reason why a *shul* must have an *aron kodesh* (ark) containing a *sefer Torah*. In the *Beis HaMikdash*, the holiest place was the *Kodesh HaKodashim* in which rested the *Aron* and its *Luchos.* The place of the *Kodesh HaKodashim* was — and still is — the Gateway to Heaven,[27] the place from which all our prayers ascend before Hashem.

Because a *shul* is a miniature *Beis HaMikdash,* it must contain a miniature *Kodesh HaKadoshim.* This is the purpose of the *aron kodesh.*

In *Mishnah Berurah,* the Chofetz Chaim speaks very severely of those who do not accord a *shul* proper reverence, saying that they "transform it into a place of idol worship."[28] Perhaps the Chofetz Chaim means that when a person behaves in a disrespectful manner when in *shul,* it is as if he is saying that he does not truly believe that Hashem's Presence resides there and that *tefillos* which are recited there have special power. This is denying a basic truth and thus is akin to idol worship.

Also in *Mishnah Berurah,* the Chofetz Chaim states that to speak *lashon hara* in a *shul* is an especially severe sin.

> In doing so, one shows lack of regard for the Shechinah... there is no comparison between someone who sins in private and someone who does so in the palace of the King...[29]

In *Sefer Chofetz Chaim,*[30] the Chofetz Chaim leads us through such a conversation and shows how terrible it can be:

> A person sitting in *shul* has an interesting piece of news to tell the fellow who is sitting next to him. He chooses a most "convenient" time for this: immediately prior to the Torah reading. But when the congregation is ready to begin the Torah reading, our storyteller is not finished. He and his friend continue their conversation right through the reading of the Torah and the *Kaddish* which follows.

The Chofetz Chaim tallies the list of sins that these two have committed — all because of gossip:

They have transgressed the commandment to show proper reverence for a *shul.* They are also guilty of public *chillul Hashem* (desecration of Hashem's Name) as they ignore Hashem's Presence in the *shul* and show disregard for the Torah.

They have spoken and listened to *lashon hara,* which involves many sins.

They have ignored the Torah reading. We are required to listen attentively to the Torah reading. Even to *study Torah* during the Torah reading is forbidden.[31] Certainly to speak *lashon hara* at such a time is a grave sin.

It is absolutely forbidden to speak during *Kaddish.*[32]*

---

*In *Mishnah Berurah* (56:1), the Chofetz Chaim writes at length of the severity of talking during *Kaddish.* The following is among his many comments there: "... *Sefer Mateh Moshe* (411) cites a *Midrash* that states that a certain scholar (after he had died) appeared to his student in a dream with a stain upon his forehead. The student asked, "Why did this happen to you?" The scholar answered, "Because I was not careful to refrain from speaking during *Kaddish.*"

Furthermore, reciting *Amein, Yehei Shmei Rabbah...* with proper concentration has the power to break severe Heavenly decrees. How unfortunate for this to be sacrificed in exchange for some forbidden talk!

❧ The Tosafos Yom Tov's Prayer

R' Yom Tov Lipman Heller was one of the towering Torah personalities of seventeenth-century Europe. His classic commentary to Mishnah, *Tosafos Yom Tov*, is but one of his many contributions to Hashem's people and its Torah.

As *Rav* of a large Jewish community, the *Tosafos Yom Tov* (as he has become known) composed a *tefillah* to be recited in *shul* before *Mussaf* on Shabbos morning for the sake of those who uphold the *halachah* by not engaging in conversation during *davening* (prayers). There are *shuls* which recite it today.

מִי שֶׁבֵּרַךְ אֲבוֹתֵינוּ אַבְרָהָם יִצְחָק וְיַעֲקֹב מֹשֶׁה וְאַהֲרֹן דָּוִד וּשְׁלֹמֹה, הוּא יְבָרֵךְ אֶת כָּל מִי שֶׁשׁוֹמֵר פִּיו וּלְשׁוֹנוֹ שֶׁלֹּא לְדַבֵּר בְּעֵת הַתְּפִילָה. הַקָּדוֹשׁ בָּרוּךְ הוּא יִשְׁמְרֵהוּ מִכָּל צָרָה וְצוּקָה וּמִכָּל נֶגַע וּמַחֲלָה, וְיָחוּלוּ עָלָיו כָּל הַבְּרָכוֹת הַכְּתוּבוֹת בְּסֵפֶר תּוֹרַת מֹשֶׁה רַבֵּינוּ וּבְכָל סִפְרֵי הַנְּבִיאִים וְהַכְּתוּבִים, וְיִזְכֶּה לִרְאוֹת בָּנִים חַיִּים וְקַיָּמִים, וִיגַדְּלֵם לַתּוֹרָה וּלְחוּפָּה וּלְמַעֲשִׂים טוֹבִים, וְיַעֲבוֹד אֶת ה' אֱלֹקֵינוּ תָּמִיד בֶּאֱמֶת וּבְתָמִים וְנֹאמַר אָמֵן.

He Who blessed our forefathers Avraham, Yitzchak, Yaakov, Moshe, Aharon, David and Shlomo — may He bless everyone who guards his mouth and tongue from speaking during prayers. May the Holy One, Blessed is He, protect him from every trouble and distress, from every plague and illness. May all the blessings written in the Torah transmitted by Moshe our teacher and the Books of the Prophets and Writings come to rest upon him; may he merit to see offspring who will live and endure and may he raise them to Torah, the marriage canopy and good deeds; and may he serve Hashem, our G-d, always, in truth and perfection. Now let us respond: Amen.

May we all merit to be included in this blessing.

Chapter Twenty-two

Nothing but the Truth

*T*he year was 1975 and the place was Camp Torah Vodaath, a popular boys' summer camp in upstate New York. It was the Senior Division All-Star Baseball Game of Color War and hundreds of campers and staff members were sitting on bleachers and standing on the sidelines watching a very exciting game.

The score was tied 1-1 and David Tepper (not his real name) was on second base. David was fifteen years old, in the camp's senior bunk and possibly the best player on his team. His team was in high spirits as he took a lead off second while the next pitch headed towards home plate.

The batter swung and hit a line drive into the outfield. David rounded third and headed for home plate as the crowd roared. There was a play at the plate; as David slid into home, the catcher caught the throw and tagged him. "Safe!" the umpire shouted.

The catcher was obviously upset. He told the umpire, a member of the camp administration, that he had tagged the runner *before* he had touched home plate. But the umpire stood by his call.

David's team was jubilant. They had taken the lead and were now in a position to pick up some crucial Color War points. And perhaps a victory in the All-Star game would give them the momentum to win Color War.

David had been slow in standing up and dusting himself off. As he walked away from home plate, his teammates surrounded him, pounded him on the back and congratulated him. Strangely, he was the only one who did not seem to be excited. Quietly, he made his way through the crowd and approached the umpire.

"I was out," he said quietly.

The umpire was not sure that he had heard correctly. "What did you say?" he asked. "I said that I was out," David replied. "I am positive that he tagged me before I touched home plate."

Suddenly, everyone grew silent. Many people had been close enough to hear the conversation and word of David's admission made its way quickly through the crowd.

The umpire pondered the matter silently. This was not a situation which is discussed in the Major League Baseball rulebook. It would never happen in professional sports. No professional ballplayer would admit that he was out after being called "safe" by the umpire.

After what seemed like a very long time, the umpire cleared his throat and said, "Well, I'm human and I can make a mistake. If you're positive that he tagged you before you reached home plate, then you're out."

The game ended in a tie.

On the last night of camp, before the night activity got underway, the head counselor addressed campers and staff: "There are a lot of memories that we take home after an eight-week camp season. But if there's one memory above all that we should take home with us, it's that of David Tepper speaking the truth after being called 'safe.'"

Our Sages teach that "the seal of *HaKadosh Baruch Hu* is truth."[1] The first, middle and last letters of the *Aleph-Beis* form the word אֱמֶת, *truth,* indicating that Torah is the ultimate truth and that the more a person develops the quality of truth within himself, the more he can attach himself to Torah and merit to understand it in all its beauty and depth.[2]

In our days, R' Yaakov Kamenetsky, of blessed memory, was know for his strict adherence to truth in every situation. As a young man in Russia, he came before the draft board and was accused by an army officer of having appeared the day before under a different name. "I have never told a lie my entire life," R' Yaakov said emphatically. The manner in which he spoke convinced the officer that he was telling the truth.

A woman once asked him whether or not it was permissible to lie about one's earnings in order to obtain certain government benefits. R' Yaakov responded that this was absolutely forbidden. The woman asked, "But aren't there gentiles who cheat about these things?" R' Yaakov responded, "But they did not stand at the foot of *Har Sinai* (Mount Sinai) — *we did.*"

R' Yaakov lived to age ninety-five. When in his nineties, he was asked in what merit he had lived so long. "I never said a lie," was his reply.

People from around the world would seek the blessings of the Manchester *Rosh Yeshivah,* R' Yehudah Zev Segal. This *tzaddik* once confided that because of this, he was especially careful with his words at all times — for how could his blessings be effective if his lips were guilty of improper speech? "Improper speech" includes not only *lashon hara,* but also falsehood and other forms of forbidden speech. R' Segal was constantly on guard that his every word should be absolutely true.

He would often study with *talmidim* before *Maariv.* One evening, they had to stop for *Maariv* while in the middle of a paragraph. R' Segal said, "We will continue after *Maariv.*" By the time *Maariv* was over, R' Segal was thoroughly exhausted. Only one thought prevented him from retiring for the night: he had said that the learning would resume. He therefore studied with his *talmidim* for a few minutes before retiring.

Once, on a visit to America, R' Segal agreed to visit the home of a certain individual. Circumstances beyond his control made it impossible for him to keep the appointment. When he returned to America *a few years later,* he made a point of visiting this man.

On a journey from Manchester to the city of Bournemouth, R' Segal stopped off in London to attend a gathering to which he had been personally invited. In his remarks, the chairman thanked R' Segal for having made a special trip to attend the gathering. When the chairman mentioned this a second time, R' Segal's passion for truth forced him to speak up. "Actually," he said before the entire assemblage, "I did not make a special trip; I stopped off here on my way to another destination."

A couple who had been married for some years without children frequently requested R' Segal's blessings and advice. On the eighth of Tishrei, 5752 (1991), the couple came to Manchester to request his blessing before Yom Kippur. This time, R' Segal responded in a most unusual way: "Do not worry — next year you will return to me with your baby."

Four months later, R' Segal passed away. By that time, the young woman was expecting a child. A few days into the year (5753), the couple returned to Manchester with their baby to be present at the *hakamas matzeivah* (unveiling) at R' Segal's grave. It was the eighth of Tishrei, exactly one year to the day from when R' Segal had uttered the words: "Next year you will return to me with your baby."

ℒ *Language of the Heart*

R' Shraga Frank was one of the wealthiest Jews in Lithuania.* He owned a leather factory, a leather goods store,

---

*R' Shraga merited four sons-in-law who were all outstanding *talmidei chachamim.* They were: R' Moshe Mordechai Epstein, *Rosh Yeshivah* of Yeshivas Knesses Yisrael in Slobodka; R' Isser Zalman Meltzer, *Rosh Yeshivah* in Slutzk and later in Yeshivah Eitz Chaim in Jerusalem (and father-in-law of R' Aharon Kotler); R' Baruch Hurwitz, *Rav* in Alexot, Lithuania and Chairman of Agudath Israel in Lithuania; and R' Sheftel Kramer, a *Rosh Yeshivah* in Slutzk and later *Mashgiach* of one of America's first yeshivos, located in New Haven, Connecticut. (He was the father-in-law of R' Yaakov Yitzchak Ruderman.)

and a great deal of real estate. More important, he was a *talmid chacham* and *tzaddik,* and he was held in high esteem by the founder of the *Mussar* Movement, R' Yisrael Salanter.

Once, a merchant came to purchase a large quantity of leather from R' Shraga. The man requested a reduction in the price, since he was making a large purchase.

R' Shraga replied that his profit margin was fixed, regardless of the size of the order, and therefore he could not offer a reduction. He told the man, "Feel free to purchase your leather from another dealer. In fact, I will give you a list of other dealers whom you can approach." And he handed the man such a list.

The man made the rounds of the leather dealers and found that R' Shraga's price was the cheapest. He returned to R' Shraga and informed him that he wished to make his purchase at the price which had been quoted.

To the man's surprise, R' Shraga said, "I will be happy to sell you the goods — but at a cheaper price than I had originally quoted.

"You see, after you left I thought it over and I realized that I really *could* offer you a reduction, since as you maintained, you were making an unusually large purchase. And although you returned to me prepared to accept my original price, I will sell it to you for less, in keeping with the verse,[3] "Hashem, who may reside in Your tent?.... One who speaks truth in his heart."[4]

Chapter Twenty-three

Fine-tuning

S ome of the nicest children I know like lizards.

And why not? They *are* kind of cute, like little alliga-
tors, only more colorful.

But our Sages had a problem with the word "lizard."
It all depends on how the word is used.
Allow me to explain.

✍ A Hidden Flaw

Once, there was a person who everyone assumed was a
qualified *Kohen*. He performed the service in the *Beis
HaMikdash* and received his portion of the Temple sacrifices.

It happened one day that three *Kohanim* were discussing the
size of their respective portions from the week's *Lechem*

HaPanim (Show Bread). One said, "The portion I received was the size of a bean."

The second one said, "The portion I received was the size of an olive."

The third one said, "I received a portion the size of a lizard's tail."

The Sages were shocked by this last statement. How could a *Kohen* express himself so coarsely? How could he compare the sanctified bread which sat upon the Golden Table in the *Beis HaMikdash* to the tail of a non-kosher reptile?

The Sages were convinced that something was wrong. This fellow could not be a pure *Kohen*. No one who himself was sanctified with the holiness of *Kehunah,* who was fit to serve in the *Beis HaMikdash,* could possible have expressed himself in such a way.

They investigated and discovered that their suspicion was correct. His lineage was flawed and he was unfit to serve in the *Beis HaMikdash.*[1]

Kohanim are not the only ones who are expected to speak in a refined manner. The entire Jewish people are a מַמְלֶכֶת כֹּהֲנִים וְגוֹי קָדוֹשׁ, *kingdom of priests and a holy nation.*[2] *Rambam* learns from this verse that it is not enough for a Jew to avoid using obscene language; we are obligated to use only language which is noble and pure.[3]

Rabbi Avraham Pam, revered *Rosh Yeshivah* of Mesivta Torah Vodaath, often speaks about the importance of speaking בְּלָשׁוֹן נְקִיָּה, *in a refined manner of speech.* He says that words such as "stupid" or "crazy" do not belong in a Torah Jew's vocabulary. R' Pam did not find it necessary to mention the term "s-h-u-t u-p." It is obvious that this expression is coarse and unbecoming those who are Hashem's ambassadors on this earth.

✎ The Right Expression

It is told that the Chazon Ish once heard someone exclaim, "That's a lie!" The Chazon Ish said, "It is better to say, 'That's not true,' " a more refined way of speaking. Similarly, R' Yehudah Zev Segal would tell a child, "Your hands are not clean," rather than, "Your hands are dirty."

Someone once showed R' Segal a public letter in which the writer questioned whether a certain popular food item which bore a *kashrus* symbol was actually kosher. The letter stated that whoever ate this food had "eaten ham." R' Segal found this offensive and said that it made him wonder whether the writer was someone whose word could be trusted.

There was a certain *chasid* of Ger whom people would refer to as "The Yellow One," because of his yellowish complexion. When the *Imrei Emes* of Ger, R' Avraham Mordechai Alter, heard this, he became upset. "Is that how one refers to a Jew?" he demanded.

Sometimes, a carelessly used expression can cause tremendous hurt. In an Orthodox summer camp, a staff member lost his temper and punched another staff member, causing him to bleed. This was cause for wonder, because the attacker was known to be mild mannered. When the head counselor confronted him, the young man explained: "I know that I should not have done that, but I just lost myself. You see, the fellow that I punched got angry at someone else and said to him, 'You're retarded!' Now, I happen to have a brother who is mentally retarded and I can't take it when people get into arguments and try to get even with one another by calling the other party 're-tarded'..."

৯ *A Tzaddik's Wish*

Our Sages relate that R' Shimon bar Yochai once expressed the wish that man would have been created with two mouths, one to use for the study of Torah and one for other purposes.[4] This great sage, who authored *Sefer HaZohar*, had a deep understanding of the holiness of each word of Torah, and how the words of Torah which we utter can be contaminated by a mouth which sometimes utters improper words.

Of course, R' Shimon was not questioning the wisdom of Hashem, Who created man with only one mouth. It is Hashem's will that we learn to become masters over our power of speech, so that nothing improper escapes our lips. In this way, the words of Torah and *tefillah* which we utter will have their maximum effect in the Upper Worlds.

In Jerusalem there lived a saintly Jew named R' Shmuel Yaakov Weinberg. In his younger years, R' Shmuel Yaakov lived in Russia and was drafted into the Czar's army for an indefinite period. A few months after his induction, R' Shmuel Yaakov's wife gave birth to their first child, a boy. His wife asked the city's *rav,* a renowned *tzaddik* named R' Yosef Lowenstein, to serve as *sandak* at the *bris.*

The joy of the *bris* was marred by the weeping of the baby's mother, for her husband who was not present. Seeing her distress, the *Rav* offered her words of comforts. "You will see, your husband will return home in time for the *pidyon haben* (redemption of the first-born)."

Soon after, R' Shmuel Yaakov was court-martialed, having been falsely accused of breaking an army regulation. He was brought before a military court for trial. The judge, who happened to be a relative of the Czar, had a menacing look about him. When R' Shmuel Yaakov entered the courtroom and took one look at the judge, he found himself too frightened to even collect his thoughts and prepare some sort of defense.

Hashem planted an idea in R' Shmuel Yaakov's mind just as he was summoned to stand before the judge. He stood up from his seat in the back of the courtroom and began to walk with an exaggerated limp. The judge watched the Jew limp for a few moments and then hopped off the platform and went behind R' Shmuel Yaakov. The assemblage watched with great amusement as the judge proceeded to imitate the way R' Shmuel Yaakov was walking. Everyone roared with laughter at the way the judge was ridiculing the hapless Jew.

R' Shmuel Yaakov stood before the judge's table and the judge ascended the platform. The judge banged the gavel and the courtroom fell silent. "This is a military court!" the judge roared. "And a military court is for soldiers — not clowns. We don't need soldiers like you!" He sent R' Shmuel Yaakov out in disgrace — and with a note discharging him from the army.

R' Shmuel Yaakov arrived home in time for his son's *pidyon haben*. When his wife told him about the *Rav's* promise, R' Shmuel Yaakov went to see him. "Does the *Rav* actually possess *ruach hakodesh* (Divine Inspiration)?" he asked.

R' Lowenstein replied, "No, I do not possess *ruach hakodesh*. But I am extremely careful with my words and nothing improper escapes my lips. I believe that it is in this merit that Hashem fulfills whatever I say."[5]

Shlomo *HaMelech* said: "The tongue of a righteous person is choice silver."[6] A *tzaddik's* every word is measured and he is careful to express himself in only the finest way. Therefore, the effect of his words are long-lasting, like choice silver which remains for generations.[7]

Chapter Twenty-four

The Right Word

A person should learn Torah, be honest in the way he does business and speak gently to people. Then what will people say of him? Fortunate is his father who taught him Torah, fortunate is his rebbi who taught him Torah. This person who learned Torah — see how beautiful are his ways, how pleasant is his behavior. It is concerning such people that Hashem says[1], "You are My servants, Yisrael, in whom I shall be glorified."[2]

We are accustomed to hearing inspiring stories of great *roshei yeshivah* and Chassidic *rebbeim* whose every action was *leshem Shamayim* (for the sake of Heaven) and resulted in *kiddush Hashem* (sanctification of Hashem's Name). It is not often, though, that we read of an individual whose work brought him in daily contact with non-religious Jews and gentiles, with congressmen, senators and even the President of the United States — and whose every word and deed were guided by one barometer: whether or not the result would bring *kiddush Hashem.*

His name was Rabbi Moshe Sherer, late President of Agudath Israel of America. He glorified Hashem and His Torah by earning a reputation as an exceptionally gifted, honest, and straightforward ambassador of Torah. He also glorified Hashem's Name by the way he spoke to people.

He was a person who was always able to find the right word to say at any occasion. This was certainly true when he spoke in public, such as when he delivered the invocation at Mayor Rudolph Giuliani's inauguration in New York City. Equally important, he always found the right word when speaking privately with someone.

He knew how to make a person feel good.

℘ *"Good Morning"*

The annual dinner of Agudath Israel in the spring of 1999 was dedicated to the memory of R' Sherer, who had passed away one year earlier on the day of that year's annual dinner. In preparation for the dinner, R' Sherer's distinguished son R' Shimshon visited Agudah headquarters in lower Manhattan. He entered the huge office building and walked across the lobby to the receptionist, a gentile woman. R' Shimshon wished her a "Good morning," and asked if he had to sign in. "If you're here to visit Agudath Israel, it's not necessary," she replied. R' Shimshon said that indeed, he had come to visit Agudath Israel. He added, "Rabbi Sherer, the late President of Agudath Israel, was my father. Did you know him?"

"Did I know him?" the woman responded. "I smile every day because of him." She explained:

"Among all those who occupied offices in this building, Rabbi Sherer was always the first to arrive for work each morning. He would enter the building briskly, as if he was in a hurry to do something important. He would press the button for the elevator and then, as he waited for the elevator to descend, he would hurry across the lobby to my desk. 'Good morning — and keep on smiling,' he would tell me. And I knew that he meant it.

"Tears are welling up in my eyes as I say this. At times, my life is rough, but then I remember your father's words and I smile."

Hearing this, R' Shimshon was reminded of an incident which happened in his youth. As a young boy, he would walk through the streets of Boro Park on Shabbos morning together with his father as they made their way to *shul*. R' Sherer wished a *"Gut Shabbos"* to every Jew he passed and a "Good morning" to every gentile.

One Shabbos morning, young Shimshon asked his father, "Daddy, are you running for president? Why must you say 'Good morning' to every single person whom we pass?"

R' Sherer replied, "As you know, when I was a student at Mesivta Torah Vodaath, I had the great privilege of serving as an assistant of sorts to the *gaon* and *tzaddik* R' Elchonon Wasserman when he visited America in 1938.* I first met R' Elchonon when I reported to his room one morning at the Broadway Central Hotel. I greeted the *tzaddik* with a *"Shalom Aleichem"* and then we headed for the elevator to go downstairs.

"As we waited for the elevator, R' Elchonon turned to me and asked, *'Vi azoi zogt men 'Gut morgen' oif Einglish?'* ('How does one say *"Gut morgen"* in English?') I replied, 'Very much like we say it in Yiddish — "Good morning."

"R' Elchonon then paced back and forth and practiced saying 'Good morning.' The elevator arrived and as we entered it, R' Elchonon wished the gentile elevator attendant, 'Good morning.' He then turned to me and asked, *'Hob ich gut gezokt?'* ('Did I say it well?')

---

*This was arranged by the legendary founder of Mesivta Torah Vodaath, R' Shraga Feivel Mendlowitz, who recognized R' Sherer's talents and wanted him to spend time in the company of R' Elchonon, a spiritual giant and expositor of *daas Torah* (the Torah viewpoint). R' Sherer would say that his decision to devote his life to serving *Klal Yisrael* was largely due to R' Elchonon's influence.

"And so," concluded R' Moshe Sherer, "I learned from R' Elchonon that saying 'Good morning' to everyone is something that a Jew should do."

A thoughtful word at the right time can have enormous impact. Yes, even a simple 'Good morning' can give a person a feeling of self-worth and change his entire day.

And words, when used correctly, are themselves "ambassadors" of Hashem and His Torah. A person who speaks wisely and thoughtfully, in a calm and respectful manner, demonstrates that the Torah's ways are "ways of pleasantness and all its paths are peace."[3] This is a great *kiddush Hashem*.

✍ A Letter to Ben

We have learned that one can transgress the laws of *shemiras halashon* through writing something negative about someone. By contrast, one should never underestimate the power of a kind letter. A thoughtful note to a friend or relative can be tremendously meaningful and appreciated.

Sometimes, a kind letter to a total stranger can change the person's life for the better, as the following story illustrates:

Yosef Hartman* manages the New York office of YellowOnline.com, a yellow page company on the Internet which uses the display ad format. One day, he received an e-mail communication which indicated that the sender wanted to have his company listed by YellowOnline. Yosef called the phone number which accompanied the communication and instead of talking business with a potential customer, found himself listening to a very apologetic mother.

Her son, Ben, is mentally retarded and spends most of his

---

*This name has been changed by request. All other names and details of this story are authentic.

day sending out e-mail messages on his computer. It was Ben who, without his parents' knowledge, had sent the communication to Yosef's office, hoping to receive some sort of response. The woman apologized profusely for having wasted Yosef's time with what was nothing but a false lead.

Yosef, a fine, G-d-fearing young man, did not consider the matter a waste of time. He decided to do something which might brighten Ben's life a bit. He composed a letter and had his entire office staff sign it. The letter read:

Dear Ben:

Thank you very much for your e-mail to us here at YellowOnline.com. It is always a pleasure to hear from people who have interest in our company. I spoke to your mom today, and she mentioned that you surf the web a lot. How did you reach us? Did you link to us from another website? I would be very interested in hearing from you on this. If you have the time, please drop us a line or two.

Take care and regards to your mom.

Sincerely yours,
Joseph Hartman
and the New York sales team
YellowOnline.com

Six days later, the owners of YellowOnline, Robert and Pesie Davis of Los Angeles, received the following communication from Ben's mother:

If Joseph Hartman and the YellowOnline New York sales team are any indication, YellowOnline must be a very rare and special organization.

Today, my son Ben received the warmest letter, signed by Joseph and his colleagues, acknowledging an e-mail he had sent to them while surfing the net. Ben is twenty-five years old and mentally handicapped. He spends most of his time alone at home and the computer helps him to pass the time.

For some reason, Ben had included my business number in his e-mail, so Joseph Hartman called it looking for

Ben, to follow up on what I believe he thought was a business lead. I explained the situation and apologized for the confusion, but he wouldn't hear of it. In fact we both had a good chuckle over the whole thing.

The letter today was a complete surprise. Ben has few real friends to speak of and has only received a couple of personal letters in his entire lifetime. He was so excited to see his name on the envelope that he was shaking when he opened it. He's still phoning relatives and reading the letter to them, word for word. In all honesty, I was moved to tears when I read it myself. We're going to have it framed and hang it in his room.

This was a demonstration of public relations at its finest, which is why I felt it should be brought to your attention.

✒ A Good Listener

Listening, too, is an art. We have learned that the Torah strictly forbids us from listening to *lashon hara*. A person can sin and cause others to sin by lending an ear to gossip and other forbidden speech. He can cause untold harm to individuals or cause feuds to erupt by serving as a willing audience to the wrong kind of talk.

On the other hand, a person can actually perform a *mitzvah* by being a good listener in the right situation.

When the previous Gerrer *Rebbe,* R' Pinchas Menachem Alter, was *Rosh Yeshivah* of Yeshivah Sfas Emes, his students became aware that once a month he would be paid an unusual visit. On *erev Rosh Chodesh,* a simple beggar would come to the *Rosh Yeshivah's* home and converse with him for a quarter of an hour or more. The students asked the beggar about this and he explained to them that years before, the *Rosh Yeshivah* had asked that he visit him every *erev Rosh Chodesh* to receive a donation. The *Rosh Yeshivah* would prepare a cup of tea for the man — but that was not all. The beggar explained to the amused students that he was something of an "expert" on current events. As the man sipped his tea, the *Rosh Yeshivah* would ask him for his analysis of the latest news in Israel and around the world. Of course, the beggar was only too happy to provide the *Rosh Yeshivah* with this vital information.

The students understood that the *Rosh Yeshivah* was doing this for only one reason — to make the beggar feel important and needed. They were amazed that R' Pinchas Menachem, who spent every available moment immersed in Torah study, would give of his precious time for this purpose.

On *erev Rosh Chodesh Av*, 5752 (1992), two weeks after R' Pinchas Menachem succeeded his brother as *Rebbe,* the beggar made his way as usual toward the *Rebbe's* home — but this time, he was stopped by some students. "Surely you know that the *Rosh Yeshivah* has become the *Rebbe* of thousands of *chassidim.* As busy as he was until now, he is far more busy now. And he can be visited by the public only at specific hours," they informed him.

The beggar was not perturbed. He informed the students, "Well, it just so happens that I met the *Rebbe* yesterday in the street — and he told me to make sure that I come today as on every *erev Rosh Chodesh!*" With that, he made his way up the steps to the *Rebbe's* residence.

He emerged a short while later, his face aglow. The students crowded around him, eager to hear what had transpired.

"The *Rebbe* gave me an extra-large donation. He told me that since he has become *Rebbe,* key advisers keep him informed as to the latest developments around the world. Therefore, it is no longer necessary for me to go through the bother of preparing news reports and opinions.

"However, the *Rebbe* said that I must continue to come to him on *erev Rosh Chodesh* to receive my usual donation!"

May we merit to follow in the ways of our Torah leaders, and thus bring glory to Hashem, His people and His Torah.

The Mitzvah of
Ahavas Yisrael

When we think into it, we will discover that the mitzvah to judge one's fellow Jew favorably and the quality of shemiras halashon are dependent on our fulfillment of וְאָהַבְתָּ לְרֵעֲךָ כָּמוֹךָ, *Love your fellow as yourself. If we truly love our fellow Jew, then surely we will not speak lashon hara of him, and we will seek every possible point in his favor — just as we would want others to do for us.*

(The Chofetz Chaim in Sefer Shemiras HaLashon,
Shaar HaTevunah Ch. 5)

Chapter One

"...As Yourself"

Sefer HaChinuch[1] entitles his discussion of וְאָהַבְתָּ לְרֵעֲךָ כָּמוֹךָ as, "The *Mitzvah* of *Ahavas Yisrael*." We are commanded, he explains, to develop a deep-rooted love for every Jew to a point where we are concerned about each person and his possessions in the same way that we are concerned about ourselves and our own possessions. To love our fellow Jew also means to praise him, show concern for his dignity and not glorify ourselves by degrading him. Our Sages teach, "One who derives honor from his friend's shame has no share in the World to Come."[2]

Rambam puts it this way: "My compassion and love for my fellow Jew should be like my compassion and love for myself... Whatever I desire for myself I should desire for Him, and whatever I detest for myself or for those who cling to me, I should detest for him. This is what is meant by וְאָהַבְתָּ לְרֵעֲךָ כָּמוֹךָ."[3]

The Chofetz Chaim asks us to take an honest look at what we would want for ourselves:

> If I were to do something which appeared to be improper and others were talking about it, I would hope that someone would speak up in my defense and explain that I had done nothing wrong. This is exactly what we should do when our fellow Jew is incorrectly suspected of wrongdoing.
>
> Furthermore, to love one's fellow Jew is to help him avoid situations which would result in his suffering shame or criticism.
>
> Consider the following: You find yourself for an extended period of time in a city whose customs are foreign to you. You seek out a loyal friend in the city who familiarizes you with local custom and informs you privately when you are about to do something which might arouse bad feelings among the local populace. In this way, you are forewarned of anything which might cause you distress or embarrassment.
>
> We should act towards our fellow Jew in exactly this manner. If we see someone doing something which might lead to his distress or embarrassment, then we are obligated to warn him of this.[4]

The Talmud relates how one of the Sages went even beyond this:

> It happened once that Rabban Gamliel said: "Awaken seven judges for me and have them come to the attic." The next morning, Rabban Gamliel found that eight judges had gone up to the attic. He declared, "Whoever ascended without permission should descend."
>
> Shmuel *HaKattan* arose and said, "I am the one who ascended without permission."
>
> In fact, it was not Shmuel *HaKattan* who ascended without permission, but someone else. It was only to save the other person from embarrassment that Shmuel *HaKattan* declared himself as the guilty one.[5]

One who develops within himself the trait of *ahavas Yisrael* is deserving of the highest praise, as *Sefer HaChinuch* states:

> If we act towards our fellow Jew with love, peace and friendship, seek to help him and are happy when things go well for him — then Hashem says of us, "You are My servant Israel, in whom I am glorified."[6]

✍ A Heartless Request

The level of *ahavas Yisrael* which *tzaddikim* attain allows them to sense the troubles within another Jew's heart in a very real sense.

Under the Czar, life for a Jew in the Russian Army was fraught with physical and spiritual danger. Anti-Semitic soldiers would persecute their Jewish "comrades" and army rules and regulations made it virtually impossible to observe *mitzvos.*

Upon receiving the dreaded draft notice some Jewish young men would actually inflict themselves with permanent injury so that they would be declared unfit for army service.

It is not surprising that *tzaddikim* in Russia were often visited by young men or by their parents with a request for a blessing that somehow the draftee should be rejected by the army.

One day, a man and woman came before the Chortkover *Rebbe,* asking for his blessing that their son should not have to serve in the Russian Army.

The *Rebbe* paused for a moment and responded, "I do not understand the request — let him serve!"

The man and woman — and others who were present — were dumbfounded. "But *Rebbe,*" the man pleaded, "he is my son. I don't want him to die!"

The *Rebbe* seemed unmoved by this appeal. "As I have already told you, *let him serve!*"

A short while later, the *Rebbe* received a letter from the government:

To the Rabbi of Chortkov:

Some time ago, we had been informed that certain comments attributed to you indicated a lack of loyalty to our Motherland. The most serious accusation was that you discouraged young Jewish men from serving their country as soldiers.

A few weeks ago, we sent a man and woman to you, posing as parents of a draftee. Though they pleaded with you for a blessing that their "son" be freed from army service, you refused to do so.

We are pleased that the reports concerning you are false and that indeed, you are a loyal servant of the Czar.

When the *Rebbe's* followers learned of what had transpired, they assumed that the story was yet another proof that their *Rebbe* possessed *Ruach HaKodesh* (Divine Inspiration). The Chortkover *Rebbe,* however, disagreed.

"It is really quite simple," he explained. "You see, whenever someone comes to pour out his or her troubles to me, I feel the person's pain in the depths of my heart — just as if it were my very own worry. But when this man and woman told me about their son, I felt unmoved. No pain, no distress, no feeling of empathy. Nothing. This indicated to me that something suspicious was going on, and so I thought it wise not to grant them their request."

R' Avraham Yehoshua Heschel, the *Rebbe* of Kapyshnitz, had a place in his heart for every Jew. Numerous stories relate the lengths to which the *Rebbe* would go to help someone in need.

Early one morning, the *Rebbe* was walking in the Lower East Side, accompanied by a distinguished *rav.* Suddenly, the *Rebbe* stopped short and said, "Why is someone sitting in front of that building across the street?"

An old Jewish woman was sitting forlornly on the steps of an apartment building. The two *rabbanim* crossed the street to ask her what was wrong. "I could not pay this month's rent," the woman cried. "The landlord threw me out this morning."

The Kapyshnitzer *Rebbe* entered the building and rang the landlord's bell. The landlord came to the door and defended his action, saying that he could not have a situation where people were not paying their rent and he would not allow the woman to return to her apartment unless he received two months' rent.

The *Rebbe* withdrew money from his pocket and paid one month's rent. "Please let the woman return to her apartment," he said, "and I will return later with the second month's payment." The landlord agreed to this arrangement.

In relating this story, the other *rav* said, "The Kapyshnitzer *Rebbe* was not looking across the street when that woman was sitting there in distress. So how, then, did he notice her? I will tell you how. His heart was so sensitive to the plight of every Jew that he was able to sense a Jew in distress without his eyes seeing the person."

❧ A Helping Hand

Rambam informs us that when we perform an act of *chesed* (kindness) for a fellow Jew, we are fulfilling the *mitzvah* of *ahavas Yisrael*.

> It is a positive Rabbinic commandment to visit the sick, to comfort mourners, to escort the dead, to help marry off a bride, to escort guests, to involve oneself in burying the dead... to gladden a bride and groom and to provide them with all their needs. These are acts of lovingkindness that one performs with his body and which have no limit.
>
> Though these commandments are Rabbinic, they are actually encompassed in the commandment of וְאָהַבְתָּ לְרֵעֲךָ כָּמוֹךָ, [which means that] whatever you wish that others should do for you, you should do for others in Torah and *mitzvos*.[7]

The chassidic master R' Chaim of Sanz was a leader to many thousands. His days were filled with studying Torah and responding to halachic questions from all over the world, and he devoted much of his time to prayer. Yet he found time every morning and evening to receive scores of needy people, none of whom ever went away empty-handed. He also found the time to brighten a poor man's day with a friendly word and to attend the weddings of orphans.

He once said, "...and as for me, if I haven't any money to give to the needy, I pine away from distress."

The Sanzer *Rav* (as he was known) lived in a most simple home with the plainest furnishings. The room in which he would receive people privately contained a plain table and a few chairs. For years, the *Rav* sat on an old, rickety chair, until a wealthy *chasid,* who could not bear to see the *Rav* sitting in such discomfort, purchased a new comfortable chair and pleaded with the *Rav* to use it.

He would not even buy a *sefer* for himself, saying that it was more important to use the money for *tzedakah,* since *sefarim* could always be borrowed. The moment a penny would reach his hand, he would immediately give it to a poor person. When he had no money to give, he secured loans to use for *tzedakah* by pawning his Chanukah *menorah* (until Chanukah), and his *kiddush* cup (from Shabbos to Shabbos).

Once, a poor person came to him for assistance, but the *Rav* had nothing to give him. The *Rav's* distress was so obvious that one of his guests, a man of modest means, emptied all the money from his wallet and gave it to the *Rav.*

There was a poor woman in Sanz, a widow with young children, who sold fruit in the local market place. Once, she came to the *tzaddik* weeping bitterly. "*Heilige Rebbe* (Holy Rabbi)," she said, "I do not usually ask for *tzedakah,* but ill fortune has struck me. I bought a wagonload of apples and a false rumor has spread that they are rotten and sour. No one seems interested in buying them."

"Go bring the apples to the market place," the Sanzer *Rav* instructed her, "and I shall come immediately." As the woman left, the *Rav* called to his *gabbai* (attendant), "Come, we shall go sell apples." The *Rav* was lame in one leg, and he limped all the way to the marketplace.

He placed himself alongside the wagonload of apples and called out like a typical fruit merchant, "Buy apples, good sweet apples, as fine as they come!" Before long, hundreds of *chassidim* had surrounded the wagon and the entire stock was snatched up at a good price.

As the last customer left, the woman wiped away tears of joy. "You see," the Sanzer *Rav* told her, "there was nothing wrong with your apples at all."

✋ *Visitors for Bentzy*

It is a positive rabbinic commandment to visit the sick... Though these commandments are rabbinic, they are actually encompassed in the commandment of וְאָהַבְתָּ לְרֵעֲךָ כָּמוֹךָ...

Bentzy Minzer is a bright, affable boy with a charming smile and a kind heart. He is a beloved student at Mesivta Chaim Shlomo in Far Rockaway. He has muscular dystrophy and is confined to a wheelchair.

One day, the yeshivah learned that Bentzy had been rushed to Cornell Medical Center, suffering from a serious breathing problem which caused his doctors great concern. The yeshivah's faculty and students gathered to recite *Tehillim,* and the *Rosh HaYeshivah,* R' Yaakov Bender, hurried to the hospital. Bentzy was wearing an oxygen mask, but R' Bender noticed that his breathing seemed to improve as the visit progressed.

R' Bender and the mesivta's *Menahel,* R' Zevi Trenk, wanted to arrange for Bentzy to have around-the-clock visits from his fellow *talmidim* at the mesivta. They consulted a renowned Torah personality, who told them that this was the highest form of *bikur cholim* and that it was worthwhile for students to alternate taking precious hours from their Torah study schedule in order to fulfill this *mitzvah.*

A system was arranged through which Bentzy was visited twenty-four hours a day by groups of friends who stayed with him for eight-hour shifts. Car services transported the students from Far Rockaway to mid-Manhattan.

After three weeks, Bentzy was discharged from the hospital, able to breathe on his own. His mother said, "The doctors attributed my son's miraculous recovery to the love and concern he received for three consecutive weeks, twenty-four hours a day."

On the first *Motza'ei Shabbos* following his discharge, Bentzy was brought to the mesivta's dining room to participate in a spirited *melavah malkah.* To faculty and students alike, it was also a *seudas hoda'ah,* a meal of thanksgiving to Hashem for Bentzy's recovery.

ℒ *Prayer Preparation*

How well we master the quality of *ahavas Yisrael* can have a pronounced effect on the power of our prayers. R' Chaim Vital (a primary disciple of the *Arizal*) writes:

> Prior to praying in the synagogue, a person should accept upon himself the *mitzvah* of *ahavas Yisrael,* to love every Jew like his very own self, for through this his prayers will become a part of the collective prayers of Israel and will ascend ever higher and bear fruit.
>
> This is especially true among those who study Torah together. Each member of the group should see himself as a part of the others. He must feel his friends' pain and pray for them. In all his prayers, deeds and words, he should have his friends in mind.
>
> My Master [the *Arizal*] cautioned me regarding the brotherly love that should exist among our group.[8]

Whenever a Jew prays, he should have in mind others who are in need of special salvation.

The Steipler *Gaon* referred to R' Yehudah Zev Segal as the *"amud hatefillah"* ("pillar of prayer") in our generation. Each week, scores of requests came to him from all over the world, asking that he pray for the sick, for the childless and for others with specific needs. Amazingly, he never forgot an individual's situation; when he was given the name of someone who was ill, he would continue to pray for him or her long after he had been informed of the person's condition.

When a young boy was stricken with a serious illness, R' Segal visited his parents in the hospital, though he did not know the family. Nine years later, the boy, who by then was fully cured, visited R' Segal at his home. When the boy mentioned his full Hebrew name (including his mother's Hebrew name), R' Segal asked, "Are you the boy who was sick nine years ago...?"

Chapter Two

Three Levels of Love

*T*he Holy One, Blessed is He, said to Israel: "My beloved children! Is there anything that I lack that I should have to ask of you? All I ask of you is that you should love one another, honor one another and respect one another." [1]

R' Eliyahu Dessler[2] writes that the *mitzvah* of *ahavas Yisrael* can be understood on three levels.

Ramban understands the *mitzvah* as follows: People, by nature, seek uniqueness; that is, they seeks some quality, no matter how minute, in which they excel above others. To each person, the quality in which he excels represents his very life and he struggles with all his might to make himself recognized in this way...

However, the Torah reveals to us that this attitude is actually a sign of lowliness and jealousy, for what does one really lack if his neighbor enjoys the same quality that he possesses?

Therefore, the Torah commands us to love our fellow Jew to the point where this supersedes our need for uniqueness. For example, if someone is rich and is superior to others in this regard, then it is a *mitzvah* for him to desire that his neighbor should also attain such wealth. If he is wise, then he should desire that his neighbor should also attain such wisdom — and he should recognize that his essential worth is not lessened by his neighbor's success.

Recently a book was written by an Orthodox Jew in which he describes, step by step, how he attained wealth through business investments so that today, he is able to live off those investments and dedicate himself to the study of Torah. His purpose in writing this book was so that others could follow his example so that they, too, can attain a level of financial security, live off their investments and devote their day to learning.

This is true *ahavas Yisrael*.

𝒜 Good Friend

The Mishnah teaches: "Acquire for yourself a friend."[3] A good friend can change one's life in a very real sense.

Roy was a rugged-looking sensitive type who grew up with everything he could have wanted in the way of materialism. He was raised amid affluence and by the time he was in his early twenties, he had two university degrees, a pilot's license and had traveled overseas many times. And yet he could not help feeling that there was more to life; he sensed that he was not on this world merely to "live it up."

He had attended a non-Jewish school where he needed a special exemption to be excused from attending prayer services. His family was basically non-observant, though they did observe certain laws, such as building a *succah* for the holiday. When some families in the Torah community befriended Roy, he showed genuine appreciation for their way of life.

Howard was Roy's good friend. He and his family were very

close to their rabbi and were closely connected with their Orthodox *shul*. When Howard was in his teens and preparing for a vacation trip to Israel, the rabbi had suggested that he spend some time in a yeshivah there. However, Howard found this idea a bit frightening, and opted instead to spend time on a *kibbutz* picking fruit.

A few years later, he experienced a change of heart. Like Roy, he was a thinking person and he, too, had had some good experiences with the Torah community in his area. He had the feeling that if he did not give himself the opportunity to study in a yeshivah at that time, there might not be another chance.

He got in touch with Roy and told him that he was prepared to join a yeshivah for a six-month trial period — on condition that Roy accompany him. Roy agreed.

They began their preparations for their journey to Yeshivah Ohr Somayach in Jerusalem. The problem was Max. The three had been inseparable since childhood and had a deep bond of understanding with one another. Their closeness was such that words were often unnecessary; a glance was enough to share a thought or experience. When Roy and Howard invited Max to join them, he declined. He had become an instructor in a new method of body-building and physical fitness training, and he wanted to travel overseas to investigate job offers.

Howard and Roy loved yeshivah almost from the start. Within six months, they were both diligent *Gemara* students, to a degree which startled Max when he arrived at Ohr Somayach to pay them a short visit. But that visit was a failure, as Roy and Howard saw it. Max had arrived during *bein hazemanim* (intercession) when most of the faculty and students were away. However, there was one bright spot in the visit, an encounter with one of the generation's great Torah personalities.

The three had gone to visit R' Simcha Wasserman, late *Rosh Yeshivah* of Yeshivah Ohr Elchonon, who had been one of the pioneers of Torah outreach during his years in Los Angeles. R' Simcha sized up Max, taking in his muscular build, and asked him in a quiet voice, "And what do you do?" Max proceeded to explain his occupation as a fitness trainer and builder of bodies.

"Fine," said R' Simcha, looking him in the eye, "and what about your mind?"

Max was speechless.

Max returned to Australia, where he was directing a fitness program. But R' Simcha's words were an important factor when months later, his friends called him from Jerusalem to invite him once again to join them. This time Max accepted.

One of the first things they did as a threesome was to contact two other close friends, also living in Australia, to ask them to come to Ohr Somayach. They were initially unsuccessful, but they would not stop trying.

In a true friendship, each one hopes that his friend will achieve the same success and happiness as himself — especially, that his friend should lead a life that is spiritually meaningful.[4]

ℒ Level Two

Our Sages teach that performing *chesed* (acts of kindness) is the basis of genuine *ahavas Yisrael*. "If you truly desire to attach yourself to [the quality] of love of one's fellow Jew, then occupy yourself with helping him."[5]

The word אַהֲבָה, *love,* writes R' Samson Raphael Hirsch, is related to the word הַב, *give.* To love is to give, to share.

R' Elyah Lopian said that when a person says, "I love fish," he does not really love fish; he loves himself and he eats fish because of the pleasure that he derives from it. This is not love, said R' Elyah, for this is taking. To love is to give.

R' Dessler explained it this way: When a person gives, he gives of himself, and therefore he loves the recipient, for he sees the recipient as containing a part of himself. If he is exceptional in his *chesed* (lovingkindness) towards his neighbor, then he will see his entire being bound up with the recipient.

Someone who performs kindness for all Jews with every fiber of his being is entirely united with them, to the point that he feels it impossible to bear a grudge toward someone who hurts him in any way. He feels that all Jews are limbs of a single body, and therefore it was not someone else who hurt him, but his very own self — and can he bear a grudge toward his very own self? This is the extent of כָּמוֹךָ, *[Love your fellow] like yourself* which the *mitzvah* of *ahavas Yisrael* represents.

This, then, is the secret of the boundless, sincere *ahavas Yisrael* which Torah leaders display towards others. Those who are outstanding in their way of *chesed,* who despite their hectic schedules make time to help others with every sort of need, develop a boundless love for their fellow Jews.

♫ Never Too Busy

R' David Feinstein, *Rosh Yeshivah* of Mesivtha Tifereth Jerusalem, once said of his illustrious father, the *gaon* and *tzaddik* R' Moshe: "My father never wasted a minute, but if a poor or troubled person took an hour to pour out his heart, my father could spare an hour." R' Moshe, whose *hasmadah* (diligence) in Torah study was legendary, gave of his precious time for anyone who needed him.

As Executive Vice-President of Tifereth Jerusalem, R' Yisrael Eidelman often had occasion to visit R' Moshe at his apartment on New York's Lower East Side. Once, R' Eidelman approached R' Moshe's door and heard the sounds of singing coming from inside. As far as R' Eidelman knew, there was no *simchah* (festive celebration) scheduled for that afternoon. Hesitatingly, he knocked and was ushered into the small dining room by one of R' Moshe's grandchildren.

At the head of the dining room table sat R' Moshe. To his right sat an elderly man, a *chazzan* (cantor), who seemed to be entertaining R' Moshe with a cantorial rendition. When he completed a piece, the man turned to R' Moshe and ask, "Was it good?" and R' Moshe replied, "Yes, yes, it *was* good!" The man appeared pleased and happily took leave of R' Moshe.

When the apartment door closed, R' Moshe said to R' Eidelman, "Every person has his own individual needs. This man needs me to listen to him sing and give my approval."

A young *rav* arrived at a wedding where he had been asked to serve as *mesader kiddushin* (one who officiates). How shocked he was to see R' Moshe Feinstein among the guests! The *rav* hurried over to the fathers of the bride and groom. "How could you ask me to be *mesader kiddushin* when you invited R' Moshe? I would not have the nerve to officiate in his presence!" Both fathers insisted that they had not invited R' Moshe and that they had no idea why he had come to the wedding.

The *rav* approached R' Moshe and after exchanging greetings, he said, "May I ask what is the *Rosh Yeshivah's* connection to this *simchah* (celebration)?"

R' Moshe replied, "This morning, I was riding the elevator in the apartment building in which I live, when a man turned to me and said, 'The *Rosh Yeshivah* does not know me, but I have been residing in this building for a number of years. My granddaughter is getting married tonight and it would mean a lot to me if the *Rosh Yeshivah* would attend.'

"That is why I am here."

ஜ *A Model for All*

R' Moshe's *ahavas Yisrael* was a model for all to emulate.

One Shabbos afternoon, he sat in the *beis midrash* of Mesivtha Tifereth Jerusalem, reciting *Tehillim* as a mildly retarded boy stood watching him. The boy went over and turned R' Moshe's *Tehillim* on an angle to the right, and R' Moshe continued reciting. The boy took the *Tehillim* and turned it completely around and R' Moshe continued reciting. Not satisfied, the boy turned the page, but R' Moshe still did not become upset.

A man sitting nearby had watched all this and, although people went out of their way to be patient with the boy, the man had seen what he felt was too much. "Stop it already!" he snapped. "Let the *Rosh Yeshivah daven!*"

R' Moshe turned to the man and said, "He is only playing with me. I *enjoy* it when he plays with me! I love him like my own child!" With those words, R' Moshe embraced the boy and kissed him.

R' Moshe lived in a high-rise apartment building on Manhattan's FDR Drive. One *erev* Yom Kippur, a few years before his passing, R' Moshe was taken from his apartment by wheelchair to a waiting car, which was to bring him to Yeshivah of Staten Island for Yom Kippur. In the elevator on the way downstairs stood a non-religious Jew. The man bent down towards R' Moshe and with a touch of hesitation, said, "A happy new year, Rabbi."

R' Moshe looked up and smiled with genuine warmth. "A good year to you," he responded. The man was touched by R' Moshe's obvious sincerity. He bent down again and said, "And a healthy year, too, Rabbi." With his sparkling eyes, R' Moshe looked back at the man and said, "May you also be blessed with a healthy year, one filled with success and *nachas* from your children. And may you live to witness *Mashiach's* arrival."

As R' Moshe was being wheeled to the car, the man turned to R' Moshe's daughter-in-law, Rebbetzin Sheila Feinstein, and said, "It is obvious that I am not religious — my head is not covered — yet, to the Rabbi, I am a 'Somebody!'" Later, Rebbetzin Feinstein repeated these words to R' Moshe. R' Moshe did not see his behavior towards the man as something unusual. "אבער ער איז א איד! But he is a Jew!" R' Moshe said simply.

ℒ *The Highest Level*

There is a level of *ahavas Yisrael,* says R' Dessler, which surpasses even that which was previously mentioned. This is *ahavas Yisrael* which is a product of drawing close to Hashem. Someone who humbles himself totally before Hashem and nullifies his own personal desires for Hashem's sake, will do the same towards his fellow, who was created in the Divine image.

In his writings, R' Aryeh Levine discusses different levels of *ahavas Yisrael*:

> What is *ahavas Yisrael*? It is enormous, boundless love of Hashem towards His people, the Nation of Israel, a love which was expressed when He designated us as His Chosen People.
>
> Perfect *ahavas Yisrael,* with no blemish at all, can be attributed only to Hashem. We can only attempt to emulate His ways, to pride ourselves on having attained some level of *ahavas Yisrael.*
>
> Clearly, there are many levels of *ahavas Yisrael.* The greater the level a person has attained in Torah and good deeds, the greater is his *ahavas Yisrael.*
>
> Consider this: One needs to attain a very high spiritual level to fulfill the teaching, "Let your fellow's honor be as dear to you as your own."[6] Now, can a person [reach yet a higher level where he can] rejoice over his friend's honor as he would rejoice over his own? This is not easily attained.
>
> Therefore, the Talmud relates that Hillel the Elder ran a distance of three *mil* (approx. 2 miles) in front of a poor man who had once been rich.[7] Hillel perceived that the man felt deprived of this honor, therefore he did whatever was in his power to bring it about. Such perception, which Hillel attained through humility, tolerance, understanding, and especially through proper *ahavas Yisrael,* is [indicative of] the highest level of *ahavas Yisrael.*[8]

ℒ Hillel's Rule

Hillel the Elder explained the *mitzvah* to love one's fellow Jew as: "What is hateful to you, do not do unto others."[9] According to this, it would seem that if we do not mind being treated with disrespect, then we would be allowed to treat others disrespectfully. This, however, is incorrect.

When Hillel explained *ahavas Yisrael* to mean, "What is hateful to you, do not do unto others," he was speaking to a gentile who asked that he be taught "all of Torah while standing on one foot." As R' Yehudah Zev Segal explained:

> A Jew should strive to love and admire his fellow Jew's every redeeming quality... he should rejoice in his neighbor's success as he would in his own, while feeling the pain of his neighbor's misfortune... However, there is a step that precedes this: First, one must avoid doing to others that which he himself detests. In responding to the gentile, Hillel told him only the initial step of this *mitzvah*.[10]

Chapter Three

The Great Rule

"Love your fellow as yourself" — *Rabbi Akiva said: "This is a great rule in the Torah." (Rashi citing Torah Kohanim)*

❧ All-encompassing

According to *Sefer HaChinuch*,[1] the *mitzvah* of *ahavas Yisrael* encompasses all *mitzvos* between a Jew and his fellow. If I truly love my neighbor, then I will not steal from him, damage his property, speak *lashon hara* about him, seek revenge against him, etc.

Yam HaTalmud (quoting his father) writes that *ahavas Yisrael* will also lead to fulfillment of *mitzvos* which are between man and Hashem. All Jews are responsible for one another[2] and in Heaven, all Jewish souls are connected. "All the souls of the

House of Yaakov who came to Egypt, seventy."[3] The Torah's use of נֶפֶשׁ, [lit. *soul*], as opposed to נְפָשׁוֹת, [*souls*], alludes to the fact that in Heaven, the souls of the Jewish people are like one.[4]

When a Jew performs a *mitzvah,* he benefits not only himself, but the entire world, and especially the Jewish people. When he sins, he causes harm to the Jewish people. This is why our Sages teach that before deciding on a proper course of action, a Jew should imagine that the world is being judged in Heaven and that one deed can tip the scale in either direction.[5]

If, for example, a Jew with true *ahavas Yisrael* were to be tempted to eat some non-kosher food, he might say to himself: "If I eat this food, I will get some momentary pleasure — but at what price? I will have caused harm to my friends, family and neighbors; to all Jews, in fact. Am I so selfish as to hurt so many whom I love, because I want to eat this sandwich? Hasn't the *galus* (exile) lasted long enough? Need I be the one to prolong the suffering of our people even one additional moment?"

℘ *The Totality of Torah*

Ksav Sofer writes that there are many *mitzvos* which an individual cannot fulfill personally. For example, some *mitzvos* apply only to men, some only to women, some only to *Kohanim,* and some only to those living in Eretz Yisrael. How, then, can a person fulfill all of Torah?

By fulfilling the *mitzvah* of *ahavas Yisrael,* one unites himself with his fellow Jews and shares in the benefits of their *mitzvah* accomplishments. In this way, it is as if he fulfilled all of Torah. This is why the *mitzvah* of *ahavas Yisrael* is the "great rule in the Torah."

The word יִשְׂרָאֵל (Israel) forms the initial letters of יֵשׁ שִׁשִׁים רִבּוֹא אֹתִיוֹת לַתּוֹרָה, *There are six hundred thousand letters in the Torah.* Another name of the Jewish people, יְשֻׁרֻן (Jeshurun), forms the initials of יֵשׁ שִׁשִׁים רִבּוֹא נְשָׁמוֹת, *There are six hundred thousand [Jewish] souls.* This teaches us that each Jewish soul is represented by a letter in the Torah.

For a *sefer Torah* (Torah scroll) to be fit for use, it cannot be missing even a single letter. Furthermore, each letter of the *sefer Torah* is unique, for it contains meanings and teachings — both revealed and hidden — which are unlike any others in the Torah. Similarly, every Jew is unique and special. Hashem placed him or her on this world to accomplish a mission which no other *neshamah* (soul) can accomplish.

The Mishnah teaches:

> A man mints many coins from one mold and they are all alike, but the King of kings, the Holy One, Blessed is He, minted all men from the mold of Adam and not one is like the other. Therefore, everyone is obligated to say, "For my sake was the world created."[6]

The *mitzvah* of *ahavas Yisrael* is a "great rule in the Torah" in that the "rule" (i.e. the "law") of the Torah scroll requiring that it be complete, hints to the uniqueness of every Jew. By recognizing this uniqueness, one will surely come to love his fellow Jew.

❧ *Love Your Fellow, Love Hashem*

Shach writes that when a person develops within himself genuine *ahavas Yisrael,* it is only natural that he will come to love Hashem, Who gave us His precious Torah, and granted each of us a lofty *neshamah* through which we can fulfill our life's mission. And through *ahavas Hashem,* one will come to fulfill all of Torah.

The reverse is true as well. *Ahavas Yisrael* is an extension of *ahavas Hashem;* if one truly loves Hashem, then he will come to love His Chosen People of whom the Torah states: "You are children to Hashem, your G-d."[7] This is alluded to in the words which conclude the command to love one's fellow Jew: אֲנִי ה, *I am Hashem.*

R' Moshe Wolfson notes that the *gematria* (numerical value) of וְאָהַבְתָּ אֵת ה אֱלֹקֶיךָ (*And you shall love Hashem, your G–d*[8]) is equal to that of וְאָהַבְתָּ לְרֵעֲךָ כָּמוֹךָ אֲנִי ה (*You shall love your fellow as yourself — I am Hashem*) — 907.

✒ The Power of Unity

The power of unity is awesome, which may be another reason why "Love your fellow…" is the "great rule in the Torah." R' Aharon Kotler[9] quotes a teaching of the Sages:

Peace is precious, for even if Israel worships idols but enjoys peace among its people, Hashem says, as it were: "I cannot punish them, for there is peace among them."[10]

This was the difference between the דּוֹר הַמַּבּוּל (Generation of the Deluge[11]) and the דּוֹר הַפְּלָגָה (Generation of the Dispersion[12]). The former were immersed in robbery [a symptom of disunity] and therefore nothing remained of them, while the latter loved one another, as it says, "The whole earth was of one language and common purpose."[13] This is why they were not totally destroyed.

This, says R' Aharon, teaches us the power of unity. The unity of the דּוֹר הַפְּלָגָה was directed *against* Hashem, yet it ensured the people's survival. We should bear in mind that just as a *mitzvah* is greater when performed by a community,[14] so too, is a sin worse when performed by a community. Of course, the sins of the דּוֹר הַפְּלָגָה were recorded in Heaven and were not ignored. In Heaven they would be held accountable for their sins. Nevertheless, because of their unity, Hashem said, as it were, "I cannot exercise My power over them." As long as they remained unified, there was still time to repent.

If such is the power of *sinful* unity, can we imagine how great is the power of a community that is unified for the sake of Heaven?

"Love your fellow as yourself" — *This is a great rule in the Torah.*

The level of a generation's Torah learning is very much intertwined with its level of *ahavas Yisrael.*

Our Sages inform us that when the Jewish people received the Torah, they were united "like one man with one heart."[15] It was at that time that Hashem said: "Since Israel rejected strife and embraced harmony, dwelling as one, the time is ripe for Me to give them the Torah."[16]

R' Chaim Shmulevitz explains:[17]

Torah was not given to individuals. It was given to a single unified nation; their being "like one man with one heart" transformed six hundred thousand individuals into one entity.

Our Sages teach that at the time of the Purim miracle, the Jewish people experienced a reacceptance of Torah, on a deeper level than at Sinai.[18] The source of this reacceptance was that Haman's decree reunited the people as never before. In times of danger, petty quarrels and personal grudges disappear and people focus their concerns on the welfare of the community, not on their personal differences. Therefore, at the time of the Purim miracle, the Jewish people were able to receive the Torah in its deepest and fullest sense.

We are taught that the Torah learning of the generation of R' Yehudah bar Ilai was on a higher level than that of the generations of Moshe *Rabbeinu* and King Chizkiyahu.[19]

The generation of Moshe stood at Sinai to receive the Torah, with all its accompanying miracles. King Chizkiyahu imbued his people with a spirit of study so powerful that every child in Israel was expert in the difficult laws of purity. How could R' Yehudah bar Ilai's generation surpass their level of Torah learning?

His generation was unique. "Six *talmidei chachamim* would cover themselves with one blanket."[20]

Let us ask ourselves, says R' Chaim Shmulevitz: If six people cover themselves with one blanket, can any of them stay warm? The answer is that if each one pulls the blanket to himself, no one will be covered. But if each one pushes the blanket to the other, to ensure that his neighbor is sufficiently covered, then all six of them will be warm.

It was this sort of unity that allowed R' Yehudah bar Ilai's generation to receive the Torah on the highest level.

"Love your fellow as yourself" — This is a great rule in the Torah.

⁀

It is most fitting that the above thought was said by R' Chaim Shmulevitz, who combined greatness in Torah with a level of *ahavas Yisrael* that was legendary.

In the 1970's, a passenger plane filled with Jews was hijacked by terrorists to Entebbe, Uganda. Jews around the world joined in prayer for the hostages' well-being. (After a few weeks, Israeli forces staged a surpise raid which freed them.) The Mirrer Yeshivah *beis midrash* in Jerusalem was filled to capacity as everyone waited for R' Chaim, the *Rosh Yeshivah,* to address the assemblage before the recital of *Tehillim.*

A hush fell over the crowd as R' Chaim entered. But instead of making his way to the front of the *beis midrash,* he collapsed into a chair near the door and began to sob. After a few minutes, he calmed down, made his way to the *aron kodesh* and ascended the platform to speak. But before he could utter a word, he was once again overcome by weeping, for the plight of his fellow Jews being held hostage by vicious terrorists, who were threatening to kill them if their demands were not met.

R' Chaim was unable to speak and he descended the platform. But no words were necessary. The sight of this *tzaddik* crying as he did inspired everyone to recite *Tehillim* with great fervor as never before.

On a day when one of R' Chaim's children was getting married, he summoned a *talmid* who had been trying unsuccessfully for many years to find his *shidduch* (marriage match). "Tonight," R' Chaim told the young man, "I will, *b'ezras Hashem,* be taking one of my children to the *chuppah.* And so I thought to myself, 'Who should I be thinking of on such a day?'

You were the person who came to mind. So I just want you to know that I am thinking of you."

On *Hoshanah Rabbah* 5739 (1978), R' Chaim, stricken by the disease from which he would not recover, was lying in bad racked by pain. A young man entered the room and asked that he pray for someone who was ill.

After the young man left, R' Chaim said to his son, "Please help me get dressed. I must go to the *Kosel* to pray."

"But Father," his son protested, "you can hardly turn over in bed. How can you go to the *Kosel?*"

But R' Chaim was insistent. If a Jew was sick, he had to pray for him at the *Kosel.*

Reluctantly, his son helped him to dress. At the *Kosel* plaza, R' Chaim emerged from the car with barely enough strength to stand. He prayed, was driven home and returned to his sickbed.

Reb Chaim would often tell his *talmidim,* "What is the purpose of life if not to give of oneself to others?"

Our Sages teach[21] that a *tzaddik* is considered living even after death, because the living still benefit from his words and deeds. He is still giving, so he is still alive.

After R' Chaim died, his classic *Sichos Mussar* was used as a primary text for the *baal teshuvah* movement in Russia, which operated in secret under the Communists. To this day, his *shmuessen* (discourses) are studied and cherished by Torah students everywhere.

And his way of caring for others remains a shining example for all to follow.

R' Chaim is still giving; he is very much alive.

❧ "*I Am Hashem*"

To explain why the commandments, "You shall not take revenge or bear a grudge... love your fellow as yourself," are followed by "I am Hashem," the Chofetz Chaim offers a parable:[22]

Reuven was upset with his neighbor Shimon over something

which Shimon had done. One day, Yehudah, a respected man known for his truthfulness, tells Reuven, "I was present recently when Shimon paid a visit to one of our generation's greatest Torah personalities, who is known for his wisdom and piety. This *tzaddik* accorded Shimon great honor and showed him genuine love. After witnessing this, my friend, I must conclude that your opinion of Shimon is grossly incorrect."

After taking a few moments to digest this information, Reuven responds, "It may well be that I am mistaken. My feeling that Shimon has wronged me may very well be a result of a person's natural inclination to see himself as right in any argument.

"On the other hand, it may be that Shimon is so clever and deceiving that he is able to deceive even a *tzaddik* into thinking that he is a good person. In other words, your report has given me food for thought, but I'm not fully convinced. In any case, for the time being I will refrain from speaking badly about Shimon."

Some time later, Yehudah tells Reuven, "I was privileged to be present when Shimon met with the Sages of the Mishnah — Rabbi Yehudah *HaNassi* (the Prince), Rabbi Meir and others — men endowed with *Ruach HaKodesh* (Divine Inspiration), who are akin to angels and cannot possibly be deceived! I saw how they accorded Shimon great honor and showed him deep love and admiration."

A shaken Reuven responds, "I have erred. Obviously, my personal prejudices caused me to bear ill will towards Shimon."

Yehudah then adds, "The Sages of the Mishnah are often visited by Eliyahu *HaNavi* (the Prophet). They mentioned that Eliyahu had related how he heard Hashem express His deep love of Shimon."

"Woe is me!" exclaimed Reuven. "I have borne a grudge and spoken *lashon hara* against someone whom Hashem loves! I now see things differently. Either I totally misunderstood Shimon's actions, or I failed to realize that he acted unintentionally. Surely such a good person would not have wronged me intentionally!"

This, says, the Chofetz Chaim, is the meaning of "I am Hashem." Hashem loves every Jew with a deep, unfathomable love. And just as His love for us is deep and unwavering, so too should we develop within ourselves this sort of love for one another.

Chapter Four

Children of One Father

In *Leshichno Sidreshu*,[1] R' Yitzchak Koledetsky writes:

The *mitzvah* of *ahavas Yisrael* includes all Jews, regardless of affiliation, party or community. To our misfortune, Satan has succeeded in dividing our people into groups and sub-groups and he [Satan] has succeeded in implanting a wrong feeling that, "If someone does not belong to my group, and especially if he is an opponent of my group, then it is a *mitzvah* to ostracize him and to denigrate him." Many forget a foundation of Judaism upon which all of Torah is dependent, for our Sages taught that the *mitzvah* of *ahavas Yisrael* is a "great rule in the Torah." The divisions within the Torah community have created great confusion and have separated one Jew from another, to the point where they have forgotten that "we are all children of one Father."[2]

We must always bear in mind: Everyone seeks to serve Hashem in the way that he learned from his ancestors and teachers. Our common denominator is that all of us are faithful to the same Torah and the same *Shulchan Aruch*. The Chofetz Chaim would say that when *Mashiach* will arrive, Hashem will grasp a Torah scroll in His hand, as it were, and *He will not ask us,* "To which group did you belong?" Rather, He will ask each of us, "How much of the Torah did you fulfill?"

All this is obvious and well known.

❧ Those Who Are Distant

R' Koledetsky continues:

All Jews, regardless of personal affiliation, are like precious children to Hashem. Even those unfortunate souls who are distant from Torah and *mitzvos* are considered "children of Hashem," and regarding all of them we have been assured, "that no one will be banished from Him."[3] No Jewish soul will be lost, ל"ר; all will return in the end with complete repentance. We must pray for our dear estranged brethren, pray that Hashem will inspire them soon with a spirit of purity from Above, so that they will repent completely and "they will all become a single society, to do Your will wholeheartedly."[4]

It is the obligation of every Jew who is fortunate enough to be Torah observant to relate toward our non-religious brethren with true *ahavas Yisrael.* By showing them genuine love and concern, while sanctifying Hashem through exemplary speech and behavior, we may inspire them to embrace the Torah — the Torah which every Jewish *neshamah* that would ever be born accepted at Sinai.

❧ A Praiseworthy Jew

On a visit to Vilna, the Chofetz Chaim arrived at an inn to spend the night. As he entered the dining room, he noticed a boorish-looking fellow being served a large portion of meat and a drink. The Chofetz Chaim looked on in dismay as the man devoured the meat in a few bites, gulped down his drink and then addressed the waiter in an unbecoming way as he asked for more food.

The Chofetz Chaim rose from his seat and was about to make his way to the fellow's table, when the innkeeper stopped him. "*Rebbi*," said the man, "this boor is a lost Jewish soul, a Cantonist. He was taken from his home by force at age seven and worked on a Siberian farm until age eighteen. Then he spent twenty-five years in the Czar's army. Is it any wonder that he is nothing but an ignorant, uncivilized boor to whom life means nothing but eating and drinking? Please, do not attempt to correct his behavior. I fear that he may become angry and could even respond by striking you."

"So that is his story!" exclaimed the Chofetz Chaim. "Do not worry, I am hopeful that I will speak to him in a way that will not upset him."

The Chofetz Chaim approached the man, extended his hand in greeting and said, "Is what I hear true, that you were snatched from your home at age seven, grew up among gentiles and never had the opportunity to study a word of Torah? You have suffered *Gehinnom* on this world! I am sure that the wicked people who persecuted you forced you to eat non-kosher foods and transgress other *mitzvos* as well. Yet you remained a Jew and did not let the Czar achieve his goal of convincing you to convert. Praiseworthy are you! For thirty years, you bore suffering at the hands of your oppressors, and here you are, a Jew who clings to his faith in the A-mighty. What a source of merit you have earned for yourself!"

The Chofetz Chaim's sincere words, spoken from a mouth that was holy and pure, touched the Cantonist to the depths of his soul. Tears flowed from his eyes and he embraced the Chofetz Chaim. The Chofetz Chaim then spoke to the man about returning to the path of Torah, the path which his parents had been prevented from teaching him. Under the Chofetz Chaim's guidance, he became a complete *baal teshuvah*.

In the early 1900's, a fierce struggle raged between the secularists and the Torah community in Eretz Yisrael over who would determine the nature of Jewish life in our precious land. The leader of the Torah community was Jerusalem's beloved *Rav,* the legendary R' Yosef Chaim Sonnenfeld.

It happened that one of the secularist leaders, known for his vicious anti-religious attacks, suddenly became critically ill and was hospitalized in the English Missionary Hospital. A ban on entering this hospital had been decreed by the *rabbanim* of Jerusalem, since, as its name implied, it was run by Christian missionaries. After four weeks in this hospital, the man's condition worsened and doctors gave up all hope for his recovery.

His family knew that their only hope was to transfer him to the best hospital in the country at that time, Shaarei Zedek, headed by Dr. Moshe Wallach, a G-d-fearing man whose every move was guided by the cities' *tzaddikim.* However, since the family had ignored the ban on the Missionary Hospital, they feared that the patient would be refused admittance to Shaarei Zedek.

A close friend of the family, Amnon (not his real name), suggested that they contact Rabbi Sonnenfeld, whose heart overflowed with love for every Jew. They agreed to this and the person who had made the suggestion hurried to the Old City where R' Chaim (as he was known) resided.

Amnon found R' Chaim deeply immersed in Torah study. R' Chaim recognized his visitor, and surely recalled that he had abandoned the path of Torah, yet he smiled and greeted him warmly.

Amnon apologized for the interruption and explained why he had come. He included every detail, including the fact that the patient had spent four weeks in the Missionary Hospital. The man concluded his report and appealed to R' Chaim to write a letter to Dr. Wallach urging him to admit the patient to Shaarei Zedek.

R' Chaim creased the page he was studying, donned his coat

and prepared to leave for the hospital. Outside a fierce thunderstorm raged; Amnon blocked the door, refusing to allow R' Chaim to venture forth in such treacherous weather. "All I asked for was a letter," he insisted. "I did not intend that the *Rav* should walk out in such weather."

R' Chaim responded: "When a Jewish life is in danger, a letter is *not* enough. I must personally attend to fulfilling this great *mitzvah*."

R' Chaim dashed out of the room and in a moment he was up the steps of his basement apartment. Though Amnon was a young man, he had a hard time keeping pace with the seventy-five-year-old *tzaddik*. As they walked, the rain intensified. Amnon said, "Perhaps we should wait until the rain lets up a bit?" In response, R' Chaim quickened his pace, exclaiming, "How can someone going to save a life be deterred by a few drops of rain?"

At the entrance to the Old City, they boarded a horse-drawn carriage and headed for the hospital. R' Chaim withdrew his worn *Tehillim* and became immersed in his prayers, while Amnon sat transfixed by the glow on the *tzaddik's* face.

They arrived at the hospital and R' Chaim sprang from the carriage while Amnon paid the driver. By the time Amnon entered the hospital, R' Chaim was already in Dr. Wallach's private office, telling him that the patient should be admitted immediately.

Two weeks later, the patient was released from Shaarei Zedek, fully recovered from his illness. Knowing that the patient considered R' Chaim his "adversary" the family decided not to tell him who had been responsible for his gaining admission to Shaarei Zedek.

A year passed and the patient was asked to deliver the keynote address at the groundbreaking ceremony for a new *kibbutz*. As he reached the climax of his speech, he shouted, "We will build this land in our own way, with our own strength! We will wage a fight to the death against the black arm of Rabbi Sonnenfeld and his cronies!"

Amnon, who was sitting in the audience, could not contain himself. He shouted towards the podium, "How dare you! Have a little respect for the saintly rabbi to whom you owe your very life!"

The speaker was shocked into silence and asked Amnon to explain himself. Amnon took the podium and told the story of how the *tzaddik* from Jerusalem had saved the life of the man who had vowed to destroy him.[5]

✒ *"Reb Shmuel"*

In the early days of the Second World War, after Poland had been invaded by Germany and Russia, thousands of yeshivah students and their *rebbeim* streamed from Poland to Vilna. This city, known as "the Jerusalem of Lithuania," was for the time being not under either Russian or German rule.

Their flight to Vilna and survival there was orchestrated by the great *gaon* and *posek hador,* R' Chaim Ozer Grodzensky, who served as Vilna's *Rav* and who was looked at as the devoted father of the yeshivah world.

The *Vaad Hatzalah* (Rescue Committee) which was founded by the Torah leaders of America was dedicated to doing whatever possible to help the suffering Jews of Europe. The *Vaad's* very first project, in the early days of the war, was to raise funds to help support the thousands of yeshivah students in Vilna and its suburbs.

Rabbi Eliezer Silver, a renowned *gaon* who served as Chief Rabbi of Cincinnati, among many illustrious credentials, had been elected by his colleagues to serve as *Vaad* President. R' Silver decided to send a representative to Vilna to get a firsthand look at the situation and to get a detailed assessment from R' Chaim Ozer as to what the refugees needed.

The man chosen for this was Dr. Samuel Schmidt, Editor of Cincinnati's *Every Friday* Jewish weekly. Dr. Schmidt had been an ardent and influential secular Zionist-Socialist until he came in contact with R' Silver. From then on, he began to adopt certain religious practices and develop an appreciation for the Torah way of life. His meeting with R' Chaim Ozer in Vilna inspired him to become a complete *ba'al teshuvah.*

Dr. Schmidt later recounted:

> It was shortly after I arrived in Vilna on a Shabbos after-noon, that I entered R' Chaim Ozer's bedroom at his request. (R' Chaim Ozer was ill and was confined to bed.) The *gaon* was sitting up and smiling pleasantly, and the at-mosphere was peaceful, for he was officially not seeing people at that hour.
>
> He began to ask me about myself and listened carefully to every detail of my history. I told of my mission to Poland in the 1920's as a medical expert, to help immunize my Jewish brethren against various epidemics... of my mis-sion to Israel some years later... R' Chaim Ozer, the genius in Torah and other wisdom, asked me all about myself. He listened with rapt attention and then, with a look of true friendship, said, "Allow me, Dr. Schmidt, to address you in a familiar way, by your first name — Reb Shmuel."
>
> His words touched my heart and my tears flowed freely. "I am not worthy of this!" I protested. He replied, "*Chas v'shalom* (Heaven forfend)! For a Jew living in the securi-ty of America, to undertake a dangerous mission and travel under wartime conditions to a faraway land in order to assist his fellow Jews and rescue the yeshivos — this is proof of his worth!"
>
> He continued to offer me encouragement. The next morning, I donned a *tallis* and put on *tefillin* for the first time... And I became observant in Torah and *mitzvos* in all their fine details."[6]

❧ A Higher Purpose

When the beloved Lakewood *Rosh Yeshivah* R' Shneur Kotler arrived in Memphis, Tennessee, on a fund-raising trip, he visited his longtime friend, the distinguished *Rav,* R' Ephraim Greenblatt. R' Shneur went over his list of potential donors with R' Greenblatt, who provided him with some background information on each person. R' Greenblatt, who had been R' Shneur's *chavrusa* (study partner) when they were both *talmidim* of the Lakewood Yeshivah, had graciously agreed to call for appointments and accompany R' Shneur to them.

When they came to the name "Marc Schaeffer" (not his real name) R' Greenblatt said, "I don't recommend that you visit Mr. Schaeffer. Unfortunately, he makes no secret of the fact that he does not contribute to charity. His attitude is, 'I don't believe in it.' "

"In that case," said R' Shneur, "We will *definitely* visit him."

R' Greenblatt repeated that he did not think that the visit would yield results, but he respected R' Shneur's wishes and called for an appointment.

"No problem," Mr. Schaeffer said on the phone. "I'll be glad to see you, but please remember that I don't give charity."

Mr. Schaeffer welcomed the two *rabbanim* cordially and invited them to be seated. "But please remember," he added, "that I won't give you a dime."

"Don't worry about that; I'm here to visit a fellow Jew," R' Shneur replied warmly. "But I'm intrigued by your attitude. Why don't you give charity?"

Mr. Schaeffer explained that he was a Holocaust survivor; the war had left him full of questions and anger. He was no longer a practicing Jew and this included not giving *tzedakah*.

"Mr. Schaeffer," R' Shneur replied in his gentle, caring way, "you had a terrible experience. But we are only human and therefore we cannot fathom G–d's ways, nor may we question them.

"On the other hand, you might try looking at matters from a different perspective. So many perished in the Holocaust; it was only through the grace of G–d that you and some others survived. That alone calls for gratitude to the One Above!"

Mr. Schaeffer appeared thoughtful. R' Shneur went on to discuss other topics and the two conversed for about two hours.

"Mr. Schaeffer," R' Shneur finally said, "In the amount of time that I spent here, I could have visited a few people — people who support Torah. Instead, I chose to visit you... because I wanted to give you the opportunity to merit a portion in the

World to Come through the *mitzvah* of *tzedakah*."

Tears welled up in Mr. Schaeffer's eyes. "Thank you, Rabbi," he whispered. He withdrew his check book, wrote a check for fifty dollars and handed it to R' Shneur.

R' Shneur wished him well and the two *rabbanim* left.

On the way home, R' Shneur told R' Greenblatt the following story:

With the outbreak of the Second World War and the German invasion of Poland, everyone who had the necessary papers attempted to flee across the border into neighboring Lithuania. R' Shneur's illustrious father, R' Aharon Kotler, crossed the border together with his family. However, he soon realized that amidst all the tumult, he had left his *tefillin* behind. He was determined to return to Poland to retrieve them. That night, R' Aharon crossed the border and safely made his way to the *beis midrash* where his *tefillin* still lay.

By then it was morning. R' Aharon decided to remain in hiding until nightfall, when he would attempt to cross back into Lithuania. He headed to a border village and knocked on the door of a farmhouse.

"May I stay here overnight?" he asked.

"Certainly, Rabbi," was the farmer's reply.

They spoke for a while and R' Aharon discovered that the farmer was Jewish, though totally ignorant of his heritage. When R' Aharon donned his *tefillin* and *davened Shacharis,* the farmer watched him intently. After he had completed his prayers, R' Aharon asked the man if he had ever worn *tefillin,* to which the man replied, "No, never."

R' Aharon gave the man a brief introduction to the *mitzvah* of *tefillin* and told him that by fulfilling this *mitzvah,* he could earn reward in the World to Come. The man was agreeable to the suggestion that he don the *tefillin,* and R' Aharon helped him.

That night, R' Aharon safely crossed the border once again.

Years later, the farmer appeared to R' Aharon in a dream. He said, "When I was called before the Heavenly Court, the evidence against me was overwhelming and I was sure that I was doomed. But one angel came to my defense, saying that I had once put on *tefillin*. For that *mitzvah,* I was granted reward.

"Thank you, *Rebbi.*"

The next morning, R' Aharon related the dream to his family. He remarked, "At the time, I thought that I had gone back to retrieve my *tefillin*. Now I see that Hashem sent me back to help a Jew earn a bit of *Olam Haba* (the World to Come)."

"And so," R' Shneur concluded, "I was more interested in changing this man's attitude towards *tzedakah* and faith in Hashem than I was in receiving a check from him. With his new outlook, he will merit a share in *Olam Haba,* and that is what I hoped to accomplish."[7]

Chapter Five

Lessons of Greatness

R' Avraham Yehoshua Heschel, the *Rebbe* of Kapyshnitz, had a place in his heart for every Jew. People who were lonely and distressed, whose life experiences left them somewhat odd and difficult to deal with, felt at home and welcome at the *Rebbe's* table.

The *Rebbe* enjoyed a close relationship with the Ponovezher *Rav,* R' Yosef Shlomo Kahaneman. In fact, it was the Ponovezher *Rav* who arranged the *shidduch* (marriage match) between the son of R' Shlomo Zalman Auerbach and the *Rebbe's* granddaughter. The *Rebbe* once said, "Do you think that the mitzvah of וְאָהַבְתָּ לְרֵעֲךָ כָּמוֹךָ *(Love your fellow Jew as yourself)* means to love the Ponovezher *Rav*? Of course not! How could one *not* love the Ponovezher *Rav*! Rather, the mitzvah is to love the Jew whom it is difficult to deal with, the one who might not earn our love naturally. *That* is what *ahavas Yisrael* means."

In the Lower East Side, where the *Rebbe* resided after he arrived in America, there lived a fellow named Moshe, an angry, embittered, lonely soul who would make unreasonable demands on others and would never trouble himself to help someone else. Moshe lived with a certain family for a while until the family members could not bear it any longer. They asked him to leave, but Moshe refused! The family brought their problem to a local *rav* who asked the Kapyshnitzer *Rebbe* if he could intervene.

The *Rebbe* met with Moshe and got straight to the point. "The family has asked you politely to leave — why do you refuse to cooperate?" Moshe replied honestly, "Because there I can get three meals a day, a bed, and clean clothing. If I move out, I will have to care for myself!"

The *Rebbe* replied, "Moshe, I think you know that I am a man of my word. Move out of that house and you can move in with my family."

Moshe would do things which infuriated everyone around him — except the Kapyshnitzer *Rebbe*. Whenever he would conduct a *tish*, the *Rebbe* would keep a towel on his lap on which he would wipe his hands. Sometimes, Moshe would reach over to take the towel out of the *Rebbe's* lap in order to mop his own brow. The *chassidim* were furious at this obvious show of disrespect and lack of basic decency, but the *Rebbe,* keenly aware that Moshe was set in his ways and would not change, let such matters pass without a word.

It was the *Rebbe's* custom to recite the Friday night *Kiddush* and partake of his meal at his *tish* (public chassidic gathering) which commenced some two hours after *Maariv* had ended. One Friday night, the *Rebbe* entered the room to recite *Kiddush* and noticed that someone was missing. "Where is Moshe?" he demanded to know. The *chassidim* looked at one another until someone told the *Rebbe* the truth: Moshe had done something which everyone had agreed was outrageous and he had been ordered to leave the *beis midrash.*

The Kapyshnitzer *Rebbe* was dismayed beyond words. "A *Yid* was told that he was not welcome in my *beis midrash*? *Oy vey!* I will not recite *Kiddush* until Moshe is found and brought back to the *tish*!"

There was one problem. No one had any idea where Moshe might have gone. The *Rebbe* was not perturbed by this. "Search the streets until you find him," he instructed his sons. After searching for almost two hours, they found Moshe and convinced him to return with them. The *Rebbe* greeted Moshe warmly and then recited *Kiddush*.

ℒ *The Hostage Crisis*

In the summer of 1970, Arab terrorists hijacked three TWA jets, forcing the pilots to land the planes in the Jordanian desert, where the passengers were held hostage for some time. Among the hostages were R' Yitzchak Hutner, *Rosh Yeshivah* of Mesivta Rabbi Chaim Berlin and one of the generation's leading Torah personalities, and his family. While Jews everywhere prayed for the safe release of *all* the hostages, there was particular concern for R' Hutner, to whom so many turned for guidance and inspiration and whose advanced age made prolonged captivity especially dangerous.

When with Hashem's help R' Hutner and some others were released, hundreds of *bnei Torah* and their *roshei yeshivah* went to Kennedy Airport to greet the *Rosh Yeshivah* upon his arrival. A popular Jewish band was also on hand and their lively music added to the festive atmosphere as everyone waited for the plane to touch down.

Among those present was R' Moshe Feinstein. R' Moshe approached the band leader and said, "I'm sorry, but you will have to stop the music. You see, six hostages are still being held by the terrorists. As long as even *one* hostage is being held, we cannot celebrate."

R' Hutner himself did not forget the remaining hostages for a moment. R' Moshe Sherer, late President of Agudath Israel of America, recorded some of his memories of that ordeal. During the three weeks that R' Hutner and the others were held hostage, R' Sherer's many projects for the sake of Jewry came to a standstill, as he and others worked around the clock contacting leaders of governments and trying to devise a way to resolve the crisis peacefully.

R' Hutner, along with thirty-one other hostages, arrived at Kennedy Airport on Monday evening, September 28, 1970. The next morning, R' Sherer received an urgent phone call from R' Hutner, saying that he was "tormented" by the uncertain fate of the remaining six hostages — among them R' Yosef and R' Baruch Harari-Raful, who today are distinguished leaders of New York's Sephardic community. For the next five hours, R' Sherer was on the phone with the State Department, Agudath Israel's Knesset members in Jerusalem and other important contacts. At 2:00 P.M., R' Sherer phoned R' Hutner with the wonderful news that the hostages had been freed and would soon be in the hands of the International Red Cross.

But there was still one major hurdle to overcome. The next day was *erev* Rosh Hashanah. In addition to the two *rabbanim,* there was one other hostage, a Dr. Berkowitz, an Orthodox Jew who resided in New York. Was there any way that they could be reunited with their families before Rosh Hashanah?

Thus began a new around-the-clock effort, involving activists from Jerusalem, London, Washington and New York. At the same time, R' Sherer was in contact with the administration of R' Hutner's yeshivah, who were keeping the Raful families informed of developments. At 12:30 A.M., R' Sherer phoned TWA Chief of Operations, to plead with him to place the hostages on the earliest possible flight out of Athens.

The plane carrying the six special passengers took off from Athens at 6:45 A.M. New York time. It met strong headwinds and had to stop in Lisbon, Portugal for refueling. Its scheduled arrival time in New York was 6:10 P.M. Sunset was 6:38 P.M.

The Mayor's office arranged for police helicopters to be on hand at the airport to fly the passengers to Brooklyn and the Bronx, respectively. But this was not necessary. The plane touched down one-half hour ahead of schedule. Rabbis Raful and Dr. Berkowitz were escorted to waiting police cars and were driven home. R' Sherer phone R' Hutner with the news that everyone had arrived home safely before sunset.

And that is when R' Hutner — and everyone else involved — were able to rejoice.

ଓ *Everyone's Friend (I)*

R' Aryeh Levin was famous for his *ahavas Yisrael*. He saw only the good in people, even those for whom others rarely had a kind word. "That man," R' Aryeh would say, "is such a good person. You simply don't know him like I know him..."

"But, R' Aryeh," his listener would protest, "people say that he...."

R' Aryeh would interject. "People also say things about me that are not true. One has to train himself to hear only the good, otherwise his ears will be so stuffed with evil talk that there will be no room for truth to enter!"

Once, a demonstration was held by a group which believed that it is forbidden for Orthodox Jews to recognize the secular government of Israel or to associate with any of its members. The police arrested some of the demonstrators.

When R' Aryeh learned that some of the demonstrators had been imprisoned, he immediately brought a Torah scroll to the prison so that the prisoners could hear the Torah reading on Shabbos. When he saw that their cell was rather dark, he requested of the officer in charge that they be moved to brighter quarters.

One of the prisoners refused to look at R' Aryeh, because R' Aryeh was known to be on friendly terms with government sympathizers. "Why do you help this man?" the officer asked R' Aryeh. "He doesn't even consider you worthy of looking at!"

"But that is to his credit," R' Aryeh replied softly. "He takes strong issue with my willingness to associate with certain individuals. His feelings over this are so strong that he considers it forbidden to look at my face. And he will not be 'bribed' into compromising his beliefs! Nothing, not even the favors which I have just done for him, will sway him in any way.

"Now there's a man of truth!"

For sixty years, R' Aryeh rose early each morning to pray at one of Jerusalem's many *vasikin minyanim,* which pray the *Shacharis Shemoneh Esrei* at sunrise, the preferred time. On his way to *shul,* he would greet everyone he met — especially the Jerusalem street cleaners who rose early to begin their work.

He once told someone, "I have a special love for the street cleaners. Just look: While everyone else is sleeping, they are busy cleaning the streets of Jerusalem, and earning an honest living to support their families. Their work is not respected, they are not held in high esteem and they are paid a meager salary. Nevertheless, they go about their work faithfully."

During the last years of British rule over Eretz Yisrael (then called "Palestine"), many Jews were imprisoned on various charges relating to the political situation. R' Aryeh took it upon himself to become the unofficial "prison rabbi," visiting the inmates regularly to offer them his friendship and sympathetic ear. He became their link to the outside world, carrying scores of messages to and from family members.

When R' Aryeh was preparing to marry off his daughter, the prisoners managed to pass word to one another about presenting him with a cash gift to help pay for the wedding. Somehow, a collection was made within the prison walls which totaled twenty-five Israeli pounds, an appreciable sum in those days. One of the prisoners had a check written for the amount and attached to it a note expressing the prisoners' deep appreciation to R' Aryeh for all that he had done for them.

R' Aryeh responded with a beautiful letter of thanks in which he explained why he could not cash the check. He considered this *mitzvah* of helping the prisoners and their families exceedingly precious and he did not want to benefit from it in any way on this world. In this way, the *mitzvah* would remain whole and perfect in his Heavenly account.

However, he requested that he should be allowed to keep the check as a remembrance, for it represented the love and appreciation which the prisoners felt towards him.[1]

ℒ *Everyone's Friend (II)*

R' Shlomo Zalman Auerbach knew virtually everyone in his Shaarei Chesed neighborhood personally — including a young boy who was born handicapped. Every Friday night after *davening,* this boy would wish R' Shlomo Zalman a *"Gut Shabbos."* If ever the boy did not come over, R' Shlomo Zalman made sure to inquire about him.

When a grandchild of R' Shlomo Zalman passed away, this boy decided that it was not the proper time to wish the *tzaddik* a *"Gut Shabbos."* But as the boy headed for home, R' Shlomo Zalman came towards him with his hand extended, smiling as usual. "Where is my *'Gut Shabbos'*?" he wanted to know.

After R' Shlomo Zalman's funeral, the boy was inconsolable. As his father explained, "My son has lost one of his best friends."

There was an old, sick woman in Shaarei Chesed who lived a lonely existence. The highlight of her day was when R' Shlomo Zalman would pass her house on his way to *Shacharis* and wish her a warm "Good morning." At the funeral, this woman wailed, "Who will wish me 'Good morning' now...?"

A number of taxi drivers visited the Auerbach family during the week of *shivah.* They said that they felt a special bond with R' Shlomo Zalman because he treated them with such respect. In fact, it was not uncommon to see a taxi driver pat R' Shlomo Zalman on the back, as if they were old friends.

He surely could have spent his time riding in a taxi engrossed in Torah thoughts. Instead, he chose to make conversation with the driver, in the hope that this would leave the driver with a favorable impression of Orthodox Jews and their way of life.

✌ For Those Who Caused Him Pain

Fire raged through a home in Jerusalem's Shaarei Chesed neighborhood. It was with great difficulty that firefighters managed to salvage but a few of the homeowner's possessions.

The couple that occupied this home were a pair of embittered souls. They seemed jealous of the family of the famed *maggid* and *tzaddik*, R' Sholom Schwadron, and over the years, they caused R' Sholom and his family untold distress.

Yet after the fire, when the neighborhood residents united to discuss how to help the couple, R' Sholom led the effort.

"You had to see him in action," R' Sholom's son-in-law recalled. "The energy which he invested in this effort was incredible. You would have thought that the man was his relative or close friend. That man had no idea that my father-in-law was thinking about him day and night. Had they told him, he probably would have not believed it."

During that period, R' Sholom was asked to speak at *Kollel Chazon Ish* in Bnei Brak. The study hall was filled to capacity. In the middle of his impassioned speech, R' Sholom suddenly raised his voice and cried, "My brethren! Something has happened in Jerusalem! A fire has destroyed a family's home... Charity! Support for the unfortunate! This is a *mitzvah* in the Torah!"

He then did something even more unusual. He announced, "I am going to circulate among you. Everyone give what you can."

R' Sholom removed his hat from his head, turned it upside down and began to make his way through the crowd. People contributed generously. R' Sholom himself was astounded at the sum that he collected that night for his "friend."

With that money, R' Sholom bought the man a new stove, other appliances and there even was some cash left over to give the man. The appliances and money were given through a third party and the couple never learned that their true benefactor was R' Sholom.[2]

ℒ No Time to Rest

It was 1:00 A.M. when the phone rang at the home of Yaakov Reiner* in Lakewood, New Jersey. On the line was the venerable *Mashgiach* of the Lakewood Yeshivah, R' Nosson Wachtfogel. R' Nosson spoke with obvious distress. "Please, Yaakov, come to my house. I must see you right now!"

Yaakov hurried to dress and soon was knocking on the *Mashgiach's* door. R' Nosson welcomed him inside and got straight to the point. "I called you here concerning the situation of your friend Daniel. As you well know, his home situation right now is extremely delicate and I fear that things may deteriorate unless something is done soon. And I wanted you to know that his situation allows me no rest! That is why I summoned you in the middle of the night."

"What does the *Mashgiach* suggest that I do?" asked Yaakov.

"You will know what to do," R' Nosson replied.

Yaakov went home and mulled over the situation. By now, it was close to 2:00 A.M. Nevertheless, he picked up the phone and called his close friend, Simchah. "The *Mashgiach* called me an hour ago to come and see him. He says that he cannot rest until something is done to help Daniel."

A few minutes later, Yaakov's phone rang for the second time that night. This time it was Simchah calling him. "The *Mashgiach* just called me to tell me the same thing he told you. We've got to do something fast."

Two days later, Simchah flew out of state to speak to someone on Daniel's behalf. His mission was successful and as a result, a potentially tragic situation was averted.

ℒ For Every Jewish Child

In the winter of 1995, R' Moshe Sherer was diagnosed with a serious illness which would require months of difficult treatments.

---

*All names of *talmidim* have been changed.

With Hashem's help his health was restored, and he regained his old vigor and enthusiasm. R' Sherer took ill again some three years later and passed away in the spring of 1998 (5758) on the day of the annual dinner of Agudath Israel of America, the movement which he had led for decades with heart and soul.

At his first appointment with the doctor who would administer his treatments, R' Sherer was told that it would be virtually impossible for him to appear in public for the next six months. R' Sherer had but one request: that the treatments should not interfere with his annual visit to the summer camps of Agudath Israel — Camp Agudah, Camp Bnos and Camp Chayil Miriam — whose campers were so very dear to him.

From the day of that appointment until the summer, R' Sherer appeared in public only once — at the annual dinner of Agudath Israel, where he addressed the gathering as he did every year. When he entered the hall, it was announced that no one should shake his hand, to prevent contact with germs which might cause infection. Everyone obeyed this instruction.

In the summer, R' Sherer visited his doctor prior to his trip to the summer camps. He had lost weight and did not look well at all. The doctor cautioned him that during his visits, he was not to shake anyone's hand. R' Sherer said nothing after the doctor completed his instructions.

R' Sherer was driven to the camps by his distinguished son, R' Shimshon. As they headed towards Camp Agudah, R' Sherer said, "I hope that the children won't be scared when they see how I look. Maybe I'm being selfish for wanting to visit them." R' Shimshon assured his father that the campers would be thrilled to see him, as indeed they were.

R' Shimshon then reminded his father of the doctor's warning not to shake anyone's hand. "Shimshy," R' Sherer responded, "it's too much to ask of me. How can I be deprived of hugging the people in camp whom I love so?" "Daddy," R' Shimshon pleaded, "please listen to the doctor."

As they entered the jam-packed dining room of Camp Agudah, R' Sherer was greeted, as always, with thunderous singing and clapping. The love which everyone, young and old, felt for him was palpable, as was their excitement at seeing this very great, very humble individual.

After being introduced by the Head Counselor, R' Simcha Kaufman, R' Sherer took the microphone. He quoted the Steipler *Gaon,* who used to say that often, the source of a person's problems is that he is too concerned with the אֲנִי, the "*I.*" "I need this," or "I need that." He is too preoccupied with himself and not concerned enough with helping others. R' Sherer told the campers that if we truly want this *galus* (exile) to end and the *Beis HaMikdash* to be rebuilt, then we have to focus less on our own needs and more on the needs of our fellow Jews.

As R' Sherer spoke, his face became flushed and his old fire returned. He finished speaking and the camp's Director, Meir Frischman, prepared to escort R' Sherer out the kitchen exit, which was only a couple of feet from where he had delivered his speech. This way, he would not have to shake anyone's hand.

But that is not what happened. Instead, R' Sherer took R' Meir by the hand and began to walk with him through the length of the dining room. As he hugged R' Kaufman, the hundreds of campers crowded around him — and he began to shake everyone's hand! R' Shimshon could not believe what was happening. "Daddy — what are you doing?" he asked in dismay, but R' Sherer seemed not to have heard him. He continued to shake hands with campers and staff, smiling the entire time, until he reached the last table in the huge dining room. It was the table of Bunk ל"ב, a bunk of special children. R' Sherer made a point of shaking the hand of every boy in this bunk, and he smiled at each child with a special warmth.

When R' Sherer finally walked through the dining room's double door to the building's lobby, his son asked him, "Daddy, the doctor begged you not to shake hands with anyone — what did you just do?"

"Shimshy," R' Sherer replied, "do you understand the torture of a father who is not able to hug his children? These campers are my children — why do you think I told the doctor that I wanted to schedule the treatments in a way that would allow me to visit my camps? These are my *kinderlach* (children)!"

R' Shimshon responded, "Well, if that's the case, then I'm also entitled to a hug," and he hugged his father for the first time since the treatments had begun many months before. Tears flowed down R' Shimshon's cheeks. "Why are you crying?" R' Sherer asked. "I'm getting better! Our Merciful Father is making me better! I was able to speak to my *kinderlach*!"

"I'm crying," R' Shimshon replied, "because I have such a father."

R' Sherer then said: "Do you know why every year I walk through the camp dining room? Do you think that I'm running for the position of Color War General? Do I need to have everyone jumping all over me trying to shake my hand? I do it for one reason: to teach the campers how precious every Jewish child is, and how special the campers in Bunk ל״ב are. Let every camper see how Moshe Sherer walks through the dining room and stops by the last table to shake the hand of every boy in Bunk ל״ב."

✒ A Hug for Life

In an address on the topic of *Ahavas Yisrael*, Rabbi Paysach Krohn related the following story:

The year was 1945, and the place was a Nazi concentration camp which had just been liberated by Allied forces. A boy named Herschel, starving and battered both physically and emotionally, was rummaging through garbage cans desperately seeking something to eat. The degradation of searching through garbage did not bother Herschel. He was a mere skeleton of his former self, and he would do anything for a scrap of food. And his pride was not a factor, because he had none. By treating him and his fellow Jews as sub-human, the Nazis had left the young boy without a trace of self-worth. The fact that he was a Jew, a member of G-d's Chosen People, meant very little to him at that point.

Herschel's search for food was unsuccessful. As he lifted his head up from yet another trash heap, he noticed another survivor, a man whom he did not know.

"Please," Herschel begged, "please, give me something to eat... anything — I'm starving!"

"I wish I had something to give you," replied the man, whose name was R' Yisrael. "But I, too, am starving and do not have a morsel of food. There is only one thing that I can give you" — and with those words, R' Yisrael drew Herschel close to him and hugged him tightly. "I want you to know that I love you," he said, his voice choked with emotion. "I love you because you are a Jew. Always remember this hug from someone who loved you simply because you are a Jew."

Eventually, both survivors made their way to Eretz Yisrael and began their lives anew. More than fifty years after his encounter with Herschel, R' Yisrael passed away in Jerusalem. When Herschel came to fulfill the *mitzvah* of *nichum aveilim* (comforting mourners), he related that in the years immediately following the war, he endured much trauma and suffering and there were moments when he contemplated abandoning the Torah way of life. "At those moments," he told R' Yisrael's children, "one memory kept me going: your father — a total stranger — hugging me tightly and telling me, 'I love you because you are a Jew.' It is thanks to that hug and those words that I, my children and grandchildren are living a Torah life today."[3]

There are other kinds of "hugs," encounters of kindness and love which leave lifelong impressions.

A young man related to R' Moshe Sherer that his decision to devote his life to Torah study had its roots in a two-minute encounter at an airport with R' Yaakov Kamenetsky years earlier, when he was a boy.

He had been trying to snap a picture of R' Yaakov when someone motioned to him to go away. The boy's face fell as he started to walk away, but R' Yaakov stopped him. "That's all right," the *tzaddik* said as he smiled warmly, "you can take the picture." R' Yaakov straightened his frock, smiled and said, "Shoot!"

"The warmth which R' Yaakov displayed towards me," the young man recalled, "simply made a tremendous impression on me. I never forgot it."

May we merit to master the golden quality of *ahavas Yisrael* and thereby draw others closer to Hashem and His Torah.

Sources

The Gift of Speech

1: Word Power

1. *Mishlei* 18:21.
2. *Vayikra Rabbah* 33:1.
3. *Arachin* 15b.
4. *Sefer Shemiras HaLashon, Shaar HaZechirah* Ch. 7. This is further elaborated upon in Chapter Twenty-one.
5. *Mishnah Negaim* 3:2.
6. *Ohel Yaakov, Parashas Metzora.*

2: Destruction and Rebuilding

1. *Berachos* 10a.
2. *Yerushalmi Pe'ah* 1:1.
3. *Yerushalmi Yoma* 1:1.
4. *Chovas HaShemirah* Ch. 8.
5. From *Silent Revolution: A Torah Network in the Soviet Union* by Miriam Stark Zakon (Mesorah Publications).
6. See *Bereishis* 23:8 with *Rashi.*
7. *Yerushalmi Pe'ah* 1:1. For the Chofetz Chaim's explanation of this teaching, see *A Lesson A Day*, Day 11.
8. In his ethical letter.
9. *Parashas Shelach.*
10. *Sefer Shemiras HaLashon, Shaar HaZechirah* Ch. 1.
11. *Hilchos Lashon Hara* 2:11.
12. *Sefer Maalos HaMidos* ch 24.
13. *Chofetz Chaim: A Daily Companion* follows this schedule for *Sefer Chofetz Chaim. Chofetz Chaim: A Lesson A Day* follows its own schedule, but includes study of both *Sefer Chofetz Chaim* and *Sefer Shemiras HaLashon.* Both are published by Mesorah.

3: The Truth Hurts

1. *Vayikra* 19:16.
2. Ibid. v. 18.
3. *Rashi* ad loc.
4. *Shabbos* 31a.
5. Preface to *Sefer Chofetz Chaim*, Positive Commandment 2.
6. From the *Minchah Shemoneh Esrei* of Shabbos.
7. *Be'er Mayim Chaim, Hilchos Lashon Hara* 7:24.
8. *Shaarei Teshuvah* 217.

4: The Benefit of the Doubt

1. *Vayikra* 19:15.
2. *Rashi* from *Toras Kohanim* 4:4.
3. *Shabbos* 127b.
4. *She'iltos D'R' Achai* 40.
5. 6:6.
6. *Mishnas R' Aharon*, vol. I, p. 62
7. The complete account appears in *More Shabbos Stories*, p. 142.
8. *Hilchos Lashon Hara*, footnote to 6:8.
9. *Shabbos* 127b.
10. *Atarah L'Melech* p. 81.

5: A Shameful Mistake

1. *Avos* 3:15.
2. *Bava Metzia* 59a.
3. *Shaarei Teshuvah* 3:139.
4. Though a person generally turns red when he is embarrassed, this is because the blood gathers in his face before draining from it (*Tosafos* to *Bava Metzia* 58b).
5. Footnote to *Hilchos Lashon Hara* 9:5.
6. *Orach Chaim* 142.
7. R' Avraham Yeshayahu Karelitz of Bnei Brak (1878-1953), author of the multi-volumed *Chazon Ish* and a leader of Torah Jewry in the period immediately following the Second World War.
8. From *Maaseh Ish* (Vol. II) by Rabbi Zvi Yabarov.

6: Painful Words

1. *Vayikra* 25:17.
2. Preface to *Sefer Chofetz Chaim*, Negative Commandment 14.
3. *Shemos* 22:21.
4. Published by Feldheim.
5. *Choshen Mishpat* 176.
6. *Shemos* 22:21.
7. *Atarah L'Melech* pp. 83-84.
8. *Mishlei* 10:12.
9. *Bava Basra* 16b.

7: Put-downs

1. *Hilchos Lashon Hara* 5:7.
2. See *Beitzah* 16a.
3. From *Tuvcha Yabi'u*, Vol. I, pp. 367-368.
4. See *Sforno* to *Bereishis* 4:6.
5. *Avos* 4:24.
6. *Berachos* 28b.
7. *Vayikra* 19:18.
8. *Taanis* 22a.
9. *Hilchos Lashon Hara* 3:3.
10. *Atarah L'Melech* pp. 194-195.
11. *Mishlei* 3:17.

8: Not-So-Innocent Remarks

1. *Hilchos Lashon Hara* 5:2.
2. See Chapter Fourteen.

9: "In My Opinion..."

1. *Hilchos Lashon Hara* 5:7.
2. Ibid. 5:2.
3. Ibid. 9:1-2.

10: Common Misconceptions

1. *Hilchos Lashon Hara* 1:9.
2. Ibid. 4:1. By proudly relating the incident, thus giving the impression that he did nothing wrong, the speaker may be guilty of *chillul Hashem* (desecration of Hashem's Name).
3. Ibid. 9:3.
4. *Mishlei* 27:14.
5. *Hilchos Lashon Hara* 2:2.
6. In a footnote to *Hilchos Lashon Hara* 9:3, the Chofetz Chaim writes that according to some *Rishonim*, such statements are actual *lashon hara*.
7. *Hilchos Lashon Hara* 9:1.
8. Ibid. 9:3, based on *Shaarei Teshuvah* 3:227.
9. *Mishlei* 6:13-14.
10. *Rashi* to *Vayikra* 19:16.
11. *Hilchos Lashon Hara* 1:8.
12. *Be'er Mayim Chaim* 14 to *Hilchos Lashon Hara* Ch. 1.
13. *Hilchos Lashon Hara* 3:4.
14. *Pe'ah* 1:1, cited in *Be'er Mayim Chaim* to Chapter 3 of *Hilchos Lashon Hara*, 3.
15. *Hilchos Lashon Hara* 3:4.

11: Bad News

1. See Chapter 2.
2. Based on *Hilchos Lashon Hara* 2:3 with *Be'er Mayim Chaim* 6.

3. *Yoreh De'ah* 243:6 cited in *Hilchos Lashon Hara* 8:4.
4. *Shabbos* 119b.
5. *Rashi* to *Devarim* 19:17.
6. *Hilchos Lashon Hara* 8:4.
7. *Yevamos* 14b.
8. See *Avos* 5:20.
9. He applied to R' Aharon the comment of *Rashi* to *Bamidbar* 8:3 regarding Aharon HaKohen.
10. *I Shmuel* Ch. 24. Shaul, like David, was a great *tzaddik*. A discussion of why he pursued David is beyond the scope of this work. The interested reader should study the relevant chapters in *I Shmuel* with commentaries.
11. *Berachos* 62b.
12. *I Shmuel* 24:6. David felt that it was disrespectful to have damaged the king's garment.
13. *Mishnas R' Aharon*, Vol. I, p. 51.
14. *Makkos* 22b.

12: *Wholesale Destruction*

1. By Malky Lowinger, a free-lance writer in Brooklyn. Copies of the article are available from the *Am Echad* office at 38 William St., New York, N.Y. 10038.
2. By Blimie Friedman; it appeared in *The Jewish Observer.*
3. Fur-rimmed hat worn by many *chassidim* on Shabbos and the Festivals.
4. Also called a *yarmulka.*
5. High fur hat worn by some chassidic sects on Shabbos and the Festivals.
6. *Hilchos Lashon Hara* 10:12.

13: *Playing with Fire*

1. *Avos* 4:1.
2. *Mishnah Uktzin* 3:12.
3. *Sefer Shemiras HaLashon, Shaar HaZechirah*, ch. 15.
4. *Bamidbar* ch. 16.
5. See *Shemos* 2:13 with *Rashi.*
6. *Shemos* 16:20 with *Rashi.*
7. *Rashi* to *Bamidbar* 16:12, citing *Tanchumah* 12.
8. *Bamidbar* 17:5.
9. *Sefer Shemiras HaLashon, Shaar HaZechirah* 17.
10. *Sifri* to *Devarim* 13:7.
11. See *Rashi* to *Vayikra* 19:3 and *Shulchan Aruch, Yoreh De'ah* 240:15.
12. *Mishlei* 21:23.
13. *Leshichno Sidreshu*, Vol. II, pp. 157-158.
14. *Tehillim* 34:15.
15. *Vayikra Rabbah* 9:9.
16. *Shabbos* 127a.

14: *When Bad is Good*

1. *Hilchos Rechilus* 5:3-4.

2. *Vayikra* 19:16.
3. *Hilchos Lashon Hara* 10:1-2.
4. See *Shulchan Aruch, Yoreh De'ah* 247:2.
5. *Koheles* 9:17.
6. *Mishlei* 3:17.
7. *Shemos* 23:7.
8. See *Rashi* to *Bereishis* 18:13.

15: Family Talk

1. Preface to *Sefer Shemiras HaLashon*.
2. *Hilchos Lashon Hara* 8:1.
3. See previous chapter.
4. See "Bad Humor" in Chapter Seven.
5. *Hilchos Lashon Hara* 8:10.
6. See footnote to *Hilchos Lashon Hara* 10:14; see also Hebrew note 113 to Laws in *A Lesson a Day.*
7. Sotah 17a; see Rashi.
8. Yoma 9b.
9. *Hilchos Lashon Hara* 9:5 with footnote.
10. Ibid. 8:14.

16: Rechilus

1. *Hilchos Rechilus* 1:2.
2. *Vayikra* 19:16.
3. *Hilchos Rechilus* 1:3.
4. ibid. 4.
5. ibid. 5.
6. ibid. 6.
7. From *All for the Boss* by Ruchoma Shain (published by Feldheim).
8. *Hilchos Rechilus* 1:8.
9. *Bereishis* 18:13.
10. In *Be'er Mayim Chaim* (14), the Chofetz Chaim points out that from this episode we derive that while for the sake of peace one may alter the truth, he should avoid an outright lie if possible. Here, Hashem altered Sarah's words by omitting part of them.
11. *Hilchos Rechilus, Be'er Mayim Chaim* 8:6.
12. *Hilchos Rechilus* 1:7.
13. *Shabbos* 88b.
14. *Shoftim* 5:31.
15. Footnote to *Shaar HaTevunah* Ch. 8. The story is found in *Sefer Toldos Adam* on the life of R' Zalman of Volozhin.

17: Shades of Ill Will

1. *Hilchos Rechilus* 1:10.
2. *Rambam, Hilchos De'os* 7:5.

3. Based on *Hilchos Rechilus* 2:4.
4. Ibid. 8:3.
5. Ibid. 8:2.
6. Ibid. 8:1.
7. Ibid. 1:11.
8. Ibid. 3:2.
9. Ibid. 6:3-4.

18: *Repairing the Damage*

1. *Hilchos Lashon Hara* 4:12.
2. *Hilchos Teshuvah* 2:2.
3. *Shaarei Teshuvah* 1:11.
4. *Bamidbar* 5:6-7.
5. *Horeb* 514.
6. This explanation was reportedly said some twenty years ago by a *baal teshuvah*, who died suddenly hours after he had thought of it while learning with a study partner. It is told that R' Shneur Kotler, ז״ל, spoke at the man's funeral and said that he died a *baal teshuvah* in the fullest sense.
7. *Mishnah Yoma* 8:9 and *Shulchan Aruch, Orach Chaim* 608:1.
8. *Hilchos Lashon Hara* 4:12. The Chofetz Chaim states that when the *lashon hara* was accepted as truth, the person must seek forgiveness even if the subject of his words is unaware of the *lashon hara* spoken against him. It is told that R' Yisrael Salanter (who kept a *Sefer Chofetz Chaim* in his *tallis* bag) asked on this: Does one's desire to repent give him a right to cause the victim of his words emotional pain by informing him that he had spoken against him? The Chofetz Chaim is reported to have responded that while R' Yisrael's question is a good one, the *halachah* still stands, for it is based on the words of *Rabbeinu Yonah* (*Shaarei Teshuvah* 3:207) who was one of the great *poskim* of earlier generations.
9. 606:3.
10. Ibid. 1.
11. From *Reb Elyah: The Life and Accomplishments of Rabbi Eliyahu Lopian* by Rabbi David J. Schlossberg, published by Mesorah.
12. From *Voice of Truth* [Heb. *Kol Chotzev*]: *The Life and Eloquence of Rabbi Sholom Schwadron*, published by Mesorah.

19: *The Art of Not Listening*

1. *Shemos* 23:1
2. *Hilchos Lashon Hara* 6:1.
3. Ibid. 2.
4. Ibid. 5.
5. In *Be'er Mayim Chaim*, the Chofetz Chaim speculates that the person may be rabbinically required to close his ears. To avoid this problem, he strongly advises that one pick himself up and leave whenever possible.
6. *Hilchos Lashon Hara* 6:6.
7. *Pirkei D'R' Eliezer, Tzavaas R' Eliezer HaGadol.*

8. *Devarim* 23:13-14.
9. *Kesubos* 5a-b.
10. See *Rambam, Hilchos De'os* 7:3.
11. Footnote to *Hilchos Lashon Hara* 6:3.
12. *Mishlei* 25:23. Apparently, *Rabbeinu Yonah* understands the word תְחוֹלֵל, *drives away* as related to יְחוֹלֵל in *Tehillim* 29:9 and וַתִּתְחַלְחַל in *Esther* 4:4.
13. Published by Mesorah.
14. *Devarim* 23:10.
15. Chapter One.
16. *Be'er HaGolah*, The Third Well.
17. From *Reb Elchonon: The Life and Ideals of Rabbi Elchonon Bunim Wasserman of Baranovich* published by Mesorah.
18. *Karyana D'Igarta*, vol. I, 11.
19. *Kesubos* 8a.
20. *Chiddushei Aggados* ad loc.

20: Listening vs. Accepting

1. Footnote to *Hilchos Lashon Hara* 6:11.
2. *Niddah* 61a.
3. *Hilchos Lashon Hara* 6:11.
4. Ibid. 2.
5. *Be'er Mayim Chaim* 6:3.
6. *Hilchos Lashon Hara* 6:2.
7. Ibid. 4.
8. Ibid. 3.

21: Squandering One's Wealth

1. *Mishlei* 13:7.
2. *Sefer Shemiras HaLashon*, Afterword, Part II.
3. *Shaar Ha'Keniah* Ch. 7.
4. By R' Raphael Hamburger (eighteenth century).
5. *Tehillim* 34:14-15.
6. See Chapter 1.
7. *Vayikra* 13:46.
8. Ibid. v. 45.
9. *Moed Katan* 5a.
10. Such as *zav* and *zavah* (*Vayikra* Ch. 15).
11. *Sefer Shemiras HaLashon, Shaar HaZechirah* Ch. 7.
12. *Bereishis Rabbah* 65:20.
13. *Sefer Shemiras HaLashon, Shaar HaZechirah* Ch. 10.
14. *Esther Rabbah* 9:4.
15. An auspicious time for prayer; see *Berachos* 3a.
16. *Esther* 6:1.
17. *Shabbos* 119b.
18. *Sefer Shemiras HaLashon, Shaar HaZechirah* ch. 8.

19. *Mishnah Berurah* 124:27.
20. חֲזָרַת הַשַּׁ"ץ is the repetition of the *Shemoneh Esrei* by the שְׁלִיחַ צִבּוּר (emissary of the congregation, popularly known as the *chazzan*).
21. *Shulchan Aruch, Orach Chaim* 124:7.
22. *Bereishis* 4:13.
23. *Berachos* 10a.
24. *Zohar, Shemos* 5b. While *Zohar* makes mention of the Temple's western wall, commentators apply the statement to the wall of the Temple Mount.
25. *Vayikra* 26:2.
26. *Yechezkel* 11:16; see *Megillah* 29a.
27. *Bereishis* 28:17.
28. *Mishnah Berurah* 151:1, citing *Semak*.
29. Ibid. 2.
30. Introduction, Positive Commandments.
31. *Shulchan Aruch, Orach Chaim* 146:2.
32. Ibid. 56:1.

22: Nothing but the Truth

1. *Shabbos* 55a.
2. *Rashi* (ibid.) writes that the word אֱמֶת alludes to the verse, "I am the first and I am the last, and beside me there is no G-d" (*Yeshayahu* 44:6).
3. *Tehillim* 15:1-2.
4. From *BeDerech Eitz Chaim* by Yedael Meltzer.

23: Fine-tuning

1. *Pesachim* 3b.
2. *Shemos* 19:6.
3. *Moreh Nevuchim* 3:8. See *Pesachim* 3a-b.
4. *Yerushalmi Berachos* 1:2, *Yerushalmi Shabbos* 1:2.
5. From *Sipurim Yerushalmiyim* by Nun ben Avraham (Jerusalem 1994).
6. *Mishlei* 10:20.
7. *Ralbag ad loc.*

24: The Right Word

1. *Yeshayahu* 49:3.
2. *Yoma* 86a.
3. *Mishlei* 3:17.

The Mitzvah of Ahavas Yisrael

1: "...as Yourself"

1. 243.
2. *Yerushalmi Chagigah* 2:1.
3. *Sefer HaMitzvos* 206.
4. *Shemiras HaLashon, Shaar HaTevunah* Ch. 5.
5. *Sanhedrin* 11a.
6. *Yeshayahu* 49:3.
7. *Rambam, Hilchos Aveil* 14:1.
8. *Shaar HaKavanos, Birchos HaShachar.*

2: Three Levels of Love

1. *Tana D'vei Eliyahu Rabbah* Ch. 28.
2. *Michtav M'Eliyahu, Vol. III*, pp.88-90.
3. *Avos* 1:6.
4. Adapted from *Anatomy of a Search* by Akiva Tatz, published by Mesorah.
5. *Derech Eretz Zuta* Ch. 2.
6. *Avos* 2:15.
7. *Kesubos* 67b.
8. *R' Aryeh Hayah Omer*, p. 301.
9. *Shabbos* 31a.
10. *Inspiration and Insight, Vol. I*, p. 190.

3: The Great Rule

1. 243.
2. *Shavuos* 39a.
3. *Bereishis* 46:27.
4. *Sefer Shemiras HaLashon, Shaar HaTevunah* ch 6.
5. *Kiddushin* 40b.
6. *Mishnah Sanhedrin* 4:5.
7. *Devarim* 14:1.
8. *Devarim* 6:5.
9. *Mishnas R' Aharon, Vol. I*, p. 73.
10. *Bereishis Rabbah* 38:6.
11. *Bereishis* Ch.6-8.
12. Ibid. Ch. 11.
13. Ibid. v. 11.
14. *Rashi* to *Vayikra* 26:8.
15. *Rashi* to *Shemos* 19:2 citing *Mechilta*.
16. *Derech Eretz Zuta* 11.
17. *Sichos Mussar [R' Chaim's Discourses]*, 5733, 22.
18. *Shabbos* 88a.

19. *Sanhedrin* 20a.
20. Ibid.
21. *Berachos* 18a.
22. *Sefer Shemiras HaLashon, Shaar HaTevunah* Ch. 6.

4: Children of One Father

1. Vol. I, pp. 298-299.
2. An expression borrowed from *Bereishis* 42:11.
3. *II Shmuel* 14:14.
4. From the prayers of Rosh Hashanah and Yom Kippur.
5. From *Guardian of Jerusalem* [Heb. *HaIsh al HaChomah*] by R' Shlomo Zalman Sonnenfeld (Mesorah Publications).
6. From *Reb Chaim Ozer: The Life and Ideals of Rabbi Chaim Ozer Grodzensky*, published by Mesorah.
7. Adapted from *Visions of Greatness* by R' Yosef Weiss.

5: Lessons of Greatness

1. Adapted from *A Tzaddik in Our Time* by Simcha Raz, published by Feldheim.
2. From *Voice of Truth [Heb. Kol Chotzev]: The Life and Eloquence of Rabbi Sholom Schwadron*, published by Mesorah.
3. This story will appear in a forthcoming book by Rabbi Krohn.

This volume is part of
THE ARTSCROLL SERIES®
an ongoing project of
translations, commentaries and expositions
on Scripture, Mishnah, Talmud, Halachah,
liturgy, history, the classic Rabbinic writings,
biographies and thought.

For a brochure of current publications
visit your local Hebrew bookseller
or contact the publisher:

Mesorah Publications, ltd

4401 Second Avenue
Brooklyn, New York 11232
(718) 921-9000
www.artscroll.com